Advance Praise for
Battlefield America

"Just like acknowledging the nature of the problem is the first step in an individual's recovery from alcoholism, acknowledging the fascist nature of modern America is a necessary step toward restoring American liberty. *Battlefield America* does not turn away from naming the true nature of the American regime. Mr. Whitehead draws comparisons not just from history but from dystopian fiction to illustrate how America has lost its way. The very fact that books like this can still be written and published shows that we have not lost all our freedoms. John Whitehead's work should motivate us all to redouble our efforts to reclaim our freedoms."

> **—Dr. Ron Paul,** twelve-term U.S. Congressman
> and former presidential candidate

"Government surveillance, militarized police, sneak-and-peek searches, SWAT team raids, asset forfeiture schemes, overcriminalization, private prisons: these are all pressing concerns that transcend partisan politics and render the citizenry not merely suspects but criminals. Unfortunately, too many Americans have embraced the government's call to give up some freedom in return for greater safety, only to find that in doing so, they have lost freedom without gaining safety. Constitutional attorney John W. Whitehead makes a compelling and urgent case in *Battlefield America* for Americans to unite under one common goal: in defense of our freedoms. The danger is clear: if the government has the power to violate one right for one person, then no right is safe for anyone."

> **—Nadine Strossen,** former president of the ACLU and
> constitutional law professor at New York Law School

"In his compelling book, *Battlefield America*, John W. Whitehead describes the danger posed to liberty and humanity itself by the control impulse of government and technology. American 'Democratic Capitalism' is not liberating us; it is enslaving humanity."

> **—Paul Craig Roberts,** former Assistant Secretary, US Treasury,
> and former *Wall Street Journal* columnist and editor

"Once again, John W. Whitehead shows himself to be a thorough reporter, an insightful scholar and a tireless defender of the Constitution. *Battlefield America* is the most penetrating, eye-opening proof to date of the imperialist government's desecration of our constitutional personal liberties. *Battlefield America* is not only a warning of the danger ahead but also a detailed, systematic illustration of how a once freedom-loving nation can descend into tyranny. A must-read for anyone concerned about how to get us back on the road to becoming a self-governing republic. Citizens, journalists, activists, government officials—any and all Americans who have so little inkling about what it really means to be an American and actively safeguard our freedoms against all dangers, foreign and domestic—should take the time to become acquainted with this book. Students and teachers, especially, should make it a priority to debate and discuss this book in their classrooms."

—**Nat Hentoff,** syndicated columnist and historian

"John Whitehead is freedom's defense lawyer. He'll never give up, and neither must we. To join John in this fight, first read his manifesto: *Battlefield America.* You are much needed."

—**Llewellyn H. Rockwell, Jr.,** author and chairman
of Mises Institute

"The loss of personal liberty, the growth of big government, and the death of government respect for persons rarely occur overnight. It takes a fine eye and a fearless manner to discover and reveal these dangers before it is too late. No one in American today does this better than John Whitehead. In his latest magnum opus, *Battlefield America: The War on the American People,* he paints the case that Fascism is already here, liberty is already lost, we are in more danger from the government than from bomb throwers, and it is nearly too late for hope. I challenge anyone to read this book and then try to go to sleep. I found that impossible."

—**Hon. Andrew P. Napolitano**, Senior Judicial Analyst,
Fox News Channel; Distinguished Visiting Professor of Law,
Brooklyn Law School

BATTLEFIELD AMERICA

THE WAR ON THE AMERICAN PEOPLE

JOHN W. WHITEHEAD

SelectBooks, Inc.
New York

This edition published by SelectBooks, Inc.
For information address SelectBooks, Inc., New York, New York.

First Edition

ISBN 978-1-59079-309-1

Library of Congress Cataloging-in-Publication Data
Whitehead, John W., 1946-
   Battlefield America : the war on the American people / John W. Whitehead.
      pages cm
   Includes bibliographical references and index.
   Summary: "Author paints a portrait of an evolving American police state as police authority expands into extensions of the military, and government's intrusions undermine basic freedoms guaranteed to American citizens under the Constitution, turning Americans into enemy combatants who are spied upon, raided, manhandled, silenced, locked up, shot at, and denied due process of the law"-- Provided by publisher.
   ISBN 978-1-59079-309-1 (hardbound book : alk. paper) 1. Civil rights--United States. 2. Electronic surveillance--United States. 3. Abuse of administrative power--United States. 4. Police--United States. I. Title.
   JC599.U5W523 2015
   323.4'90973--dc23
                     2014048520

Cover art and illustrations by Christopher Combs
Book design by Janice Benight

Manufactured in the United States of America
10 9 8 7 6 5 4 3 2 1

To my wife, Nisha Whitehead, who keeps me in the battle
and inspires me to move forward

and

Nat Hentoff, whose dedication to freedom
has been an inspiration to me

"If liberty means anything at all,
it means the right to tell the people
what they do not want to hear."[1]

★

—GEORGE ORWELL

"Everything in our background has prepared
us to know and resist a prison when the gates
begin to close around us. . . . But what if there
are no cries of anguish to be heard? Who is
prepared to take arms against a sea of amuse-
ments? To whom do we complain, and when, and
in what tone of voice, when serious discourse
dissolves into giggles? What is the antidote
to a culture's being drained by laughter?"[2]

★

—NEIL POSTMAN
AMUSING OURSELVES TO DEATH:
PUBLIC DISCOURSE IN THE AGE OF SHOW BUSINESS

Also by John W. Whitehead

A Government of Wolves: The Emerging American Police State (2013)

The Freedom Wars: What You Can Do To Preserve Your Rights (2010)

*The Change Manifesto: Join the Block by Block Movement
to Remake America* (2008)

CONTENTS

Foreword

By Dr. Ron Paul

Most Americans react with confusion, disbelief, and even hostility when told that America is not a free country. This reaction is quite understandable. After all, we are continually bombarded with messages from politicians, the media, and even popular culture about how we are the "freest nation on Earth." We are even told that the reason people from other countries hate us is because they resent our freedom, not our drones.

But if one puts aside the propaganda and honestly looks at modern American life, the idea that we are no longer a free country does not seem so outrageous.

If Americans were truly free, then...

Would the NSA be able to "monitor" our emails and other online activity without obtaining a warrant?

Would we have to submit to the TSA's harassment every time we boarded an airplane?

Would local governments use red-light cameras to enrich themselves and deny us due process of law?

Would we hear, on an almost daily basis, stories of SWAT teams terrorizing, and even murdering, innocent Americans via no-knock raids?

Would we watch in horror as police respond to peaceful protesters with military force?

Would armed federal agents invade Amish farms because those farmers dared sell raw milk to willing consumers?

Of course, we are told these infringements on liberty are all for our own good. How else is the government supposed to protect us from terrorists or stop us from using dangerous drugs or drinking raw milk unless they have the unrestrained power to spy, harass, and even shoot us with weapons developed for use in war?

Fortunately, a growing number of Americans, including a large number of young Americans, are questioning whether we are really better off trading away our liberties for phantom security. These people are studying great libertarian thinkers like Mises, Hayek, and Rothbard. They are also organizing with other activists to spread the ideas of liberty.

Many other Americans who have not yet accepted the entire libertarian paradigm have been motivated by some outrageous examples of government abuses to speak out against the loss of our freedom. For example, Edward Snowden's revelations of the extent to which the National Security Agency was spying on Americans caused the debate on the NSA to shift in a more pro-liberty direction, while the events in Ferguson, Missouri, moved police militarization from an issue of concern for a few libertarians to the center of American political debate.

During my 2012 presidential campaign, I often said that we do not need a majority to win the battle for liberty, what we need is an "irate, tireless minority." The growing liberty movement is certainly irate and tireless. However, to make truly revolutionary change, members of the liberty movement must also have a solid understanding of the freedom philosophy as well as the communication skills to rebut the arguments thrown at us by the statists of the left and right. Liberty activists must also have the moral courage to stand by their beliefs when the establishment offers them the carrots of prestige and power or the sticks of marginalization, ridicule, smears, and even IRS audits in order to get them to "play ball" with the establishment.

Individuals who wish to move America in a pro-liberty direction must not only understand how far we have drifted from a free society, but grasp the true nature of the current system. Sadly, even many libertarians and others who acknowledge how far we have drifted from a free society fail to understand the nature of the current regime.

Some engage in the delusion that all it will take to restore our liberty is replacing a "liberal" Democrat with a "conservative" Republican or vice versa. This delusion is encouraged by the mainstream media, which exaggerates relatively minor squabbles between the parties into major ideological clashes. The rarely spoken truth is that the establishment of both parties support the welfare-warfare police state; they just disagree on how best to manage the federal leviathan.

Those who still believe there is a serious difference between the two parties should ask themselves why there is such a remarkable similarity between the foreign, civil liberties, and even economic policies of the Bush and Obama administrations.

Many libertarians and conservatives recognize that simply replacing a big government Democrat with a big government Republican will not solve what plagues our country. Even so, they too still misdiagnose the problem as being "socialism." Given the large role government plays in modern economic and personal life, this may seem an accurate label. However, technically it is quite inaccurate, as socialism describes a society in which government directly owns the major sectors of the economy. Since government does not own the "means of production," America cannot accurately be described as socialist.

In fact, the description that best fits modern America is fascist. While this description might strike some people as extreme or even kooky, anyone who considers the historical definition of a fascist regime sees that fascist may be the most accurate label to define the current American system.

Under a fascist system, property is nominally held in private hands and the economy is officially "free." All appearances to the contrary, however, the economy in a fascist system is carefully controlled by government through a labyrinth of taxes and regulations. This government control is usually exercised for the benefit of an economic elite that works to perpetuate the power of the existing political class.

Other characteristics of fascist systems include a militaristic foreign policy and a police state that abuses our civil liberties. Only the willfully ignorant could deny that America's foreign policy is militaristic, and we have already seen the myriad ways in which modern government abuses our civil liberties.

A fascist system also singles out critics of the regime for harassment. From stopping scholars who are critical of America from entering the country to harassing journalists whose works displease the current administration to siccing the IRS on organizations critical of the current administration's policies, government harassment of their political critics has become increasing common.

Just like acknowledging the nature of the problem is the first step in an individual's recovery from alcoholism, acknowledging the fascist nature of modern America is a necessary step toward restoring American liberty.

This is why John W. Whitehead's *Battlefield America: The War on the American People* is so valuable. Eschewing over-the-top hysteria in favor of pressing facts and analyses, Mr. Whitehead demonstrates the fascistic character of the current American government. One thing that makes Mr. Whitehead's work particularly valuable is the way he draws comparisons not just from history, but from dystopian fiction, to illustrate how America has lost its way. References to popular works of fiction such as *1984, Brave New World,* and even the classic *Twilight Zone* episode, "An Obsolete Man," provide a familiar point of reference for many readers and help open their minds to Mr. Whitehead's arguments.

One thing that I am particularly happy about is Mr. Whitehead's recommendation that those opposed to the current regime engage in some form of nonviolent resistance. I also endorse his recommendation that individuals seek out alternative sources of news and information and avoid what are all too often government programs that emanate from the mainstream media.

Battlefield America: The War on the American People is valuable because it does not turn away from naming the true nature of the American regime. I hope this book finds a wide audience. However, I would caution readers of this book to avoid the understandable temptation to become hopeless upon learning the magnitude of the challenges faced by the liberty movement.

The very fact that books like this can still be written and published shows that we have not lost all our freedoms. Thanks to the Internet, it is easier than ever before to spread the message of liberty and plan ways to challenge state power. John Whitehead's work should motivate us all to redouble our efforts to reclaim our freedoms.

Dr. Ron Paul
January, 2015

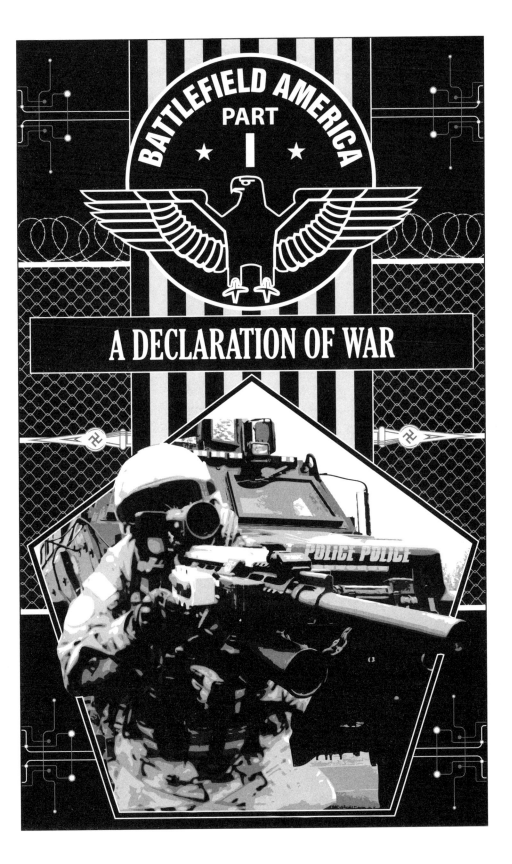

"If you want a picture of the future, imagine
a boot stamping on a human face—forever." [1]
—George Orwell

Reality Check

FACT: "Today, 17,000 local police forces are equipped with such military equipment as Blackhawk helicopters, machine guns, grenade launchers, battering rams, explosives, chemical sprays, body armor, night vision, rappelling gear and armored vehicles. Some have tanks."[2]—Paul Craig Roberts, former Assistant Secretary of the Treasury

FACT: Thanks to an overabundance of 4,500-plus federal crimes and 400,000-plus rules and regulations,[3] it is estimated that the average American actually commits three felonies a day without knowing it.[4] In fact, according to law professor John Baker, "There is no one in the United States over the age of 18 who cannot be indicted for some federal crime. That is not an exaggeration."[5]

FACT: The number of violent crimes in the country is down substantially, the lowest rate in forty years,[6] while the number of Americans being *jailed* for nonviolent crimes such as driving with a suspended license is skyrocketing.[7]

FACT: Despite the fact that we have 46 million Americans living at or below the poverty line,[8] 16 million children living in households without adequate access to food,[9] and at least 900,000 veterans relying on food stamps,[10] enormous sums continue to be doled out for presidential vacations ($16 million for trips to Africa and Hawaii[11]), overtime fraud at the Department of Homeland Security (nearly $9 million in improper overtime claims, and that's just in six of the DHS' many offices[12]), and Hollywood movie productions. ($10 million was spent by the Army National Guard on *Superman* movie tie-ins aimed at increasing awareness about the National Guard.[13])

FACT: Almost 13,000 agencies in all fifty states and four U.S. territories participate in a military "recycling" program, and the share of equipment and weaponry gifted each year continues to expand.

CHAPTER 1

It Can Happen Here

"Nonsense! Nonsense!" snorted Tasbrough. "That couldn't happen here in America, not possibly! We're a country of freedom!"[1]—SINCLAIR LEWIS, *It Can't Happen Here*

Relationships are fragile things, none more so than the relationship between a citizenry and their government. Unfortunately for the American people, the contract they entered into more than two hundred years ago—the U.S. Constitution—has been reduced to little more than a marriage of convenience and fiscal duty marked by distrust, lying, infidelity, hostility, disillusionment, paranoia, and domestic abuse.

Occupy protester arrested by NYPD
(Photography by Associated Press)

Adding insult to injury, these abuses are being perpetrated by the very government officials entrusted with ensuring the citizenry's freedom and safety.

Don't believe me? Just take a stroll through your city's downtown. Spend an afternoon in your local mall. Get in your car and drive to your parents' house. Catch the next flight to that business conference. While you're doing so, pay careful attention to how you and your fellow citizens are treated by government officials, the ones whose salaries you are paying.

You might walk past a police officer outfitted in tactical gear, holding an assault rifle, or drive past a police cruiser scanning license plates. There might be a surveillance camera on the street corner tracking your movements. At the airport you may be put through your paces by government agents who will want to either pat you down or run scans of your body. And each time you make a call or send a text message, your communications will most likely be logged and stored in a government file. When you return home, you might find that government agents have been aggressively questioning your neighbors about you as part of a "census" questionnaire. After you retire to sleep, you might find yourself awakened by a SWAT team crashing through your door (you'll later discover they were at the wrong address), and if you make the mistake of reaching for your eyeglasses, you might find yourself shot by a cop who felt threatened.

Is this the behavior of a government that respects you? One that looks upon you as having inviolate rights? One that regards you as its employer, its master, its purpose for being?

I don't think so.

A Wolf in Sheep's Clothing

While this transformation of the government into a hyper-militarized, twitchy, easily offended, suspicious, locked down, paranoid, all-seeing bureaucracy is being sold to the public as an unavoidable means of preventing terrorism and maintaining national security, it is little more than a wolf in sheep's clothing. In fact, what we are dealing with is a police state disguised as a benevolent democracy, a run-away government hyped up on its own power and afraid of its citizenry, whose policies are dictated more by paranoia, power, and control than need.

When one considers the growing list of opinions and activities which may make a federal agent or local police officer think you're a terrorist, or sympathetic to terrorist activities—advocating states' rights, believing the state to be unnecessary or undesirable, "conspiracy theorizing," concern about alleged FEMA camps, opposition to war,[2] organizing for "economic justice,"[3] frustration with "mainstream ideologies," opposition to globalization, and, ironically, ammunition stockpiling[4]—the picture becomes that much more alarming.

By the time you throw into the mix a variety of military-police training exercises that are occurring across the country, ostensibly to "train" first responders to deal with emergency situations and social unrest but overtly targeting American citizens, then it becomes that

SWAT Team members prepare for a drill.
(Source: Oregon Department of Transportation)

much harder to answer "no" when asked to consider whether "we the people" have become the enemies of our own government.[5]

Why is this happening? When did we as a nation take such a wrong turn onto such treacherous terrain? Who or what is responsible for our steady slide into tyranny? Where do we go from here? And what, if anything, can we do about it?

Here's the problem as I see it: "We the people" have become so trusting, so gullible, so easily distracted, so out-of-touch and so sure that our government will always do the right thing by us that we have ignored the warning signs all around us. In so doing, we have failed to recognize them as potential red flags to use as opportunities to ask questions, demand answers, and hold our government officials accountable to respecting our rights and abiding by the rule of law.

Unfortunately, once a free people allows the government to make inroads into their freedoms, or uses those same freedoms as bargaining chips for security, it quickly becomes a slippery slope to outright tyranny. And it doesn't really matter whether it's a Democrat or a Republican at the helm, because the bureaucratic mindset on both sides of the aisle now seems to embody the same philosophy of authoritarian government.

The Future Is Now

It doesn't take a weatherman to realize when a storm is brewing: clouds gather, the wind begins to blow, and trees bend as their leaves are violently tossed in the air. It's the same way with freedom. The warning signs are everywhere. They're staring us in the face. Sadly, most seem unaware of this, or they are all too content to attend to the daily grind and bow before the great pacifier (a.k.a. television) or stare endlessly into their cell phones, laptops, and other electronic distraction gadgets. "Who needs repression," declares philosopher Slavoj Zizek, "when one can convince the chicken to walk freely into the slaughterhouse."6 However, we have no excuse. The tentacles of the police state are now all around us. We only have to open our eyes and see through the lens of truth.

As you will see in the pages to follow, writers such as Aldous Huxley, George Orwell, Ray Bradbury, and Philip K. Dick and filmmakers such as François Truffaut, Stanley Kubrick, Ridley Scott, the Wachowski Brothers, Neill Blomkamp, John Carpenter, and others have been predicting our present state of affairs for years. They saw the lockdown coming. They predicted that freedom would fall, and how, and when.

Some of these literary and cinematic prophets were chillingly accurate: In 1932 Huxley's *Brave New World* prophesized mood-enhancing drugs and genetic engineering. Several decades later in 1950, antidepressants were first popularized to the masses, and in 1972 the first DNA manipulation was announced.7 Bradbury's *Fahrenheit 451* (1948) envisioned a world in which people were tuned into TVs and tuned out to each other. Decades later, iPods, cellphones, and earbuds would take the world by storm.8 Orwell's *1984* (1948) warned against a world in which the government spies on its citizens. It would take us only about sixty-five years to realize he was right.9

As uncanny as these "Nostradamuses" might seem, however, they were not so much attempting to foretell the future as they were documenting their concerns about their own place and time. For example, when Orwell and Huxley penned their masterpieces, they did so as commentaries on the rise of a controlling, manipulative scientific establishment, as well as the dangers of totalitarianism in the 1930s and 40s. That their dire extrapolations about the future have proven to be so accurate is less a reflection of their skills as fortunetellers as it is our unmitigated failure to heed their warnings.10

Likewise, if we fail to take notice of the alarm bells being sounded by contemporary writers, filmmakers, and activists, we will have only ourselves to blame when freedom falls.

Welcome to the Police State

Law enforcement officers block a downtown street during a protest in Tampa, Florida.
(Photography by Associated Press)

"This is not a new world: It is simply an extension of what began in the old one. It has patterned itself after every dictator who has ever planted the ripping imprint of a boot on the pages of history since the beginning of time. It has refinements, technological advancements, and a more sophisticated approach to the destruction of human freedom. But like every one of the super states that preceded it, it has one iron rule: Logic is an enemy, and truth is a menace."[1]—ROD SERLING, *The Twilight Zone*

How do you get a nation to docilely accept a police state? How do you persuade a populace to accept metal detectors and pat downs in their schools, bag searches in their train stations, tanks and military weaponry used by their small town police forces, surveillance cameras on their traffic lights, police strip searches on their public roads, unwarranted and forced blood draws at drunk driving checkpoints, whole body scanners in their airports, and government agents monitoring their communications?

Try to ram such a state of affairs down their throats, and you might find yourself with a rebellion on your hands. Instead, you bombard the citizenry with constant color-coded alerts, terrorize them with reports of shootings and bomb threats in malls, schools, and sports arenas, desensitize them with a steady diet of police violence, and mesmerize them with entertainment spectacles (what the Romans used to refer to as "bread and circus" distractions) and electronic devices, while selling the whole package to them as being in their best interests.

And when leaders like John F. Kennedy,[2] Martin Luther King Jr.,[3] John Lennon,[4] and others rise up who dare to challenge the government elite, what happens to them? Government agents carry out surveillance on them, intimidate them, threaten them, and in some cases cause them to "disappear," knowing full well that few will rise up to take their place.

Likewise, when government whistleblowers, lacking followers or name recognition, rise up and shine a spotlight on the government's misdeeds, they are labeled traitors, isolated from their friends and loved ones, and made examples of: this is what happens to those who dare to challenge the police state.[5]

Fixing the Unfixable

What is most striking about the American police state is not the megacorporations running amok in the halls of Congress, the militarized police crashing through doors and shooting unarmed citizens, or the invasive surveillance regime which has come to dominate every aspect of our lives. No, what has been most disconcerting about the emergence of the American police state is the extent to which the citizenry appears content to passively wait for someone else to solve the nation's many problems.

Yet if we don't act soon, all that is in need of fixing will soon be unfixable, especially as it relates to the police state that becomes more entrenched with each passing day. By "police state," I am referring to more than a society overrun by the long arm of the police—federal, state, and local. I am referring to a society in which all aspects of a person's life are policed by government agents, one in which all citizens are suspects, their activities monitored and regulated, their movements tracked, their communications spied upon, and their lives, liberties, and pursuit of happiness dependent on the government's say-so.

That said, how can anyone be expected to "fix" what is broken without first understanding the lengths to which the government will go in order to accustom the American people to life in a police state? Why are millions of innocent Americans being spied on by government agents, as well as by their partners in the corporate world, when they've done nothing wrong? As noted by the Brookings Institution, "For the first time ever, it will become technologically and financially feasible for authoritarian governments to record nearly everything that is said or done within their borders—every phone conversation, electronic message, social media interaction, the movements of nearly every person and vehicle, and video from every street corner."[6]

Indeed, as the trend towards overcriminalization makes clear, it won't be long before average law-abiding Americans are breaking laws they didn't even know existed during the course of a routine day. The point, of course, is that while you may be oblivious to your so-called law-breaking—whether it was collecting rainwater to water your lawn, lighting a cigarette in the privacy of your home, or gathering with friends in your backyard for a Sunday evening Bible study—the government will know each and every transgression and use them against you when convenient.

We Are the Enemy

The outlook for civil liberties grows bleaker by the day, from the government's embrace of indefinite detention for U.S. citizens and armed surveillance drones flying overhead to warrantless surveillance of phone, email, and Internet communications and prosecutions of government whistle-blowers. Meanwhile, the homeland is ruled by a police-industrial complex, an extension of the America military empire. Everything that our founding fathers warned against—a standing army that would see American citizens as enemy combatants—is now the new norm. The government—local law enforcement now being extensions of the federal government—has trained its sights on the American people. We have become the enemy. And if it is true, as the military asserts, that the key to

Pictured: the Parrot AR.Drone 2.0. At least 30,000 drones are expected to occupy U.S. airspace by 2020. (Photographer: Nicolas Halftermeyer)

defeating an enemy is having the technological advantage, then "we the people" are at a severe disadvantage.

These troubling developments are the outward manifestations of an inner philosophical shift underway in how the government views not only the Constitution and the Bill of Rights but "we the people," as well. What this reflects is a move away from a government bound by the rule of law to one that seeks total control through the imposition of its own self-serving laws on the populace.

All the while, the American people remain largely oblivious to the looming threats to their freedoms, eager to be persuaded that the government can solve the problems that plague us, whether it is terrorism, an economic depression, an environmental disaster, or even a viral epidemic.

CHAPTER 3

A State of Martial Law

Police lock down Boston in the wake of the Boston Marathon bombing.
(Photography by Associated Press)

"Totalitarian paranoia runs deep in American society, and it now inhabits the highest levels of government. . . . Since the terrorist attacks of 9/11, America has succumbed to a form of historical amnesia fed by a culture of fear, militarization and precarity. Relegated to the dustbin of organized forgetting were the long-standing abuses carried out by America's intelligence agencies and the public's long-standing distrust of the FBI, government wiretaps and police actions that threatened privacy rights, civil liberties and those freedoms fundamental to a democracy."[1]—PROFESSOR HENRY GIROUX

Caught up in the televised drama of a military-style manhunt for the suspects in the 2013 Boston Marathon explosion, most Americans failed to realize that the world around them had been suddenly and jarringly shifted off its axis—that axis being the U.S. Constitution.

For those like me who have studied emerging police states, the sight of a city placed under martial law left us in a growing state of unease. Boston was, for all intents and purposes, locked down, its citizens under house arrest[2] (officials used the Orwellian phrase "shelter in place" to describe the mandatory lockdown[3]), military-style helicopters equipped with thermal imaging devices buzzing the skies,[4] tanks and armored vehicles on the streets,[5] and snipers perched on rooftops,[6] while thousands of black-garbed police swarmed the streets and SWAT teams carried out house-to-house searches[7] in search of two young bombing suspects.

These were no longer warning signs of a steadily encroaching police state.

The police state had arrived.

Dragging the People Along

Equally unnerving was the ease with which many Americans welcomed the citywide lockdown, the routine invasion of their privacy, and the dismantling of every constitutional right intended to serve as a bulwark against government abuses. Watching it unfold, I couldn't help but think of Nazi Field Marshal Hermann Goering's remarks during the Nuremberg trials. Goering noted:

> It is always a simple matter to drag people along whether it is a democracy, or a fascist dictatorship, or a parliament, or a communist dictatorship. Voice or no voice, the people can always be brought to the bidding of the leaders. This is easy. All you have to do is tell them they are being attacked, and denounce the pacifists for lack of patriotism and exposing the country to danger. It works the same in every country.[8]

As the events in Boston made clear, it does indeed work the same in every country. The same propaganda and police state tactics that worked for Adolf Hitler continue to be employed with great success in a post-9/11 America.

Whatever the threat to so-called security—whether it's rumored weapons of mass destruction, school shootings, alleged acts of terrorism, or a serial killer on the loose—it doesn't take much for the American people to march in lockstep with the government's dictates, even if

A woman carries a girl from their home as a SWAT team searching for a suspect in the Boston Marathon bombings enters the building in Watertown, Mass. (April 19, 2013). (Photography by Associated Press)

it means submitting to martial law, having their homes searched, and being stripped of their constitutional rights at a moment's notice.

"We agreed to give up most of our enumerated rights and civil liberties in exchange for a lot of hyper-patriotic tough talk, the promise of security and the freedom to go on sitting on our asses and consuming whatever the hell we wanted to," explained *Salon* journalist Andrew O'Hehir. "The fact is that whatever dignified private opinions you and I may hold, we did not do enough to stop it, and our constitutional rights are now deemed to be partial or provisional rather than absolute, do not necessarily apply to everyone, and can be revoked by the government at any time."[9]

From Boston to Ferguson to America

The difference between what happened in Boston in the wake of the 2013 Boston Marathon bombing and what took place a year later in August 2014, in Ferguson, Missouri, where residents took to the streets protesting a police shooting of an unarmed resident,[10] is not in the government's response but in the community's response.

SWAT team in camouflage on Ferguson streets (Photography by Jamelle Bouie)

While few Americans objected when the city of Boston was locked down and placed under quasi-martial law,[11] a year later many Americans seemed shocked at the tactics being employed to quell citizen unrest in Ferguson, Missouri. Nevertheless, if you compare the tactics and equipment used in both cities, there was little difference: both employed SWAT teams, armored personnel carriers, and men in camouflage pointing heavy artillery.[12]

In commenting on the chaos surrounding the events in Ferguson, journalist Will Bunch wrote:

> I thought I was losing my capacity to be shocked—but events in Missouri over just the last couple of hours have crossed a frightening line, one that makes me pray that this assault on fundamental American values is just the aberration of one rudderless Heartland community, and not the first symptoms of nation gone mad with high-tech weaponry to keep its own citizens in line.[13]

Unfortunately, this is what happens when you ignore the warning signs.

This is what happens when you fail to take alarm at the first experiment on your liberties.

This is what happens when you fail to challenge injustice and government overreach until the prison doors clang shut behind you.

Here's the problem: in the American police state that now surrounds us, there are no longer such things as innocence, due process, or justice—at least, not in the way we once knew them. We are all potentially guilty, all potential criminals, all suspects waiting to be accused of a crime.

CHAPTER 4

The Dismal State of Our Freedoms

"What the government is good at is collecting taxes, taking away your freedoms and killing people. It's not good at much else."[1]—Author TOM CLANCY

Imagine living in a country where armed soldiers crash through doors to arrest and imprison citizens merely for criticizing government officials. Imagine that in this very same country, you're watched all the time, and if you look even a little bit suspicious, the police stop and frisk you or pull you over to search you on the off-chance you're doing something illegal. Keep in mind that if you have a firearm of any kind while in this country, it may get you arrested or, worse, shot and killed by agents of the government.

If you're thinking this sounds like America today, you wouldn't be far wrong. However, the scenario described above took place more than two hundred years ago, when American colonists suffered under Britain's prenatal version of a police state. It was only when the colonists got fed up with being silenced, censored, searched, frisked, threatened, and arrested that they finally revolted against the tyrant's fetters.

Any attempt to understand the dismal state of our freedoms in the present day must start with an understanding of where it all began.

The Founding "Terrorists"?

No document better states the colonists' grievances than the Declaration of Independence. A document seething with outrage over a government that had abused those in its care, the Declaration of Independence was signed on July 4, 1776, by fifty-six men who laid everything on the line and pledged it all—"our Lives, our Fortunes, and our sacred Honor"—because they believed in a radical idea: that all people are created to be free.

Had the Declaration of Independence been written today, it would have rendered its signers terrorists, resulting in them being placed on a government watch list, targeted for surveillance of their activities and correspondence, and potentially arrested, held indefinitely, stripped of their rights and labeled enemy combatants. (Illustration by Caroline Jonik)

Branded traitors, these men were charged with treason, a crime punishable by death. For some, their acts of rebellion would cost them their homes and their fortunes. For others, it would be the ultimate price. Yet even knowing the heavy price they might have to pay, these men dared to speak up when silence could not be tolerated. Even after they had won their independence from Great Britain, these new Americans worked to ensure that the rights they had risked their lives for would remain secure for future generations. The result: the Bill of Rights, the first ten amendments to the Constitution.

Imagine the shock and outrage our forefathers would feel were they to discover that some two hundred years later, the government they had created has been transformed into a militaristic police state in which exercising one's freedoms is often viewed as a flagrant act of defiance.

Indeed, had the Declaration of Independence been written today, it would have rendered its signers terrorists, resulting in them being placed on a government watch list, targeted for surveillance of their activities and correspondence, and potentially arrested, held indefinitely, stripped of their rights, and labeled enemy combatants.

The True State of Our Freedoms

A cursory review of the true state of our freedoms as outlined in the Bill of Rights shows exactly how dismal things have become:

The *First Amendment* is supposed to protect the freedom to speak your mind and protest in peace without being bridled by the government. It also protects the freedom of the media, as well as the right to worship and pray without interference. In other words, Americans cannot be silenced by the government. Yet despite the clear protections found in the First Amendment, the freedoms described therein are under constant assault. Whether it's a Marine detained for criticizing the government on Facebook,[2] a reporter persecuted for refusing to reveal his sources,[3] or a protester arrested for standing silently in front of the U.S. Supreme Court,[4] these are dangerous times for those who choose to exercise their right to free speech.

The *Second Amendment* was intended to guarantee "the right of the people to keep and bear arms." Yet while gun *ownership* has been recognized as an individual citizen right, Americans continue to face an uphill battle in the courts when it comes to defending themselves against militarized, weaponized government agents armed to the hilt. In fact, court rulings in recent years have affirmed that citizens don't have the right to resist police officers who enter their homes illegally, mistakenly, or otherwise.[5]

The *Third Amendment* reinforces the principle that civilian-elected officials are superior to the military by prohibiting the military from entering any citizen's home without "the consent of the owner." Unfortunately, the wall of separation between civilian and military policing has been torn down in recent years, as militarized SWAT teams are now allowed to burst into homes unannounced in order to investigate minor crimes such as marijuana possession[6] and credit card fraud.[7] With domestic police increasingly posing as military forces—complete with weapons, uniforms, assault vehicles, etc.—a good case could be made for the fact that SWAT team raids constitute the forced quartering of soldiers within the private home, which the Third Amendment was written to prevent.

The *Fourth Amendment* prohibits government agents from touching you or placing you under surveillance or entering your property without probable cause and, even then, only with a court-sanctioned warrant. Unfortunately, the Fourth Amendment has been all but eviscerated in recent years by court rulings and government programs that sanction all manner of intrusions. As a result, police now have carte blanche authority to break into homes or apartments without a warrant, conduct roadside strip searches, and generally manhandle the citizenry as they see fit. Moreover, in the so-called name of "national security," intelligence agencies like the National Security Agency (NSA) now have the ability to conduct mass unwarranted electronic intrusions into the personal and private transactions of all Americans, including phone, mail, computer, and medical records.[8] All of this data is available to other government agencies, including local police.

The *Fifth Amendment* is supposed to ensure that you are presumed innocent until proven guilty, and government authorities cannot deprive you of your life, your liberty, or your property without following strict legal guidelines. Unfortunately, those protections have been largely extinguished in recent years, especially in the wake of Congress's passage of the National Defense Authorization Act (NDAA), which allows the president and the military to arrest and imprison Americans indefinitely without due process.[9]

Protesters take issue with the NDAA's indefinite detention provision. (Source: RT)

The *Sixth Amendment* was intended to not only ensure a "speedy and public trial," but it was supposed to prevent the government from keeping someone in jail for unspecified offenses. That too has been a casualty of the so-called war on terror. Between the NDAA's indefinite detention clause and the Authorization for Use of Military Force (AUMF) legislation, which has been used to justify killing American citizens with drones in the absence of a court trial,[10] the Sixth Amendment's guarantees become meaningless.

The *Seventh Amendment* guarantees citizens the right to a jury trial. However, when the populace has no idea what's in the Constitution—civic education has virtually disappeared from most school curriculums[11]—that inevitably translates to an ignorant jury incapable of distinguishing justice and the law from their own preconceived notions and fears.

The *Eighth Amendment* is similar to the Sixth in that it is supposed to protect the rights of the accused and forbid the use of cruel and unusual punishment. However, the Supreme Court's determination that what constitutes "cruel and unusual" should be dependent on the "evolving standards of decency that mark the progress of a maturing society"[12] leaves us with scant protection in the face of a government elite lacking in morals altogether. America's continued reliance on the death penalty, which has been shown to be flawed in its application and execution, is a perfect example of this.[13]

The *Ninth Amendment* provides that other rights not enumerated in the Constitution are nonetheless retained by the people. Popular sovereignty—the belief that the power to govern flows upward from the people rather than downward from the rulers—is clearly evident in this amendment. However, it has since been turned on its head by a centralized federal government that sees itself as supreme and which continues to pass more and more laws that restrict our freedoms under the pretext that it has an "important government interest" in doing so. Thus, once the government began violating the non-enumerated rights granted in the Ninth Amendment, it was only a matter of time before it began to trample the enumerated rights of the people, as explicitly spelled out in the rest of the Bill of Rights.

As for the *Tenth Amendment*'s reminder that the people and the states retain every authority not otherwise mentioned in the Constitution, that assurance of a system of government in which power is divided among local, state, and national entities has long since been rendered moot by the centralized Washington, DC, power elite: the president, Congress and the courts. Indeed, the federal governmental bureaucracy has grown so large that it has made local and state legislatures relatively irrelevant. Through its many agencies, the federal government has stripped states of the right to regulate countless issues that were originally governed at the local level.

Brief Reprieves

Sadly, even on those rare occasions when the courts provide us with a slight glimmer of hope that all may not be lost, those brief reprieves of judicial sensibility are quickly overwhelmed by a bureaucratic machine that continues to march relentlessly in lockstep with the American police state.

CHAPTER 5

Waking Up to Reality

"The Secret Government is an interlocking network of official functionaries, spies, mercenaries, ex-generals, profiteers and superpatriots, who, for a variety of motives, operate outside the legitimate institutions of government. Presidents have turned to them when they can't win the support of the Congress or the people, creating that unsupervised power so feared by the framers of our Constitution. ..."[1]

—BILL MOYERS, journalist and White House press secretary
under President Johnson (1988)

Professor Jacques Ellul, writing years ago, argued that we appear to be living in what he called the "illusion of freedom."[2] An illusion, as everyone knows, is something that is not based on reality. As more and more Americans are coming to realize, freedom—true freedom, as we once knew it—is increasingly an illusion.

Consider the following a wake-up call to the reality of life in the American police state:

Americans no longer have any protection against police abuse. It is no longer unusual to hear about incidents in which police shoot unarmed individuals first and ask questions later, such as the 16-year-old teenager who skipped school only to be shot by police after they allegedly mistook him for a fleeing burglar.[3] Then there was the unarmed man in Texas "who was pursued and shot in the back of the neck by Austin Police ... after failing to properly identify himself and leaving the scene of an unrelated incident."[4] A 19-year-old Seattle woman was accidentally shot in the leg by police after she refused to show her hands.[5] What is becoming equally commonplace is the news that the officers involved in these incidents get off with little more than a reprimand.

Americans are no longer innocent until proven guilty. Due in large part to rapid advances in technology and a heightened surveillance culture, the burden of proof has been shifted so that the right to be considered innocent until proven guilty has been usurped by a new norm in which all citizens are suspects. This is exemplified by police practices of stopping and frisking people who are merely walking down the street and where there is no evidence of wrongdoing.[6] Likewise, by subjecting Americans to full-body scans[7] and license-plate readers[8] without their knowledge or compliance and then storing the scans for later use, the government—in cahoots with the corporate state—has erected the ultimate suspect society or, more aptly, the police industrial complex. In such an environment, we are all potentially guilty of some wrongdoing or other.

Americans are powerless in the face of militarized police. In early America, citizens were considered equals with law enforcement officials. Authorities were rarely permitted to enter one's home without permission or in a deceitful manner. And it was not uncommon for

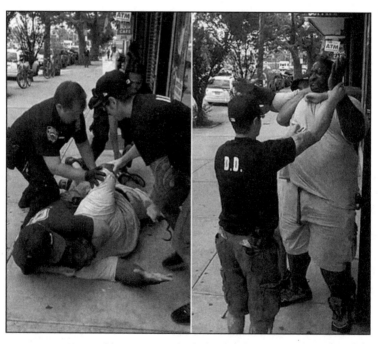

43-year-old Eric Garner died after being placed in a chokehold by New York police officers, allegedly for selling loose cigarettes.

police officers to be held personally liable for trespass when they wrongfully invaded a citizen's home. Unlike today, early Americans could resist arrest when a police officer tried to restrain them without proper justification or a warrant—which, of course, the police had to allow citizens to read before arresting them. (Daring to dispute a warrant with a police official today who is armed with high-tech military weapons and tasers would be nothing short of suicidal.) As police forces across the country acquire military-grade hardware in droves,[9] Americans are finding their once-peaceful communities transformed into military outposts, complete with tanks, weaponry, and other equipment designed for the battlefield.

Ripped Off and Victimized?

Americans are little more than pocketbooks to fund the police state. If there is any absolute maxim by which the government seems to operate, it is that the American taxpayer always gets ripped off. This is true, whether you're talking about taxpayers being forced to fund high-priced weaponry that will be used against us, endless wars that do little for our safety or our freedoms, or bloated government agencies such as the Department of Homeland Security and the NSA with its secret budgets, covert agendas, and clandestine activities. Rubbing salt in the wound, even monetary awards in lawsuits against government officials who are found guilty of wrongdoing are paid by the taxpayer.[10]

In reality, Americans no longer have a right to self-defense. In the wake of various shootings in recent years, "gun control" has become a resounding theme for government officials, with President Obama even going so far as to pledge to reduce gun violence "with or without Congress."[11] Those advocating gun reform see the Second Amendment's right to bear arms as applying only to government officials. As a result, even Americans who legally own firearms are being treated with suspicion and, in some cases, undue violence. In one case, a Texas man had his home subjected to a no-knock raid and was shot in his bed after police, attempting to deliver a routine search warrant, learned that he was in legal possession of a firearm.[12] In another incident, a Florida man who was licensed to carry a concealed firearm found himself detained for two hours during a routine traffic stop in Maryland while the arresting officer searched his vehicle in vain for the man's gun, which he had left at home.[13]

Americans no longer have a right to private property. If government agents can invade your home, break down your doors, kill your dog, damage your furnishings and terrorize your family, your property is no longer private and secure—it belongs to the government. Likewise, if government officials can fine and arrest you for praying with friends in your living room, living off the grid by collecting rainwater and solar energy on your own property, and growing vegetables in your front yard, you're no longer the owner of your property.

Americans no longer have a say about what their children are exposed to in school. Incredibly, the government continues to insist that parents essentially forfeit their rights when they send their children to a public school. This growing tension over whether young people, especially those in the public schools, are wards of the state, to do with as government officials deem appropriate, in defiance of the children's constitutional rights and those of their parents, is reflected in the debate over sex education programs that expose young people to all manner of sexual practices and terminology,[14] zero tolerance policies that strip students of any due process rights, let alone parental involvement in school discipline, and Common Core programs that teach students to be test-takers rather than critical thinkers.

Danger Ahead

Americans can no longer rely on the courts to mete out justice. The U.S. Supreme Court was intended to be an institution established to intervene and protect the people against the government and its agents when they overstep their bounds. Yet through their deference to various government agents, including local police, preference for security over freedom, and evisceration of our most basic rights for the sake of order and expediency, the justices of the Supreme Court have become the architects of the American police state in which we now live, while the lower courts have appointed themselves courts of order, concerned primarily with advancing the government's agenda, no matter how unjust or illegal.

Americans no longer have a right to bodily integrity. Court rulings undermining the Fourth Amendment and justifying invasive strip searches have left us powerless against police empowered to forcefully draw our blood,[15] strip search us,[16] and probe us intimately.[17] Accounts are on the rise of individuals—men and women—being subjected to what is essentially government-sanctioned rape by police in the course of "routine" traffic stops. A New Mexico man was subjected to a twelve-hour ordeal of anal probes, X-rays, enemas, and finally a colonoscopy because he allegedly rolled through a stop sign.[18]

Americans no longer have a right to the expectation of privacy. Despite the staggering number of revelations about government spying on Americans' phone calls, Facebook posts, Twitter tweets, Google searches, emails, bookstore and grocery purchases, bank statements, commuter toll records, and so forth, Congress, the president, and the courts have done little or nothing to counteract these abuses. Instead, the government overseers seem determined to accustom us to life in this electronic concentration camp.

As a result of the increasing militarization of the police in recent years, the police now not only look like the military but they function like them, as well.
(Source: California Highway Patrol)

Moreover, whether you're talking about police shootings of unarmed individuals, NSA surveillance, drones taking to the skies domestically, SWAT team raids, or roadside strip searches, they're all part of a totalitarian continuum—the mile markers on this common road we're traveling towards the police state.

The sign before us reads "Danger Ahead." What remains to be seen is whether we can put the brakes on and safely reverse direction before it's too late to turn back.

CHAPTER 6

Fascism American Style

"I am afraid of those who proclaim that it can't happen here. In 1935 Sinclair Lewis wrote a popular novel in which a racist, anti-Semitic, flag-waving, army-backed demagogue wins the 1936 presidential election and proceeds to establish an Americanized version of Nazi Germany. The title, *It Can't Happen Here*, was a tongue-in-cheek warning that it might. But the "it" Lewis referred to is unlikely to happen again any place. ... Anyone looking for black shirts, mass parties, or men on horseback will miss the tell-tale clues of creeping fascism. ... In America, it would be super modern and multi-ethnic—as American as Madison Avenue, executive luncheons, credit cards, and apple pie. It would be fascism with a smile. As a warning against its cosmetic façade, subtle manipulation, and velvet gloves, I call it friendly fascism. What scares me most is its subtle appeal."[1]

—BERTRAM GROSS, former presidential advisor

"Fascism, like socialism, cannot achieve its aim. So there is a way in which it makes sense to speak of a stage of history: We are in the stage of late fascism. The grandeur is gone, and all we are left with is a gun pointed at our heads. The system was created to be great, but it is reduced in our time to being crude. Valor is now violence. Majesty is now malice."[2]

—Author LLEWELLYN H. ROCKWELL, JR.

The United States of America, that dream of what a democracy ought to be, is no more.

We have moved beyond the era of representative government and entered a new age. Let's call it the age of authoritarianism. History may show that from this point forward, we will have left behind any semblance of constitutional government and entered into a militaristic state where all citizens are suspects and security trumps freedom.

Fascism, like most political shifts in history, does not scream, "I'm here." Its ascension is very subtle and incremental. (Illustration by W. B. Park)

Even with its constantly shifting terrain, this topsy-turvy travesty of law and government has become America's new normal. And it's not overstating matters to say that Congress, which has done its best to keep their unhappy constituents at a distance, may well be the most self-serving, corrupt institution in America.

Economic Elites

The results of an in-depth 2014 study of government policies conducted by Princeton and Northwestern University concluded that the U.S. government does not represent the majority of American citizens. Instead, the study found that the government is ruled by the rich and powerful, or the so-called "economic elite." As the study states:

> The central point that emerges from our research is that economic elites and organized groups representing business interests have substantial independent impacts on U.S. government policy, while mass-based interest groups and average citizens have little or no independent influence.[3]

Moreover, the researchers concluded that policies enacted by this governmental elite rarely align with the preferences of the majority of Americans. Instead, they favor special interests and lobbying groups who, of course, virtually live in the halls of Congress:

> When a majority of citizens disagrees with economic elites and/or with organized interest, they generally lose. Moreover, because of the strong status quo bias built into the U.S. political system, even when fairly large majorities of Americans favor policy change, they generally do not get it.[4]

Wait a minute. We are indoctrinated in school and by the politicians to believe that America is a government "of the people, by the people and for the people." Is this not true? Have we been hoodwinked? And if it's not *our* government, then whose government is it?

A Syzygy

We must remember history. Following World War II, President Dwight D. Eisenhower expressed grave concerns about an emerging military-industrial complex in his 1961 farewell address to the nation.[5] His concern was that powerful industrial and corporate business interests were coalescing into a new form of government that would eventually be known as the corporate state. "The corporate state, American style, exemplifies a politico-legal form of syzygy," observed constitutional law professor Arthur Miller as early as the mid-1970s.[6] Over time, this syzygy—the conjunction of two organisms without either of them losing its identity—has developed beyond what Miller could have imagined.

In fact, while most of us were going about the daily routine of work, family, and leisure time, Big Business invaded the halls of Congress, the courts, and the White House. It was a silent coup, so to speak, and the result was a fusion of government and corporate interests—a syzygy— where profit, control, and the elite began to reap the benefits and rule.

This type of rule was at first called "corporatism," meaning that vast sectors of the economy, government, and politics would be managed by private business concerns. It's what is called "privatization" today by various government politicians. And, believe it or not, it was championed initially by Italian fascist Benito Mussolini and later by Adolf Hitler.[7]

Corporatism, as the studies indicate, is where the few moneyed interests—not elected by the citizenry—rule over the many. In this way, it is not a democracy or a republican form of government, which is what the American government was established to be. It is a top-down form of government and one which has a terrifying history typified by the developments that occurred in Nazi Germany: a police state culture where everyone is watched and spied on, rounded up for minor infractions by government agents, placed under police control, and placed in detention (a.k.a. concentration) camps.

If we open our eyes and minds to see the truth, we might just learn "to see dictatorship in democracy," as philosopher Slavoj Zizek recognizes.[8]

Friendly Fascism?

Years ago, William L. Shirer, author of *The Rise and Fall of the Third Reich*, observed that America may be the first country in which fascism comes to power through democratic elections.[9] When fascism finally takes hold in America, the basic forms of government will remain. That is its subtle appeal. It will appear to be friendly. The legislators will be in session. There will be elections, and the news media will continue to cover the entertainment and political trivia. Consent of the governed, however, will no longer apply. Actual control will have finally passed to the oligarchic elite controlling the government behind the scenes.

Occasionally, those who still believe in freedom will resist by daring to exercise their rights to speak out and protest. Of course, the militarized police will be there to crack a few skulls as a warning that this is not acceptable conduct in the New America.

The Obsolete State

The warning signs of any fascistic regime are there to those who are alert. They are hinted at on television programs, the Internet, and various so-called news resources. This includes those fiction writers and filmmakers who have been warning us for years that we are on the verge of a totalitarian regime.

One such writer was Rod Serling, the creator and writer of the celebrated *Twilight Zone* television series. I was fifteen years old when I saw for the first time a *Twilight Zone* segment that I could never forget entitled "The Obsolete Man."

Serling sets the episode in a futuristic society where all books and religion have been banned by a neo-Nazi state. Romney Wordsworth, a librarian and a man of faith, is judged obsolete by the Chancellor of the State and is sentenced to be executed in a manner of his choosing. Wordsworth, granted three last wishes, requests that only his assassin know the method of his death, that he die at midnight the next day, and that his death be televised. Forty-five minutes before he is to die, Wordsworth invites the Chancellor to his room and reveals that he has chosen to be killed by a bomb, which is set to explode at midnight. He then locks the door, imprisoning the Chancellor inside with him.

At first, aware that his every move is being televised, the Chancellor hides behind a veil of bravado. However, once he realizes that no one will be coming to save him because the nation is preoccupied watching this "reality" show, the Chancellor's cool begins to unravel. While Wordsworth calmly reads aloud a passage from the Bible, the minutes slowly tick by. Still no one comes to rescue the Chancellor from his predicament. Finally the Chancellor cries out, "In the name of God, let me out!" Wordsworth hands the Chancellor the key, and he flees

Photo of Burgess Meredith as Romney Wordsworth from the television program *The Twilight Zone*. The episode is "The Obsolete Man."

the room. Within seconds, the bomb explodes, blowing Wordsworth to smithereens.

When the Chancellor returns to his court, he is judged obsolete for his loss of composure and plea in the name of an outlawed God. Wordsworth in death is victorious.

This episode ends, as always, with a voiceover by Rod Serling:

> The Chancellor, the late Chancellor, was only partly correct. He was obsolete, but so is the State, the entity he worshipped. Any state, any entity, any ideology that fails to recognize the worth, the dignity, the rights of man, that state is obsolete.[10]

CHAPTER 7

We Hired Hitler!

"If you want a picture of the future, imagine a boot stamping on a human face—forever ... And remember that it is forever. The face will always be there to be stamped upon. The heretic, the enemy of society, will always be there, so that he can be defeated and humiliated over again."[1]

—George Orwell, *1984*

"The very first essential for success is a perpetually constant and regular employment of violence."[2]

—Adolf Hitler, *Mein Kampf*

Fascism, like most political shifts in history, does not scream, "I'm here." Its ascension is very subtle and incremental.

Indeed, fascism does not seek to overthrow the major institutions of society such as businesses and commercial establishments, family, religious centers, and civic traditions.[3] It seeks to control them and the social order by "celebrating it, uplifting it, centralizing it, cartelizing it, politicizing it, and using it in the glorification of a central father figure who makes them work together toward the unified goal of building the greatness of the national identity and mission."[4]

Thus, the lure of fascism is the "planned society." And by preserving that which was politically valued by the masses, fascism presents the illusion that it does not somehow destroy democratic traditions but rather provides "a new and more scientific way of managing national life."[5]

Of course, this is fascism's appeal to the middle and corporate classes and the reason it is tolerated and even venerated by the religious establishments.[6] Fascism is generally lauded—at first, that is—for bringing all institutions under government control and because it promises financial prosperity and an array of civic and cultural improvements. As author Jeffrey Tucker argues:

> The *New York Times* profiled Benito Mussolini as a genius of central planning. Churchill praised him as the man of the hour. Fascist theorists wrote for American books and were lovingly interviewed by all the major journals. Even as late as 1941, *Harper's Magazine* was praising the glories of "the German financial revolution" and the magic of the fascist system.[7]

Think of this: by 1941, the German concentration camps were in full swing and known by the world. Germany was also on the cusp of a major world war because of its aggressive, imperialistic tendencies. At the same time, Germany was being praised for its fascist "financial revolution." What?

Contrary to public opinion today, within his own time, Hitler enjoyed great popularity and was admired as a genius by various Western leaders and rode in on the coat tails of the major corporate and business concerns.

By creating the illusion that it preserves democratic traditions, fascism creeps slowly until it consumes the political system. And in times of "crisis," expediency is upheld as the central principle—that is, in order to keep us safe and secure, the government must militarize the police, strip us of basic constitutional rights and criminalize virtually every form of behavior. Pictured: Meeting of Adolf Hitler and Benito Mussolini in Stepina (Aug. 27, 1941).

In fact, in the midst of the German depression in the early 1930s, Hitler, the only nationalist with a mass following, rose to the top of the political system by promising full employment and prosperity. As former presidential advisor Bertram Gross explains:

> Privately meeting with the largest industrialists, he [Hitler] warned, "Private enterprise cannot be maintained in a democracy." On January 30, 1933, he was invited to serve as a chancellor of a coalition cabinet. "We hired Hitler!" a conservative leader reported to a business magnate.[8]

From there, Hitler rose to the top.

Backing the Regime

The Nazi regime came into power in one of the most culturally advanced countries of its time. German art, film, painting, and writing were not only influential in their own time; they still cast a shadow on modern art today. However, the German people were not oblivious to the concentration camps that dotted the landscape. In fact, media reports concerning the concentration camps flooded the country. As professor Robert Gellately writes:

> [A]nyone in Nazi Germany who wanted to find out about the Gestapo, the concentration camps, and the campaigns of discrimination and persecutions need only read the newspapers. Nazi Germany was in fact a modern media society, and for its day was in the vanguard of modernity.... [M]oreover Hitler's regime did everything possible to put a radio·in every home, and used newsreels and movies to get across their messages.[9]

The warning signs were definitely there—incessantly blinking like large neon signs. "Still," Gellately writes, "the vast majority voted in favor of Nazism, and in spite of what they could read in the press and hear by word of mouth about the secret police, the concentration camps, official anti-Semitism, and so on.... [T]here is no getting away from the fact that at that moment, 'the vast majority of the German people backed him.'"[10]

Incredibly, a half-century later, the wife of a prominent German historian, neither of whom were members of the Nazi party, opined: "[O]n the whole, everyone felt well.... And there were certainly eighty

Within his own time, Adolf Hitler enjoyed great popularity and rode in on the coat tails of the major corporate and business concerns. Pictured: Adolf Hitler is greeted by an admiring throng (Aug. 27, 1941).

percent who lived productively and positively throughout the time. ... We also had good years. We had *wonderful* years."[11]

Even various leaders from across the world became enamored with the rise of the Nazi state. When invitations were sent out to police agencies worldwide as a way of showing off the modernity of German police, among those who accepted was Edmund Patrick Coffey, an assistant to J. Edgar Hoover of the FBI. During his 1938 visit, Coffey visited various police facilities, and expressed his "great pleasure" about the work of the German police. He hoped that Hoover would visit during the following summer. The "Nazi police," as Gellately notes, "had won the FBI's seal of approval."[12]

Indeed, so impressed was the FBI with the Nazi order that, as the *New York Times* revealed, in the decades after World War II the FBI, along with other government agencies, aggressively recruited at least a thousand Nazis, including some of Hitler's highest henchmen, brought them to America, hired them on as spies and informants, and then carried out a massive cover-up campaign to ensure that their true identities and ties to Hitler's holocaust machine would remain unknown. Moreover, anyone who dared to blow the whistle on the FBI's illicit

Nazi ties found himself spied upon, intimidated, harassed, and labeled a threat to national security.[13]

Fascism Anyone?

By creating the illusion that it preserves democratic traditions, fascism creeps slowly until it consumes the political system. And in times of "crisis," expediency is upheld as the central principle—that is, in order to keep us safe and secure, the government must militarize the police, strip us of basic constitutional rights and criminalize virtually every form of behavior. And then there are the prisons to house all of us nonviolent criminals.

What we must come to terms with is whether America could eventually evolve into a fascist state. After all, there are clear indications that we are now ruled by an oligarchic elite of governmental and corporate interests, but are we there yet?

The following are a few of the necessary ingredients for a fascist state:

★ The government is managed by a powerful leader (even if he or she assumes office by way of the electoral process). This is the fascistic leadership principle (or father figure).

★ The government assumes it is not restrained in its power. This is authoritarianism, which eventually evolves into totalitarianism.

★ The government ostensibly operates under a capitalist system while being undergirded by an immense bureaucracy.[14]

★ The government through its politicians emits powerful and continuing expressions of nationalism.

★ The government has an obsession with national security while constantly invoking terrifying internal and external enemies.

★ The government establishes a domestic and invasive surveillance system and develops a paramilitary force that is not answerable to the citizenry.

★ The government and its various agencies (federal, state, and local) develop an obsession with crime and punishment. This is overcriminalization.

★ The government becomes increasingly centralized while aligning closely with corporate powers to control all aspects of the country's social, economic, military, and governmental structures.[15]

★ The government uses militarism as a center point of its economic and taxing structure.

★ The government is increasingly imperialistic in order to maintain the military-industrial corporate forces.[16]

Do you get the drift? Just look around at modern government policies. "Every industry is regulated. Every profession is classified and organized," writes Jeffrey Tucker. "Every good or service is taxed. Endless debt accumulation is preserved. Immense doesn't begin to describe the bureaucracy. Military preparedness never stops, and war with some evil foreign foe, remains a daily prospect."[17] In other words, the government in America today does whatever it wants.

Does this sound like a republic, a democracy, or a proto-fascistic form of government? It doesn't take a political scientist to recognize that there are ominous parallels to past dictatorial or fascist regimes in America today.

Pathocracy

Curiously, those at the helm of totalitarian regimes—fascist states included—share many of the same behavior traits as psychopaths: cold-hearted, lacking in empathy, grandiose, manipulative, conning, unwilling to take responsibility for one's actions, and lacking in remorse. The two hallmarks of psychopathy are a calculating mind and a seemingly easy charm.[18]

In fact, psychopaths are peculiarly adept at politics. As James Silver writing for the *Atlantic* recognizes:

> Research has shown that disorder may confer certain advantages that make psychopaths particularly suited for life on the public stage and able to handle high pressure situations: psychopaths score low on measures of stress reactivity, anxiety and depression, and high on measurers of competitive achievement, positive impressions on first encounters, and fearlessness. Sound like the description of a successful politician and leader?[19]

What is more startling is that such leaders eventually create pathocracies—totalitarian societies bent on power, control, and destruction of both freedom in general and those who exercise their freedoms.

Worse, this mental disease is not confined to those in high positions of government but can be spread to the populace. As author James G. Long recognizes: "Mental disorders among political leadership distort perceptions, attitudes, and actions among citizens."[20] And historically psychopaths have attracted large numbers of vulnerable followers.

Once psychopaths gain power, the result is usually some form of totalitarian government or a pathocracy. "At that point, the *government operates against the interests of its own people* except for favoring certain groups," Long notes. "We are currently witnessing deliberate polarizations of American citizens, illegal actions, and massive and needless acquisition of debt. This is typical of psychopathic systems, and very similar things happened in the Soviet Union as it overextended and collapsed."[21]

Does Fear Lead to Fascism?

For the final hammer of fascism to fall, it will require the most crucial ingredient: the majority of the people will have to agree that it's not only expedient but necessary. But why would a people agree to such an oppressive regime? The answer is the same in every age: fear.

Fear is the method most often used by politicians to increase the power of government. And, as most social commentators recognize, an atmosphere of fear permeates modern America: fear of terrorism, fear of the police, fear of our neighbors, and so on.

However, is such fear rational? After all, crime, as the FBI tell us, is at a forty-year low.[22]

Let's take terrorism, for starters. While it might seem to be a rational fear, the statistics from the National Security Council and the Census Bureau, among other federal agencies, say otherwise. For example: You are 17,600 times more likely to die from heart disease than from a terrorist attack. You are 11,000 times more likely to die from an airplane accident than from a terrorist plot involving an airplane. You are 1,048 times more likely to die from a car accident than a terrorist attack. You are 404 times more likely to die in a fall than from a terrorist attack.

You are 12 times more likely to die from accidental suffocating in bed than from a terrorist attack. You are 9 more times likely to choke to death in your own vomit than die in a terrorist attack. You are 8 times more likely to be killed by a police officer than by a terrorist.[23]

The list goes on and on. The point is that the government's endless jabbering about terrorism is propaganda—the propaganda of fear—and this has been used since time immemorial by those who want to gain control.

Of course there are crises which need to be met with appropriate remedies. However, with such low risks of terrorism, there is no reason for Americans to live their lives as if they'll be wiped out any moment by a terrorist. Sporadic acts of terrorism are meant to terrorize, to cower the population.

The physical limitation on freedom, as we have seen, is growing. But there's also a psychological factor involved that government propagandists are well aware of. The emotional panic that accompanies fear actually shuts down the prefrontal cortex or the rational thinking part of our brains. In other words, when we are consumed by fear, we stop thinking. "In this light, it should not be surprising that our public figures and our cause advocates often describe tragic outcomes," reports *Reason* magazine. "Rarely do we hear them quote probabilities."[24] The truth, as they say, be damned.

Loving Big Brother?

George Orwell understood all too well how fear could—and would—be used to manipulate the populace in so-called free societies into compliance. In his classic novel *Nineteen-Eighty Four*, Orwell describes a torture scene involving the resistor Winston Smith, who has an overwhelming fear of rats. O'Brien, his government interrogator, uses this bit of knowledge in attempting to force Smith to submit and convert his hatred of the government into an uncritical love of Big Brother.

O'Brien's plan, he tells Winston, is to strap a mask on his face that has a cage with rats in it. The rats, he says, will eventually be let loose on Winston's face. As O'Brien tells Winston:

The mask will fit over your head, leaving no exit. When I press this other lever, the door of the cage will slide up. These starving brutes will shoot out of it like bullets. Have you ever seen a rat leap through the air? They will leap onto your face and bore straight into it. Sometimes they attack the eyes first. Sometimes they burrow through the cheeks and devour the tongue."[25]

As O'Brien moves the cage nearer to Winston's face, Winston goes into a spastic state of panic and fear. "The rats were coming now.... Winston could see the whiskers and the yellow teeth. Again the blank panic took hold of him. He was blind, helpless, and mindless."[26] Winston, the unrepentant resistor, was now fading. "For an instant he was insane, a screaming animal."[27]

Will Winston break? Will he love Big Brother? Will he alter his view of reality? Will he "rat" out Julia, his only true friend? The mask inches closer to Winston's face. "The wire brushed his cheek. And then—no, it was not relief, only hope, a tiny fragment of hope. Too late, perhaps too late, but he had suddenly understood that in the whole world there was just *one* person to whom he could transfer his punishment—*one* body that he could thrust between himself and the rats."[28]

That is when Winston began shouting, frantically shouting, over and over: "Do it to Julia! Do it to Julia! Not me! Julia! I don't care what you do to her. Tear her face off, strip her to the bones. Not me! Julia! Not me!"[29]

In the totalitarian future at our doorsteps, the futuristic technologies once reserved for movie blockbusters such as drones, tasers, and biometric scanners will be used by the government to track, target and control the populace, especially dissidents. ("Big Brother Is Watching You" illustration by Frederic Guimont)

George Orwell understood all too well how fear could—and would—be used to manipulate the populace in so-called free societies into compliance.

This scenario presented by Orwell is nothing new. It has been implemented in past fascistic regimes, and it now operates in our contemporary world—all of which raises fundamental questions about us as human beings and what we will give up in order to perpetuate the illusions of safety and security. In the words of psychologist Erich Fromm:

> [C]an human nature be changed in such a way that man will forget his longing for freedom, for dignity, for integrity, for love—that is to say, can man forget he is human? Or does human nature have a dynamism which will react to the violation of these basic human needs by attempting to change an inhuman society into a human one?[30]

"Never in the civilised world have so many been locked up for so little." [1]
— "Rough Justice in America,"
The Economist

Reality Check

FACT: Asset forfeitures can certainly be lucrative for cash-strapped agencies and states. In the fiscal year ending September 2012, the federal government seized *$4.2 billion* in assets. Despite the fact that 80 percent of these asset forfeiture cases result in *no charge* against the property owner, challenging these "takings" in court can cost the owner more than the value of the confiscated property itself. As a result, most property owners either give up the fight or chalk the confiscation up to government corruption, leaving the police and other government officials to reap the benefits.[2]

FACT: It is estimated that 2.7 million children in the United States have at least one parent in prison, whether it be a local jail or a state or federal penitentiary, due to a wide range of factors ranging from overcriminalization and surprise raids at family homes to roadside traffic stops.[3]

FACT: The school security industry, which includes everything from biometrics to video surveillance, is estimated to be worth $4.9 billion by 2017.[4]

FACT: Despite the fact that women only make up 8 percent of the prison population, they are more likely to be strip searched, though not more likely to carry contraband.[5]

FACT: Since 2001 Americans have spent $10.5 million *every hour* for numerous foreign military occupations, including in Iraq and Afghanistan.[6] There's also the $2.2 million spent every hour on maintaining the United States' nuclear stockpile,[7] and the $35,000 spent every hour to produce and maintain our collection of Tomahawk missiles.[8] And then there's the money the government exports to other countries to support their arsenals, at the cost of $1.61 million every hour for the American taxpayers.[9]

The Building Blocks Are in Place

"First they came for the Socialists, and I did not speak out—
Because I was not a Socialist. Then they came for the Trade
Unionists, and I did not speak out—Because I was not a
Trade Unionist. Then they came for the Jews, and I did not
speak out—Because I was not a Jew. Then they came for
me—and there was no one left to speak for me."[1]

—MARTIN NIEMÖLLER

What we are witnessing today is nothing short of a war against the American citizenry waged by a run-away government hyped up on its own power, whose policies are dictated more by paranoia than need. Making matters worse, "we the people" have become so gullible, so easily distracted, and so out-of-touch that we are ignoring the warning signs all around us and failing to demand that government officials of all stripes—the White House, Congress, the courts, the military, law enforcement, the endless parade of bureaucrats—respect our rights and abide by the rule of law.

For those who can read the writing on the wall, it's all starting to make sense: the military drills carried out in major American cities,[2] the VIPR inspections at train depots and bus stations,[3] the SWAT team raids on unsuspecting homeowners, the Black Hawk helicopters patrolling American skies,[4] the massive ammunition purchases by various federal agencies such as the Department of Homeland Security, the Department of Education,[5] the IRS,[6] and the Social Security Administration,[7] the overcriminalization, the growth in private prisons, and the endless surveillance.

Viewed in conjunction with the government's increasing use of involuntary commitment laws to declare individuals mentally ill and lock them up in psychiatric wards[8] for extended periods of time, the National Defense Authorization Act's (NDAA) provision allowing the military to lock up "detainees"—that is, American citizens—who might be deemed extremists or terrorists (the government likes to use these words interchangeably) for criticizing the government only codifies this unraveling of our constitutional framework.

The building blocks are already in place for such an eventuality: the surveillance networks, fusion centers, and government contractors already monitor what is being said by whom; government databases track who poses a potential threat to the government's power; the militarized police, working in conjunction with federal agencies,[9] coordinate with the federal government when it's time to round up the troublemakers; the courts sanction the government's methods, no matter how unlawful; and the detention facilities, whether private prisons[10] or FEMA internment camps, lock up the troublemakers.

Throw in the profit-driven corporate incentive to jail Americans in private prisons, as well as the criminalizing of such relatively innocent activities as holding Bible studies in one's home[11] or sharing unpasteurized goat cheese[12] with members of one's community, and it becomes clear that "we the people" have become enemies of the state. Thus, it's no longer a question of *whether* the government will lock up Americans for First Amendment activity but *when*. (It's particularly telling that the government's lawyers, when pressed in federal court for an assurance that those exercising their First Amendment rights in order to criticize the government would *not* be targeted under the NDAA, refused to provide one.[13])

History shows that the U.S. government is not averse to locking up its own citizens for its own purposes. One need only go back to the 1940s, when the federal government proclaimed that Japanese-Americans, labeled potential dissidents, could be put in concentration (a.k.a. internment) camps based only upon their ethnic origin, to see the lengths the federal government will go to in order to maintain "order" in the homeland. The U.S. Supreme Court validated the detention program in *Korematsu v. U.S.* (1944), concluding that the government's need to ensure the safety of the country trumped personal liberties. That decision has never been overturned.

Although Supreme Court Justice Antonin Scalia has argued that the *Korematsu* decision was "wrong," in a 2014 speech he predicted that a similar detention camp scenario might be upheld in the future:

"[Y]ou are kidding yourself if you think the same thing will not happen again. . . . In times of war, the laws fall silent." As Scalia explained:

> That's what was going on—the panic about the war and the invasion of the Pacific and whatnot. That's what happens. It was wrong, but I would not be surprised to see it happen again—in time of war. It's no justification but it is the reality.[14]

Detention Camps

In fact, the creation of detention camps domestically has long been part of the government's budget and operations, falling under the jurisdiction of the Federal Emergency Management Agency. FEMA's murky history dates back to the 1970s, when President Carter created it by way of an executive order merging many of the government's disaster relief agencies into one large agency. During the 1980s, however, reports began to surface of secret military-type training exercises carried out by FEMA and the Department of Defense. Code named Rex-84,[15] thirty-four federal agencies, including the CIA and the Secret Service, were trained on how to deal with domestic civil unrest.

Japanese Americans boarding a train bound for one of ten American concentration camps, April 1942 (Photography by Russell Lee)

FEMA's role in creating top-secret American internment camps is well documented. But be careful whom you share this information with: it turns out that voicing concerns about the existence of FEMA detention camps is among the growing list of opinions and activities which may make a federal agent or government official think you're an extremist (a.k.a. terrorist), or sympathetic to terrorist activities,[16] and thus qualify you as a detainee for indefinite detention under the NDAA. Also included in that list of "dangerous" viewpoints are advocating states' rights, believing the state to be unnecessary or undesirable, "conspiracy theorizing," opposition to war,[17] organizing for "economic justice,"[18] frustration with "mainstream ideologies," opposition to abortion, opposition to globalization, and ammunition stockpiling.[19]

Of course, if you're going to have internment camps on American soil, someone has to build them. Thus, in 2006, it was announced that Kellogg Brown and Root, a subsidiary of Halliburton, had been awarded a $385 million contract to build American detention facilities. Although the government and Halliburton were not forthcoming about where or when these domestic detention centers would be built, they rationalized the need for them in case of "an emergency influx of immigrants, *or to support the rapid development of new programs*" in the event of other emergencies such as "natural disasters."[20]

Of course, these detention camps will have to be used for anyone viewed as a threat to the government, and that includes political dissidents. So it's no coincidence that the U.S. government has, since the 1980s, acquired and maintained, without warrant or court order, a database of names and information on Americans considered to be threats to the nation. This database, reportedly dubbed "Main Core," is to be used by the Army and FEMA in times of national emergency or under martial law to locate and round up Americans seen as threats to national security.[21] As of 2008, there were some eight million Americans in the Main Core database.[22]

Fast forward to 2009, when the Department of Homeland Security (DHS) released two reports, one on "Rightwing Extremism,"[23] which broadly defines rightwing extremists as individuals and groups "that are mainly antigovernment, rejecting federal authority in favor of state or local authority, or rejecting government authority entirely," and one on "Leftwing Extremism," which labeled environmental and animal rights activist groups[24] as extremists. Both reports use the words terrorist and extremist interchangeably. That same year, the DHS launched Operation Vigilant Eagle, which calls for surveillance of military veterans returning from Iraq and Afghanistan, characterizing them as extremists and potential domestic terrorist threats because they may be "disgruntled, disillusioned or suffering from the psychological effects of war."[25]

These reports indicate that for the government, so-called extremism is not a partisan matter. Anyone seen as opposing the government—whether they're Left, Right, or somewhere in between—is a target, which brings us back full circle to where we started with the NDAA's indefinite detention provision, whose language is so broad and vague as to implicate anyone critical of the government.

Again, if history acts as a guidepost for the future, then the scenario we face is frightening. As author Richard Rubenstein writes in his analysis of the Nazi regime:

> Initially, the concentration camps were established to accommodate detainees who had been placed under "protective custody" by the Nazi regime. Those arrested were people whom the regime wished to detain although there was no clear legal justification for doing so. ... In the early stages of the Nazi regime, there was no formula in law to cover all the political prisoners the Nazis wanted to arrest. This problem was solved by holding them under "protective custody" and setting up camps outside of the regular prison system to receive them.[26]

Coming Full Circle

Unfortunately, we seem to be coming full circle on many fronts. Consider that a decade ago we were debating whether non-citizens—for example, so-called enemy combatants being held at Guantanamo Bay and Muslim-Americans rounded up in the wake of 9/11—were entitled to protections under the Constitution, specifically as they relate to indefinite detention. Most Americans weren't overly concerned about the rights of non-citizens then. Now, however, it is the citizenry in the unenviable position of being targeted as detainees for indefinite detention by our own government.

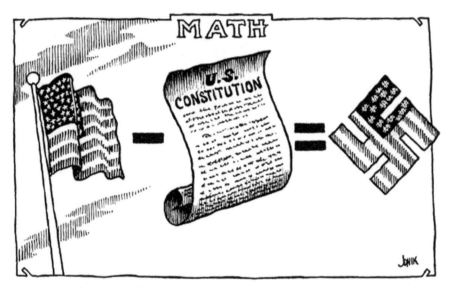

Having bought into the false notion that the government does indeed know what's best for us and can ensure not only our safety but our happiness and will take care of us from cradle to grave—that is, from daycare centers to nursing homes—we have in actuality allowed ourselves to be bridled and turned into slaves at the bidding of a corporate-run government that cares little for our freedoms or our happiness. (Illustration by Caroline Jonik)

Similarly, most Americans weren't unduly concerned when the U.S. Supreme Court gave Arizona police officers the green light to stop, search, and question anyone—ostensibly those fitting a particular racial profile—whom they suspect might be an illegal immigrant. Two years later, the cops have carte blanche authority to stop any individual, citizen and non-citizen alike, they *suspect* might be doing something illegal (mind you, in this age of overcriminalization, that could be anything from feeding the birds to growing exotic orchids).

Likewise, you still have a sizeable portion of the population today unconcerned about the government's practice of spying on Americans, having been brainwashed into believing that if you're not doing anything wrong, you have nothing to worry about. It will only be a matter of time before they learn the hard way that in a police state, it doesn't matter who you are or how righteous you claim to be—eventually, you will be lumped in with everyone else and everything you do will be "wrong," suspect, and cause to have you rounded up by government agents.

Are We Recreating the Third Reich?

Martin Niemöller learned that particular lesson the hard way. A German military officer turned theologian, Niemöller was an early supporter of Hitler's rise to power. It was only when Hitler threatened to attack the churches that Niemöller openly opposed the regime. For his efforts, Neimöller was arrested, charged with activities against the government, fined, detained, and eventually interned in concentration camps from 1938 to 1945.

As Niemöller reportedly replied when asked by his cellmate why he ever supported the Nazi party:

> I find myself wondering about that too. I wonder about it as much as I regret it. Still, it is true that Hitler betrayed me. . . . Hitler promised me on his word of honor, to protect the Church, and not to issue any anti-Church laws. He also agreed not to allow pogroms against the Jews. . . . Hitler's assurance satisfied me at the time. . . . I am paying for that mistake now; and not me alone, but thousands of other persons like me.[27]

CHAPTER 9

The Very Definition of Tyranny

"The accumulation of all powers, legislative, executive, and judiciary, in the same hands, whether of one, a few, or many, and whether hereditary, self-appointed, or elected, may justly be pronounced the very definition of tyranny."[1]

—JAMES MADISON

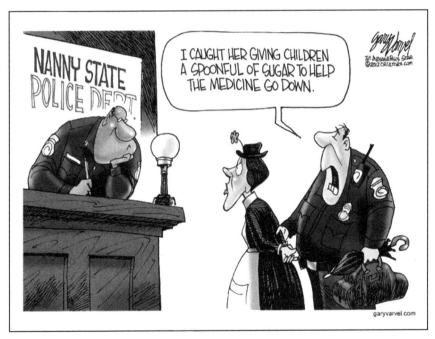

Surveillance cameras, government agents listening in on your phone calls, reading your emails and text messages and monitoring your spending, mandatory health care, sugary soda bans, anti-bullying laws, zero tolerance policies, political correctness: these are all outward signs of a government—i.e., a societal elite—that believes it knows what is best for you and can do a better job of managing your life than you can. This is the tyranny of the Nanny State: marketed as benevolence, enforced with armed police, and inflicted on all those who do not belong to the elite ruling class that gets to call the shots. (Illustration by Gary Varvel)

Surveillance cameras, government agents listening in on your phone calls, reading your emails and text messages, and monitoring your spending; mandatory health care, sugary soda bans, anti-bullying laws, zero tolerance policies, and political correctness: these are all outward signs of a fascistic government—i.e., a societal elite—that believes it knows what is best for you and can do a better job of managing your life than you can.

This is tyranny disguised as "the better good" while being marketed as benevolence, enforced with armed police, and inflicted on all those who do not belong to the elite ruling class that gets to call the shots. This is the farce that passes for law and order in America today, where crime is low,[2] surveillance is high, militarized police activity is on the rise,[3] and Americans are being penalized for living off the grid,[4] feeding wild animals,[5] growing vegetables in their front yard,[6] collecting rainwater,[7] and filming the police.[8]

To our detriment, the world is a far more dangerous place than it was a short time ago. However, it's the government that poses the gravest threat to our freedoms and way of life, and no amount of politicking, parsing, or pandering will change that.

A Two-Tiered System of Governance

Making matters worse, we now live in a two-tiered system of governance in which there is one set of laws for the government and its corporate allies, and another set for you and me.

The laws which apply to the majority of the population allow the government to do things like sending SWAT teams crashing through your door in the middle of the night, rectally probing you during a roadside stop,[9] or listening in on your phone calls and reading all of your email messages,[10] confiscating your property, or indefinitely detaining you in a military holding cell.[11] These are the laws which are executed every single day against a population which has up until now been blissfully ignorant of the radical shift taking place in American government.

Then there are the laws constructed for the elite, which allow bankers who crash the economy to walk free.[12] They're the laws that allow police officers to avoid prosecution when they shoot unarmed citizens, strip search non-violent criminals,[13] taser pregnant women on the side of the road,[14] or pepper spray peaceful protesters.[15]

These are the laws of the new age we are entering, an age of neo-feudalism, in which corporate-state rulers dominate the rest of us. We have moved into an age where we are the slaves and they are the rulers.[16]

Unfortunately, this two-tiered system of government has been a long time coming. The march towards an imperial presidency, congressional intransigence and impotence, corporate takeover of the mechanisms of government, and the division of America into have and have-nots, has been building for years.

We're All Criminals and Outlaws

Having allowed our fears to be codified and our actions criminalized, we now find ourselves in a strange new world where just about everything we do is criminalized.[17] Thanks to an overabundance of 4,500-plus federal crimes and 400,000-plus rules and regulations,[18] it's estimated that the average American actually commits three felonies a day without knowing it.[19]

The list of individuals who have suffered at the hands of a runaway legal system is growing, ranging from the orchid grower jailed for improper paperwork[20] and the lobstermen charged with importing lobster tails in plastic bags rather than cardboard boxes[21] to the former science teacher labeled a federal criminal for digging for arrowheads in his favorite campsite.[22]

Robin Speronis was threatened with eviction from her own Florida home for daring to live off the grid, independent of city utilities such as water and electricity. City officials insisted the Cape Coral resident's chosen way of life violates international property maintenance codes and city ordinances.[23]

Mary Musselman, also a Florida resident, was held in jail without bond for "feeding wild animals." The 81-year-old Musselman, on probation after being charged with feeding bears near her home, was arrested after officers discovered her leaving bread out for crows.[24]

Brandy Berning was forced to spend a night in jail after recording her conversation with an officer who pulled her over for a routine traffic stop.[25]

Nicole Gainey was arrested and charged with child neglect for allowing her 7-year-old son to visit a neighborhood playground located a half-mile from their house.[26] For the so-called "crime" of allowing her son to play at the park unsupervised, Gainey was interrogated, arrested, and

Nicole Gainey was arrested for allowing her 7-year-old son to visit a playground located a half mile from their house.
(Photography by Nicole Gainey)

handcuffed in front of her son and transported to the local jail where she was physically searched, fingerprinted, photographed, and held for seven hours and then forced to pay almost $4,000 in bond in order to return to her family. She also faced a third-degree criminal felony charge that carries with it a fine of up to $5,000 and five years in jail.[27]

Meanwhile, for Denise Stewart, just being in the wrong place at the wrong time, whether or not she had done anything wrong, was sufficient to get her arrested.[28] The 48-year-old New York grandmother was dragged half-naked out of her apartment and handcuffed after police mistakenly raided her home when responding to a domestic disturbance call. Although it turns out the 911 call came from a different apartment on a different floor, Stewart faced charges of assaulting a police officer and resisting arrest.[29]

Then there are those equally unfortunate individuals who *unknowingly* break laws they never even knew existed. For example, John Yates, a commercial fisherman, was sentenced to thirty days in prison and three years of supervised release for throwing back into the water some small fish which did not meet the Florida Fish and Wildlife Commission's size restrictions. Incredibly, Yates was charged with violating a document-shredding provision of the Sarbanes-Oxley Act.[30]

Finally, you have the rash of parents getting charged with criminal negligence and arrested for leaving their kids alone for any amount of time, whether at a park,[31] in a store,[32] in a car,[33] or in their front yard[34]—another sign of what C.S. Lewis referred to as tyranny exercised by "omnipotent moral busybodies."[35]

Following the Money Trail

As awful as these incidents are, however, it's not enough to simply write them off as part of the national trend towards overcriminalization—the overuse of criminal laws to make harmless behavior illegal—although it is certainly that. Nor can we just chalk them up as yet another symptom of an overzealous police state in which militarized police attack first and ask questions later—although it is that, too. Nor is the problem that we're a crime-ridden society. In fact, it's just the opposite. The number of violent crimes in the country is down substantially, the lowest rate in forty years,[36] while the number of Americans being jailed for nonviolent crimes, such as driving with a suspended license, are skyrocketing.[37]

So what's really behind this drive to label Americans as criminals? How did we go from enacting laws that make our worlds safer to being saddled with a government that polices our social decisions and arrests Americans for absurd "violations"? Mind you, we're not talking tickets or fines or even warnings being issued to these so-called "lawbreakers." We're talking felony charges, handcuffs, police cars, mug shots, pat downs, jail cells, and criminal records.

As with most things, if you want to know the real motives behind any government program, follow the money trail. When you dig down far enough, you quickly find that those who profit from Americans being arrested are none other than the police who arrest them, the courts which try them, the prisons which incarcerate them, and the corporations which manufacture the weapons and equipment used by police, build and run the prisons, and profit from the cheap prison labor.

Talk about a financial incentive.

First, there's the whole make-work scheme. In the absence of crime, in order to keep the police and their related agencies employed, occupied, and utilizing the many militarized "toys" passed along by the Department of Homeland Security, one must invent new crimes and new criminals to be spied on, targeted, tracked, raided, arrested, prosecuted, and jailed. Enter the police state.

Second, there's the profit-incentive for states to lock up large numbers of Americans in "private" prisons. Just as police departments have quotas for how many tickets are issued and arrests made per month[38]— a number tied directly to revenue—states now have quotas to meet for how many Americans go to jail. Having outsourced their inmate population to private prisons run by corporations such as Corrections Corp of America and the GEO Group, ostensibly as a way to save money, increasing numbers of states have contracted to keep their prisons at 90 to 100 percent capacity.[39] This profit-driven form of mass punishment has, in turn, given rise to a $70 billion private prison industry[40] that relies on the complicity of state governments to keep the money flowing and their privately run prisons full.[41] No wonder the United States has the largest prison population in the world.[42]

But what do you do when you've contracted to keep your prisons full when crime rates are falling? Easy. You create new categories of crime and render otherwise law-abiding Americans criminals. Notice how we keep coming full circle back to the point where it's average Americans like you and me being targeted and turned into enemies of the state?

That brings me to the third factor contributing to Americans being arrested, charged with outrageous "crimes," and jailed: the corporate state's need for profit and cheap labor. Not content to just lock up millions of people, corporations have also turned prisoners into forced laborers.[43]

According to professors Steve Fraser and Joshua B. Freeman, "All told, nearly a million prisoners are now making office furniture, working in call centers, fabricating body armor, taking hotel reservations, working in slaughterhouses, or manufacturing textiles, shoes, and clothing, while getting paid somewhere between 93 cents and $4.73 per day."[44] Tens of thousands of inmates in U.S. prisons are making all sorts of products, from processing agricultural products like milk and beef, packaging Starbucks coffee, and shrink-wrapping software for companies like Microsoft to sewing lingerie for Victoria's Secret.[45]

What some Americans may not have realized, however, is that America's economy has come to depend in large part on prison labor. "Prison labor reportedly produces 100 percent of military helmets, shirts, pants, tents, bags, canteens, and a variety of other equipment. Prison labor makes circuit boards for IBM, Texas Instruments, and Dell. Many McDonald's uniforms are sewn by inmates. Other corporations—Boeing, Motorola, Compaq, Revlon, and Kmart—also benefit from prison labor."[46] The resulting prison labor industries, which rely on cheap, almost free labor, are doing as much to put the average American out of work as the outsourcing of jobs to China and India.[47]

No wonder America is criminalizing mundane activities, arresting Americans for minor violations and locking them up for long stretches of time. There's a significant amount of money to be made by the police, the courts, the prisons, and the corporations.

Finally, as is the case with most of the problems plaguing us in the American police state, "we the people" are the source of our greatest problems. As journalist Gracy Olmstead recognizes, the problem arose when we looked "first to the State to care for the situation, rather than exercising any sort of personal involvement.... These actions reveal a more passive, isolated attitude. But here, again, we see the result of breakdown in modern American community—without a sense of communal closeness or responsibility, we act as bystanders rather than as stewards."[48]

Unfortunately, even in the face of outright corruption and incompetency on the part of our elected officials, Americans in general remain relatively gullible, eager to be persuaded that the government can solve the problems that plague us—whether the problem is terrorism, an economic depression, an environmental disaster, how or what we eat, or even keeping our children safe.

Jewish women from Subcarpathian Rus who have been selected for forced labor at Auschwitz-Birkenau, march toward their barracks after disinfection and headshaving. (Photography: United States Holocaust Memorial Museum, courtesy of Yad Vashem)

Auschwitz Redux?

What we're witnessing is the expansion of corrupt government power in the form of corporate partnerships that increase the reach of the state into our private lives while also adding a profit motive into the mix, with potentially deadly consequences.

This perverse mixture of government authoritarianism and corporate profits is the prevailing form of organization in American society today. We are not a nation dominated by corporations, nor are we a nation dominated by government. We are a nation dominated by corporations and government *together*, in *partnership*, against the interests of individuals, society, and ultimately our freedoms.

If it sounds at all conspiratorial, the idea that a government would jail its citizens so corporations can make a profit, then you don't know your history very well. It has been well documented that Nazi Germany forced inmates into concentration camps such as Auschwitz to provide cheap labor to BASF, Bayer, Hoechst, and other major German chemical and pharmaceutical companies,[49] much of it to produce products for European countries. Viktor Frankl, a laborer in four Nazi concentration camps, notes:

> At one time my job was to dig a tunnel, without help, for a water main under a road. I was presented with a gift of so-called "premium coupons," exchangeable for cigarettes, issued by the construction firm to which we were practically sold as slaves: the firm paid the camp authorities a fixed price per day, per prisoner.[50]

Unfortunately, we have relinquished control over the most intimate aspects of our lives to government officials who, while they may occupy seats of authority, are neither wiser, smarter, more in tune with our needs, more knowledgeable about our problems, nor more aware of what is really in our best interests. Yet having bought into the false notion that the government does indeed know what's best for us and can ensure not only our safety but our happiness and will take care of us from cradle to grave—that is, from daycare centers to nursing homes—we have in actuality allowed ourselves to be bridled and turned into slaves at the bidding of a corporate-run government that cares little for our freedoms or our happiness.

CHAPTER 10

Robbed Blind by the Government

"No power on earth has a right to take our property from us without our consent."[1]
—JOHN JAY, first Chief Justice of the United States

"This is the problem when police officers and police departments have a financial interest in doing their job. We got rid of bounty hunters because they were not a good thing. This is modern day bounty hunting."[2]
—Public Defender JOHN REKOWSKI

Under the guise of civil asset forfeiture, a revenue scheme wherein government agents (usually the police) seize private property they "suspect" may be connected to criminal activity, Americans are finding themselves robbed by the very individuals charged with protecting them from such crimes.

(Illustration by Russmo)

We labor today under the weight of countless tyrannies, large and small, carried out in the name of the national good by an elite class of government officials who are largely insulated from the ill effects of their actions. We, the middling classes, are not so fortunate. We find ourselves badgered, bullied, and browbeaten into bearing the brunt of their arrogance—paying the price for their greed, suffering the backlash for their militarism, agonizing as a result of their inaction, feigning ignorance about their backroom dealings, overlooking their incompetence, turning a blind eye to their misdeeds, cowering from their heavy-handed tactics, and blindly hoping for change that never comes.

What we have yet to come to terms with is our absolute subjugation at the hands of the government elite. Yet the reality of our oppression is undeniable. After all, if the government can arbitrarily take away your property without your having much say about it, you have no true rights. If the government can tell you what you can and cannot do within the privacy of your home, whether it relates to what you eat, what you smoke, or whom you love, you no longer have any rights whatsoever within your home.

If government officials can fine and arrest you for growing vegetables in your front yard,[3] installing solar panels on your roof,[4] and raising chickens in your backyard,[5] you're no longer the owner of your property. If school officials can punish your children for what they do or say while at home[6] or in your care, your children are not your own—they are the property of the state.

If government agents can invade your home,[7] break down your doors,[8] kill your dog,[9] damage your furnishings, and terrorize your family, your property is no longer private and secure—it belongs to the government. Likewise, if police can forcefully draw your blood,[10] strip search you,[11] and probe you intimately,[12] your body is no longer your own, either.

The End of Private Property

Long before Americans charted their revolutionary course in pursuit of happiness, it was "life, liberty, and property" which constituted the golden triad of essential rights that the government was charged with respecting and protecting.[13] To the colonists, smarting from mistreatment at the hands of the British crown, protection of their property from

Vegetable gardens have become easy targets for city officials
on the prowl for "violators." (Source: WKMG)

governmental abuse was just as critical as preserving their lives and
liberties. As the colonists understood, if the government can arbitrarily
take away your property, you have no true rights. You're nothing more
than a serf or a slave.

The Fifth Amendment to the U.S. Constitution was born of this
need to safeguard against any attempt by the government to unlaw-
fully deprive a citizen of the right to life, liberty, or property without due
process of law. Little could our ancestral forebears have imagined that
it would take less than three centuries of so-called "independence" to
once again render us brow-beaten subjects in bondage to overlords bent
on depriving us of our most inalienable and fundamental rights.

Yet slowly but surely, the yoke around the neck of the average
American has tightened with every new tax, fine, fee, and law adopted
by our so-called representatives. Meanwhile, the three branches of government (Executive, Legislative, and Judicial) and the agencies under
their command—Defense, Commerce, Education, Homeland Security,
Justice, Treasury, etc.—have switched their allegiance to the corporate state with its unassailable pursuit of profit at all costs and by any
means possible.

As a result, we are now ruled by a government consumed with
squeezing every last penny out of the population and seemingly unconcerned if essential freedoms are trampled in the process, including

the right to private property. Examples of the government's growing disregard for the sanctity of private property abound, in regard to one's home, one's possessions, and one's person. Included in the mix of profit-driven government programs are the preponderance of asset forfeiture schemes and school truancy courts. Even the traffic safety programs with red light cameras, sold to communities as a means of minimizing traffic accidents at intersections,[14] are in fact little more than a way to impose stealth taxes on drivers.

Asset Forfeiture Schemes

Under the guise of civil-asset forfeiture, a revenue scheme wherein government agents (usually the police) seize private property they "suspect" may be connected to criminal activity, Americans are finding themselves robbed by the very individuals charged with protecting them from such crimes.[15] Despite the fact that 80 percent of these asset forfeiture cases result in *no charge* against the property owner, the government keeps the citizen's property, often divvying it up with local police.[16]

As you might guess, asset forfeitures are a lucrative business for governments at all levels.[17] Often these governmental property grabs take the form of highway robbery (literally), where police officers extract money, jewelry, and other property from unsuspecting motorists during routine traffic stops. Some states are actually considering expanding the use of asset forfeiture laws to include property seized in cases of minor crimes such as harassment, possession of small amounts of marijuana, and trespassing in a public park after dark.[18]

Comparing police forfeiture operations to criminal shakedowns, journalist Radley Balko paints a picture of a government so corrupt as to render the Constitution null and void:

> Police in some jurisdictions have run forfeiture operations that would be difficult to distinguish from criminal shakedowns. Police can pull motorists over, find some amount of cash or other property of value, claim some vague connection to illegal drug activity and then present the motorists with a choice: If they hand over the property, they can be on their way. Otherwise, they face arrest, seizure of property, a drug charge, a probable night in jail, the hassle of multiple return trips to the state or city where they were

Red light camera protesters (Source: *The Newspaper*)

pulled over, and the cost of hiring a lawyer to fight both the seizure and the criminal charge. It isn't hard to see why even an innocent motorist would opt to simply hand over the cash and move on.[19]

Traffic Safety Schemes

Red light cameras, little more than intrusive, money-making scams for states, have been shown to do little to increase safety while actually contributing to more accidents. Nevertheless, they are being inflicted on unsuspecting drivers by revenue-hungry municipalities, despite revelations of corruption, collusion, and fraud.

The cameras, which are triggered by sensors buried in the road, work by taking photos of drivers who enter intersections after a traffic light turns red. What few realize, however, is that you don't actually have to run a red light to get "caught." Many drivers have triggered the cameras simply by making a right turn on red or crossing the sensor but not advancing into the intersection. Soon thereafter they receive a traffic ticket in the mail demanding payment of the fine.

Indeed, these intricate red light camera systems—which also function as surveillance cameras—placed in cities and towns throughout America ostensibly for our own good, are in reality simply another means for government and corporate officials to fleece the American people. Follow the money trail beyond the local governments working with the Australian corporation Redflex to inflict these cameras on drivers, and you'll find millions of dollars in campaign funds flowing to politicians from lobbyists for the red light camera industry.[20]

Studies show that lengthening the time of yellow lights actually serves to minimize accidents.[21] One particularly corrupt practice aimed at increasing the incidence of red light violations (and fines) involves the shortening of the time of yellow lights in intersections with red light cameras. An investigative report by a Tampa Bay news station revealed that Florida officials conspired to reduce the length of yellow light time at key intersections in order to collect more fines via red light cameras. By reducing the length of yellow lights by a mere half-second, Florida officials doubled the number of citations issued.[22] Contrast that with what happened when the yellow light time was increased from 3 seconds to the minimum requirement of 4.3 seconds at one Florida intersection: traffic citations dropped by 90 percent.[23]

Truancy Court Schemes

Yet another ploy to separate taxpayers from their hard-earned dollars and render them criminals, are school truancy laws. While disguised as well-meaning attempts to resolve attendance issues in the schools, they are nothing more than stealth maneuvers aimed at enriching school districts and court systems alike through excessive fines and jail sentences.[24] Much like the profit incentives behind privatized prisons and red light traffic cameras, there are also profit motives driving most of the state truancy laws and courts.

Under this increasingly popular system of truancy enforcement, instead of giving students detention or some other in-school punishment for "unauthorized" absences, schools are now opting to fine parents and force them or their kids to serve jail time. ("Unauthorized" is the key word here, of course, since schools retain the right to determine whether an absence sanctioned by a parent or even a doctor is acceptable.) For example, California students are fined $250 for being late to school.[25] Parents in Florida can be charged with a second-degree misdemeanor and face up to two months in jail if their kids have fifteen or more unexcused absences from school over the course of three months.[26] Truancy laws in Alabama, Texas, and North Carolina, among other states, have also resulted in parents doing jail time for their kids' absenteeism.

Serfs in Bondage

This is what a world without any real rule of law looks like—one where the lines between private and public property have been so blurred that private property is reduced to little more than something the government can use to control, manipulate, and harass you to suit its own purposes, and you, the homeowner and citizen, have been reduced to little more than a tenant or serf in bondage to an inflexible landlord. It is also a world where the government lays claim to your property, your children, and you. In other words, it is quickly becoming a totalitarian regime.

CHAPTER 11

Ravaged, Raped, and Stripped of Our Dignity

"The Fourth Amendment was designed to stand between us and arbitrary governmental authority. For all practical purposes, that shield has been shattered, leaving our liberty and personal integrity subject to the whim of every cop on the beat, trooper on the highway and jail official. The framers would be appalled."[1]—HERMAN SCHWARTZ, *The Nation*

Police carry out a roadside cavity search on a woman "suspected" of littering.

We in America get so focused on the Fourth Amendment's requirement of a warrant before government agents can invade our property (a requirement that means little in an age of kangaroo courts and rubberstamped warrant requests) that we fail to properly appreciate the first part of the statement declaring that we have a right to be *secure* in our "persons, houses, papers, and effects."

What this means is that the Fourth Amendment's protections were intended to not only follow us wherever we go but also apply to all that is ours—whether you're talking about our physical bodies, our biometric data, our possessions, our families, or our way of life. While the literal purpose of the amendment is to protect our property and our bodies from unwarranted government intrusion, the moral intention behind it is to protect our human dignity. However, at a time when the government routinely cites national security as the justification for its endless violations of the Constitution, the idea that a citizen can actually be "secure" or protected against such government overreach seems increasingly implausible.

Government-Sanctioned Humiliation and Degradation

In a judicial and bureaucratic environment in which concerns for privacy and human dignity have been largely discounted, the courts have increasingly erred on the side of giving government officials—especially the police—vast discretion when it comes to doing their jobs.

Strip searches, government-sanctioned exercises in humiliation and degradation, embody all that is wrong with the American dream-turned-nightmare. In the past, strip searches were resorted to only in exceptional circumstances where police were confident that a serious crime was in progress. In recent years, however, strip searches have become routine operating procedures in which everyone is rendered a suspect and, as such, is subjected to treatment once reserved for only the most serious of criminals.

SCOTUS Up the Wazoo (Illustration by Pat Bagley)

Thanks to the U.S. Supreme Court's ruling in *Florence v. Bd. of Chosen Freeholders of County of Burlington*, these strip searches can be carried out for a broad range of violations, no matter how minor. In that case, the justices ruled that any person who is arrested and processed at a jail house, regardless of the severity of his or her offense (i.e., they can be guilty of nothing more than a minor traffic offense), can be subjected to a virtual strip search by police or jail officials, which involves exposing the genitals and the buttocks.[2] This "license to probe" is now being extended to roadside stops, as police officers throughout the country have begun performing roadside strip searches—some involving anal and vaginal probes—without any evidence of wrongdoing and without a warrant.

Examples of minor infractions which have resulted in strip searches include individuals arrested for driving with a noisy muffler, driving with an inoperable headlight, failing to use a turn signal, riding a bicycle without an audible bell, making an improper left turn, and engaging in an antiwar demonstration (the individual searched was a nun, a Sister of Divine Providence for fifty years).[3] Police have also carried out strip searches for passing a bad check, dog leash violations, filing a false police report, failing to produce a driver's license after making an illegal left turn, having outstanding parking tickets, and public intoxication.[4] A failure to pay child support could also result in a strip search.

The cases are legion.

Leila Tarantino was subjected to two roadside strip searches during a routine traffic stop in plain view of passing traffic, while her two children—ages one and four—waited inside her car. During the second strip search, presumably in an effort to ferret out drugs, a female officer "forcibly removed" a tampon from Tarantino. No contraband or anything illegal was found.[5]

A North Carolina public school allegedly strip-searched a 10-year-old boy in search of a $20 bill lost by another student, despite the fact that the boy, J.C., twice told school officials he did not have the missing money. The assistant principal reportedly ordered the fifth grader to disrobe down to his underwear and subjected him to an aggressive strip-search that included rimming the edge of his underwear. The missing money was later found in the school cafeteria.[6]

Suspecting that Georgia Tech alum Mary Clayton might have been attempting to smuggle a Chik-Fil-A sandwich into the football stadium, a Georgia Tech police officer allegedly subjected the season ticket-holder to a strip search that included a close examination of her underwear and bra. No contraband chicken was found.[7]

Sixty-nine-year-old Gerald Dickson was handcuffed and taken into custody (although not arrested or charged with any crime) after giving a ride to a neighbor's son, whom police suspected of being a drug dealer. Despite Dickson's insistence that the bulge under his shirt was the result of a botched hernia surgery, police ordered Dickson to "strip off his clothes, bend over and expose all of his private parts. No drugs or contraband were found."[8]

In Chicago, a 15-year-old boy accused by an anonymous tipster of holding drugs was taken to a locker room by two security guards, a Chicago police officer, and a female assistant principal, and made to stand against a wall and drop his pants while one of the security guards inspected his genitals. No drugs were found.[9]

Four Milwaukee police were charged with carrying out rectal searches of suspects on the street and in police district stations over the course of several years. One of the officers was accused of conducting searches of men's anal and scrotal areas, often inserting his fingers into their rectums.[10] Half way across the country, the city of Oakland, California, has agreed to pay $4.6 million to 39 men who had their pants pulled down by police on city streets between 2002 and 2009.[11]

Thirty-eight-year-old Angel Dobbs and her 24-year-old niece, Ashley, were pulled over by a Texas state trooper on July 13, 2012, allegedly for flicking cigarette butts out of the car window.[12] Insisting that he smelled marijuana, the trooper proceeded to interrogate them and search the car. Despite the fact that both women denied smoking or possessing any marijuana, the police officer then called in a female trooper, who carried out a roadside cavity search, sticking her fingers into the older woman's anus and vagina, then performing the same procedure on the younger woman, wearing the same pair of gloves.[13] No marijuana was found.

The Reality of Our Age

The reality of our age is this: if the government chooses to crash through our doors, listen to our phone calls, read our emails and text messages, fine us for growing vegetables in our front yard, forcibly take our blood and saliva, and probe our vaginas and rectums, there's little we can do to stop them. At least, not at that particular moment.

When you're face to face with a government agent who is not only armed to the hilt and inclined to shoot first and ask questions later but also woefully ignorant of the fact that he works for you, if you value your life, you don't talk back.

This sad reality did not simply creep up on us. It came about as a result of our being asleep at the wheel. We failed to ask questions and hold our representatives accountable to abiding by the Constitution, while the government amassed an amazing amount of power over us, and backed up that power-grab with a terrifying amount of military might and weaponry, and got the courts to sanction their actions every step of the way.

However, once the dust settles and you've had a chance to catch your breath, I hope you'll remember that the Constitution begins with those three beautiful words, "We the people." In other words, there is no government without us: our sheer numbers, our muscle, our economy, our physical presence in this land. There can also be no police state—no tyranny—no routine violations of our rights without our complicity and collusion—without our turning a blind eye, shrugging our shoulders, allowing ourselves to be distracted, and our civic awareness diluted.

If there has ever been a wake-up call, it is now. But if we continue to sleep, when we do wake up, the beast that will be staring us down will be unstoppable.

CHAPTER 12

Lessons in Indoctrination and Compliance

"Is it surprising that prisons resemble factories, schools, barracks, hospitals, which all resemble prisons?"[1]

— MICHEL FOUCAULT

"[The aim of public education is not] to fill the young of the species with knowledge and awaken their intelligence.... Nothing could be further from the truth. The aim ... is simply to reduce as many individuals as possible to the same safe level, to breed and train a standardized citizenry, to put down dissent and originality. That is its aim in the United States."[2]

— HENRY MENCKEN, American Journalist (April 1924)

How do you persuade a nation of relatively freedom-loving individuals to march in lock step with a police state? You start by convincing them that they're in danger, and only the government can protect them. Keep them keyed up with constant danger alerts, and the occasional terrorist incident, whether real or staged. Distract them with wall-to-wall news coverage about sinking ships, disappearing planes, and pseudo-celebrities spouting racist diatribes. Use blockbuster movies, reality shows, and violent video games to hype them up on military tactics, and then while they're distracted and numb to all that is taking place around them, indoctrinate their young people to your way of thinking, relying primarily on the public schools and popular culture.

After all, public education the world over has always been the vehicle for statist propaganda of one sort or another, whether it's religion, militarism, democracy, or totalitarianism, and America is no exception. In fact, today's public schools, far from being bastions of free speech, are merely microcosms of the world beyond the schoolhouse gates, and increasingly it's a world hostile to freedom.

Microcosms of the Police State

Within America's public schools can be found almost every aspect of the American police state that plagues those of us on the "outside": metal detectors,[3] surveillance cameras,[4] militarized police, drug-sniffing dogs,[5] tasers, cyber-surveillance, random searches—the list goes on. Whether it takes the form of draconian zero-tolerance policies, overreaching anti-bullying statutes, police officers tasked with tasering and arresting so-called unruly children,[6] standardized testing with its emphasis on rote answers and political correctness, or the extensive use of surveillance systems cropping up in schools all over the country, young people in America are first in line to be indoctrinated into compliant citizens of the new American police state.

Zero-tolerance policies, which punish all offenses severely, no matter how minor, condition young people to steer clear of doing anything that might be considered out of line, whether it's pointing their fingers like a gun,[7] drawing on their desks,[8] or chewing their gum too loudly.[9]

Surveillance technologies, used by school officials, police, NSA agents, and corporate entities to track the everyday activities of students, accustom young people to life in an electronic concentration camp, with all of their movements monitored, their interactions assessed, and their activities recorded and archived. For example, the Department of Education (DOE), along with colleges and state agencies such as the Department of Labor and the offices of Technology and Children and Family Services, has created a system to track, archive, and disseminate data on every single part of a child's educational career. The system relies on a database called inBloom, which is funded by corporate magnates such as the Bill and Melinda Gates Foundation and Rupert Murdoch's News Corp. DOE has also received $40 million from various state and federal agencies to help fund the program.[10]

Metal detectors at school entrances and police patrolling school hallways acclimatize young people to being viewed as suspects. Funded in part by federal grants, school districts across the country have "paid local police agencies to provide armed 'school resource

America's school-to-prison pipeline is fully operational and busy churning out newly minted citizens of the American police state who have been taught the hard way what it means to comply and march in lockstep with the government's dictates.

(Illustration by Khalil Bendib)

officers' for high schools, middle schools and sometimes even elementary schools."[11] As the *New York Times* reports, "Hundreds of additional districts, including those in Houston, Los Angeles and Philadelphia, have created police forces of their own, employing thousands of sworn officers."[12] In fact, security guards now outnumber high school teachers in the United States.[13]

The problem, of course, is that the very presence of these police officers in the schools results in greater numbers of students being arrested or charged with crimes for nonviolent, childish behavior. In Texas, for example, school police officers write more than 100,000 misdemeanor tickets a year, each ticket amounting to hundreds of dollars in court fines[14]—a convenient financial windfall for the states. All too often, these incidents remain on students' permanent records, impacting college and job applications.

Weapons of compliance, such as tasers that deliver electrical shocks lethal enough to kill, not only teach young people to fear the police—the face of our militarized government—but teach them that torture is an accepted means of controlling the population. It's a problem that has grown exponentially as the schools have increasingly clamored for—and hired on—their own police forces. One high school student in Texas suffered severe brain damage and nearly died after being tasered. A 15-year-old disabled North Carolina student was tasered three times, resulting in punctured lungs. A New York student was similarly tasered for lying on the floor and crying.[15]

Standardized testing and Common Core programs, which discourage students from thinking for themselves while rewarding them for regurgitating whatever the government, through its so-called educational standards, dictates they should be taught, is creating a generation of test-takers capable of little else, molded and shaped by the federal government and its corporate allies into what it considers to be ideal citizens. Analytical thinking, once the basis of the education system, is virtually gone. Incredibly, despite the fact that the United States invests more money in public education (roughly $8,000 per child per year) than many other developed countries, America ranks 27th in the world for school educational achievement.[16]

Overt censorship, monitoring, and enforcing values of "political correctness," which manifest themselves in a variety of ways from Internet filters on school computers to sexual harassment policies, habituate young people to a world in which nonconformist, divergent, and politically incorrect ideas and speech are treated as unacceptable or dangerous. In such an environment, a science teacher criticizing evolution can get fired for insubordination,[17] a 9-year-old boy remarking that his teacher is "cute" can be suspended for sexual harassment,[18] students detected using their smart phones during class time can be reported for not paying attention in class, and those accused of engaging in "bullying, cyber-bullying, hate and shaming activities, depression, harm and self harm, self hate and suicide, crime, vandalism, substance abuse and truancy" on social media such as Twitter or Facebook, will have their posts and comments analyzed by an outside government contractor.[19]

So far I've only mentioned what's happening *within* the public schools. It doesn't even begin to touch on extracurricular activities such as the Explorers program, which trains young people—"ages 14 to 21 who have a C average"—to be future agents of the police state.[20] Explorers meet weekly, train for competitions, and spend their weekends working on service projects. In one Border Patrol training exercise, teenagers as young as 14, suited up in military gear with lethal-looking airsoft guns, were "instructed on how to quiet an obstreperous lookout," reports the *New York Times*. "Put him on his face and put a knee in his back," a Border Patrol agent explained. "I guarantee that he'll shut up."[21]

Then there's the military's use of video games and blockbuster movies to propagandize war and recruit young people. Thanks to a collaboration between the Department of Defense and the entertainment industry, the American taxpayer is paying for what amounts to a propaganda campaign aimed at entrenching the power of the military in American society.[22] As author Nick Turse points out, "Today, almost everywhere you look, whether at the latest blockbuster on the big screen or what's on much smaller screens in your own home—likely made by a defense contractor like Sony, Samsung, Panasonic or Toshiba—you'll find the Pentagon or its corporate partners."[23]

As if military propaganda weren't enough, American schools have also been eager participants in the government's surplus military recycling program. For example, a growing number of school districts have received free military surplus gear, mine-resistant armored vehicles, grenade launchers and M16 assault rifles.[24] The most common justification for such equipment is that it is necessary in order to avoid another Columbine or Newtown school shooting.[25]

The School-to-Prison Pipeline

The ramifications of training children to live in a police state are obviously far-reaching. But the trend is also to treat them like hard-core criminals, as well. As Emily Bloomenthal, writing for the *New York University Review of Law & Social Change*, explains:

> Studies have found that youth who have been suspended are at increased risk of being required to repeat a grade, and suspensions are a strong predictor of later school dropout. Researchers have concluded that "suspension often becomes a 'pushout' tool to encourage low-achieving students and those viewed as 'troublemakers' to leave school before graduation." Students who have been suspended are also more likely to commit a crime and/or to end up incarcerated as an adult, a pattern that has been dubbed the "school-to-prison pipeline."[26]

There is no shortage of examples in which children are suspended, handcuffed, arrested, and even tasered for what used to be considered childlike behavior. Case in point: in Pennsylvania, a ten-year-old boy was suspended for shooting an imaginary "arrow" at a fellow classmate, using nothing more than his hands and his imagination.[27] In Colorado, a six-year-old boy was suspended and accused of sexual harassment for kissing the hand of a girl in his class whom he had a crush on.[28] In Alabama, a diabetic teenager was slammed into a filing cabinet and arrested after falling asleep during an in-school suspension.[29] Seven North Carolina students were arrested for throwing water balloons as part of a school prank.[30]

What is particularly chilling is how effective these lessons in compliance are in indoctrinating young people to accept their role in the police state, either as criminals or prison guards. For six years, sociologist Alice Goffman lived in a low-income urban neighborhood, documenting the impact of such an environment—a microcosm of the police state—on its residents. Her account of neighborhood children playing cops and robbers speaks volumes about how constant exposure to pat downs, strip searches, surveillance and arrests can result in a populace that meekly allows itself to be prodded, poked, and stripped:

> Goffman sometimes saw young children playing the age-old game of cops and robbers in the street, only the child acting the part of the robber wouldn't even bother to run away: I saw children give up running and simply stick their hands behind their back, as if in handcuffs; push their body up against a car without being asked; or lie flat on the ground and put their hands over their head. The children yelled, "I'm going to lock you up! I'm going to lock you up, and you ain't never coming home!" I once saw a six-year-old pull another child's pants down to do a "cavity search."[31]

'Your Child Belongs to Me Already'

What's really unnerving are the similarities between our own system of youth indoctrination and that of Nazi Germany with its Hitler Youth programs and overt campaign of educational indoctrination. In fact, the United States Holocaust Memorial Museum provides some valuable

Pictured here, young "Explorers" carry out a terrorism training drill as part of a Boy Scouts-affiliated program that prepares young people for future careers in law enforcement. (Photo by Todd Krainin for *The New York Times*)

insight into education in the Nazi state, which was responsible for winning "millions of German young people … over to Nazism in the classroom and through extracurricular activities."[32] The similarities are startling, ranging from the dismissal of teachers deemed to be "politically unreliable" to the introduction of classroom textbooks that taught students obedience to state authority and militarism.[33] "Board games and toys for children served as another way to spread racial and political propaganda to German youth. Toys were also used as propaganda vehicles to indoctrinate children into militarism."[34] And then there was the Hitler Youth, a paramilitary youth group intended to train young people for future service in the armed forces and government.[35]

Hitler himself recognized the value of indoctrinating young people. As he noted, "When an opponent declares, 'I will not come over to your side, and you will not get me on your side,' I calmly say, 'Your child belongs to me already. A people lives forever. What are you? You will pass on. Your descendants however now stand in the new camp. In a short time they will know nothing else but this new community.'"[36]

CHAPTER 13

Snitches for the Police State

"There were relatively few secret police, and most were just processing the information coming in. I had found a shocking fact. It wasn't the secret police who were doing this wide-scale surveillance and hiding on every street corner. It was the ordinary German people who were informing on their neighbors."[1] —Professor ROBERT GELLATELY

If you see something suspicious, says the Department of Homeland Security, say something about it to the police, call it in to a government hotline, or report it using a convenient app on your smart phone. The "See Something, Say Something" poster has appeared for more than a decade throughout the New York City Subway system.

(Source: Dept. of Homeland Security)

The police state could not ask for a better citizenry than one that carries out its own policing. After all, the police can't be everywhere. So how do you police a nation when your population outnumbers your army of soldiers? How do you carry out surveillance on a nation when there aren't enough cameras, let alone viewers, to monitor every square inch of the country 24/7? How do you not only track but analyze the transactions, interactions, and movements of every person within the United States?

The answer is simpler than it seems: You persuade the citizenry to be your eyes and ears. You hype them up on color-coded "terror alerts," keep them in the dark about the distinctions between actual threats and staged "training" drills so that all crises seem real, desensitize them to the sight of militarized police walking their streets, acclimatize them to being surveilled "for their own good," and then indoctrinate them into thinking that they are the only ones who can save the nation from another 9/11.

As historian Robert Gellately points out, a Nazi-like order requires at least some willing collaborators to succeed.[2] In other words, this is how you turn a people into extensions of the omniscient, omnipotent, omnipresent police state, and in the process turn a citizenry against each other.

It's a brilliant ploy, with the added bonus that while the citizenry remains focused on and distrustful of each other and shadowy forces from outside the country, they're incapable of focusing on more definable threats that fall closer to home—namely the government and its cabal of Constitution-destroying agencies and corporate partners.

Community Policing

For more than a decade now, the DHS has plastered its "See Something, Say Something" campaign on the walls of metro stations, on billboards, on coffee cup sleeves, at the Super Bowl, and even on television monitors in the Statue of Liberty.[3] Now colleges, universities,[4] and even football teams and sporting arenas[5] are lining up for grants to participate in the program.

If you see something suspicious, says the Department of Homeland Security, say something about it to the police, call it in to a government hotline, or report it using a convenient app on your smart phone.

(If you're a whistleblower wanting to snitch on government wrong-doing, however, forget about it—the government doesn't take kindly to having its dirty deeds publicized[6] and, God forbid, being made to account for them.)

This is what is commonly referred to as community policing. Yet while community policing and federal programs such as "See Something, Say Something" are sold to the public as patriotic attempts to be on guard against those who would harm us, they are little more than totalitarian tactics dressed up and repackaged for a more modern audience as well-intentioned appeals to law and order and security.

This DHS slogan is nothing more than the government's way of indoctrinating "we the people" into the mindset that we're an extension of the government and, as such, have a patriotic duty to be suspicious of, spy on, and turn in our fellow citizens.

Community policing did not come about as a feel-good, empowering response to individuals trying to "take back" their communities from crime syndicates and drug lords. Rather, "Community-Oriented Policing" or COPs (short for Community Partnerships, Organizational Transformation, and Problem Solving)[7] is a Department of Justice (DOJ) program designed to foster "partnerships" between local police agencies and members of the community.[8] In reality, this program turns "local" police agencies into extensions of the federal government. (Remember, this is the same Justice Department which, in conjunction with the DHS, has been providing funding and equipping local police agencies across the country with surveillance devices and military gear. These same local police have been carrying out upwards of 80,000 SWAT team raids a year on individuals,[9] some of whom are guilty of nothing more than growing tomatoes and breeding orchids without the proper paperwork.)

What's Wrong with Community Policing?

The problem with community policing schemes is that they are not, in fact, making America any safer. Instead, they're turning us into a legalistic, intolerant, squealing, bystander nation content to report a so-called violation to the cops and then turn a blind eye to the ensuing tragedies. Curiously enough, there's rarely little indignation over the police state's partners-in-crime—the neighbors, the clerks, the utility workers—who turn in their fellow citizens for little more than having unsightly lawns and voicing controversial ideas.

Apart from the sheer idiocy of arresting people for such harmless "crimes" as letting their kids walk to the park alone, peeling the bark off a tree, and living off the grid, there's also the unfortunate fact that once the police are called in, with their ramped up protocols, battlefield mindset, militarized weapons, uniforms and equipment, and war zone tactics, it's a process that is nearly impossible to turn back and one that too often ends in tragedy for all those involved.

For instance, when a neighbor repeatedly called the police to report that 5-year-old Phoenix Turnbull was keeping a pet red hen (nickname: Carson Petey) in violation of an Atwater, Minnesota, city ordinance against backyard chickens, the police chief got involved.[10] In an effort to appease the complaining neighbor and "protect a nearby elementary school from a chicken on the loose," the police chief walked onto the Turnbull's property, decapitated the hen with a shovel, deposited the severed head on the family's front stoop, and left a neighborhood child to report the news that "the cops killed your chicken!"[11]

Community Partners in the Policing Scheme

In much the same way the old African proverb "it takes a village to raise a child" was used to make the case for an all-encompassing government program of social welfare,[12] the DHS and the DOJ are attempting to make the case that it takes a nation to catch a terrorist. To this end, the Justice Department identifies five distinct "partners" in the community policing scheme: law enforcement and other government agencies, community members and groups, nonprofits, churches and service providers, private businesses, and the media.

Together, these groups are supposed to "identify" community concerns, "engage" the community in achieving specific goals, serve as "powerful" partners with the government, and add their "considerable resources" to the government's already massive arsenal of technology and intelligence. The mainstream media's role, long recognized as being a mouthpiece for the government, is formally recognized as "publicizing" services from government or community agencies or new laws or codes that will be enforced, as well as shaping public perceptions of the police, crime problems, and fear of crime.[13]

Amazingly, the Justice Department guidelines sound as if they were taken from a Nazi guide on how to rule a nation. "Germans not only watched out for 'crimes' and other deviations" of fellow German citizens, Robert Gellately writes, "but they watched each other."[14]

CHAPTER 14

The Double Standard in Defense

"A well regulated militia, being necessary to the
security of a free state, the right of the people to keep
and bear arms, shall not be infringed."[1]
—The Second Amendment to the U.S. Constitution

"That rifle hanging on the wall of the working-class flat
or labourer's cottage is the symbol of democracy. It is
our job to see that it stays there."[2]—GEORGE ORWELL

When considered in the context of prohibitions against the government, the Second Amendment reads as a clear rebuke against any attempt to restrict the citizenry's gun ownership.
(Illustration by Yogi Love)

You can largely determine where a person will fall in the debate over gun control and the Second Amendment based on their view of government and the role it should play in our lives. Those who want to see government as a benevolent parent looking out for our best interests tend to interpret the Second Amendment's "militia" reference as applying only to the police and the military.

To those who see the government as inherently corrupt, the Second Amendment is a means of ensuring that the populace will always have a way of defending themselves against threats to their freedoms. And then there are those who view the government as neither good nor evil but merely a powerful entity that, as Thomas Jefferson recognized, must be bound "down from mischief by the chains of the Constitution."[3] To this group, the right to bear arms is no different from any other right enshrined in the Constitution, to be safeguarded, exercised prudently, and maintained in order to limit and curtail government power.

Unfortunately, while these divergent viewpoints continue to jockey for supremacy, the American government has adopted a "do what I say, not what I do" mindset when it comes to Americans' rights overall. Nowhere is this double standard more evident than in the government's attempts to arm itself to the teeth, all the while viewing as suspect anyone who dares to legally own a gun, let alone use one.

The Technicalities of Gun Ownership

Indeed, while it still technically remains legal to *own* a firearm in America, possessing one can now get you pulled over,[4] searched,[5] arrested,[6] subjected to all manner of surveillance,[7] treated as a suspect without ever having committed a crime,[8] shot at,[9] and killed. (This same rule does not apply to law enforcement officials, however, who are armed to the hilt and rarely given more than a slap on the wrists for using their weapons against unarmed individuals.)

In 2014, for example, the U.S. Supreme Court refused to hear the case of a Texas man whose home was subject to a no-knock, SWAT-team style forceful entry and raid based solely on the suspicion that there were legally-owned firearms in his household. Making matters worse, police panicked and opened fire through a solid wood door on the homeowner, who had already gone to bed.[10]

Earlier that same year, a Florida man traveling through Maryland with his wife and kids was stopped by a police officer and interrogated about the whereabouts of his registered handgun. Despite the man's insistence that the handgun had been left at home, the officer spent nearly two hours searching through the couple's car, patting them down along with their children, and having them sit in the back of a patrol car.[11] No weapon was found.

In 2011 a 25-year-old Philadelphia man was confronted by police, verbally threatened, and arrested for carrying a gun in public, which is legal within the city. When Mark Fiorino attempted to explain his rights under the law to police, a cop ordered him to get on his knees or else "I am gonna shoot ya." Fiorino was later released without charges.[12]

A provision in a Washington State bill would have authorized police to search and inspect gun owners' homes yearly.[13] Connecticut has adopted a law banning the sale of large-capacity magazines and assault weapons.[14] And a bill before the New Jersey legislature proposed to reduce the number of bullets an ammunition magazine could hold from 15 to 10.[15]

Then there's the Department of Health and Human Services, which wants anyone seeking mental health treatment—no matter how benign—to be entered into the FBI's criminal background check system and have their Second Amendment rights restricted.[16] They would join the ranks of some 175,000 veterans who have been barred from possessing firearms based solely on the fact that they received psychiatric treatment through the Department of Veterans Affairs.[17]

A Shackle on the Government's Powers

It's no laughing matter, and yet the joke is on us. "We the people" have been so focused on debating who or what is responsible for gun violence—the guns, the gun owners, or our violent culture—and whether the Second Amendment "allows" us to own guns that we've overlooked the most important and most consistent theme throughout the Constitution: the fact that it is not merely an enumeration of *our* rights but was intended to be a clear shackle on the government's powers.

When considered in the context of prohibitions against the government, the Second Amendment reads as a clear rebuke against any attempt to restrict the citizenry's gun ownership. As such, it is as necessary an ingredient for maintaining that tenuous balance between the citizenry and their republic as any of the other amendments in the Bill of Rights, especially the right to freedom of speech, assembly, press, petition, security, and due process.

Supreme Court Justice William O. Douglas understood this tension well. "The Constitution is not neutral," he remarked. "It was designed to take the government off the backs of people."[18] In this way, the freedoms enshrined in the Bill of Rights *in their entirety* stand as a bulwark against a police state. To our detriment, these rights have been steadily weakened, eroded, and undermined in recent years. Yet without any one of them, including the Second Amendment right to own and bear arms, we are that much more vulnerable to the vagaries of out-of-control policemen, benevolent dictators, genuflecting politicians, and overly ambitious bureaucrats.

When all is said and done, the debate over gun ownership really has little to do with gun violence in America. Eliminating guns will not necessarily eliminate violence. Those same individuals sick enough to walk into an elementary school[19] or a movie theater[20] and open fire using a gun *can* and *do* wreak just as much havoc with homemade bombs made out of pressure cookers[21] and a handful of knives.[22]

It's also not even a question of whether Americans need weapons to defend themselves against any overt threats to our safety or well-being, although a study by a Quinnipiac University economist indicates that less restrictive concealed gun-carry laws save lives, while gun control can endanger them.[23] In fact, journalist Kevin Carson, writing for *Counter Punch*, suggests that prohibiting Americans from owning weapons would be as dangerously ineffective as Prohibition and the War on the Drugs:

> [W]hat strict gun laws will do is take the level of police statism, lawlessness and general social pathology up a notch in the same way Prohibition and the Drug War have done. I'd expect a War on Guns to expand the volume of organized crime, and to empower criminal gangs fighting over control over the black market, in exactly the same way Prohibition did in the 1920s and strict drug laws have done since the 1980s. I'd expect it to lead to further erosion of Fourth Amendment protections against search and seizure, further

militarization of local police via SWAT teams, and further expansion of the squalid empire of civil forfeiture, perjured jailhouse snitch testimony, entrapment, planted evidence, and plea deal blackmail.[24]

Who Gets to Call the Shots?

Truly, the debate over gun ownership in America is really a debate over who gets to call the shots and control the game. In other words, it's that same tug-of-war that keeps getting played out in every confrontation between the government and the citizenry over who gets to be the master and who is relegated to the part of the servant.

The Constitution is clear on this particular point, with its multitude of prohibitions on government overreach. As author Edmund A. Opitz observed in 1964:

> No one can read our Constitution without concluding that the people who wrote it wanted their government severely limited; the words "no" and "not" employed in restraint of government power occur 24 times in the first seven articles of the Constitution and 22 more times in the Bill of Rights.[25]

As police forces across the country acquire military-grade hardware in droves, Americans are finding their once-peaceful communities transformed into military outposts, complete with tanks, weaponry, and other equipment designed for the battlefield. Pictured is the North Penn Tactical Response Team of Montgomery County, Pennsylvania, practicing Cellular Team Tactics. (Photography by Tim McAteer)

In a nutshell, then, the Second Amendment's right to bear arms reflects not only a concern for one's personal defense, but serves as a check on the political power of the ruling authorities. It represents an implicit warning against governmental encroachments on one's freedoms, the warning shot over the bow to discourage any unlawful violations of our persons or property. As such, it reinforces that necessary balance in the citizen-state relationship.

Certainly, dictators in past regimes have understood this principle only too well. As Adolf Hitler noted, "The most foolish mistake we could possibly make would be to allow the subject races to possess arms. History shows that all conquerors who have allowed their subject races to carry arms have prepared their own downfall by so doing."[26] It should come as no surprise, then, that starting in December 1935, Jews in Germany were prevented from obtaining shooting licenses, because authorities believed that to allow them to do so would "endanger the German population."[27] In late 1938, special orders were delivered barring Jews from owning firearms, with the punishment for arms possession being twenty years in a concentration camp.[28]

The rest, as they say, is history. Yet it is a history that we should be wary of repeating.

CHAPTER 15

Who's to Blame for Battlefield America?

"The tools of conquest do not necessarily come with bombs and explosions and fallout. There are weapons that are simply thoughts, attitudes, prejudices—to be found only in the minds of men. For the record, prejudices can kill and suspicion can destroy, and a thoughtless, frightened search for a scapegoat has a fallout all its own—for the children and the children yet unborn. And the pity of it is that these things cannot be confined to The Twilight Zone."[1]

—ROD SERLING, *The Twilight Zone*

So well-oiled and interconnected are the cogs, wheels, and gear shifts of the government machinery that it can be near to impossible to decipher where the fault lies when something goes awry. What some are slowly coming to realize, however, is that the mechanism itself has changed. Its purpose is no longer to keep the republic running smoothly. To the contrary, this particular contraption's purpose is to maintain control and keep the corporate police state in power. Thus, when hiccups, belches, whinges, and jams arise, they are not being caused by the mechanism itself becoming faulty—its various parts are already a corrupt part of the whole. Rather, that's the sound of someone jamming the mechanism and interrupting the smooth flow of the corporate state.

Just consider how insidious and incestuous the various "parts" of the mechanism have become.

Perhaps the most notorious offenders and most obvious culprits in the creation of the corporate state, Congress has proven itself to be both inept and avaricious,[2] oblivious champions of an authoritarian system that is systematically dismantling their constituents' fundamental rights. Congress' most grievous behavior, however, is its failure to hold

What began with the passage of the USA Patriot Act in October 2001 has snowballed into the eradication of every vital safeguard against government overreach, corruption, and abuse. (Illustration by Caroline Jonik)

the president accountable, enabling him to routinely operate above the law. The precedent set of Congress going along with senseless and illegal White House policies has turned the office of the president into an untouchable, unstoppable force.

The Executive Branch is no better, no matter which party occupies the White House. For example, despite having ridden into office on a wave of optimism and the promise of a new America free of civil liberties abuses, Barack Obama has proven to be a more effective manipulator of the American people than his predecessors. His presidency will be defined by "kill lists;"[3] the murder of civilians (including women and children) in secret drone strikes abroad, including drone strikes against at least four American citizens living outside the country;[4] the championing of warrantless surveillance of American citizens; and the funneling of arms to al-Qaeda backed rebels in Syria.[5]

The U.S. Supreme Court—once the last refuge of justice, the one governmental body really capable of rolling back the slowly emerging tyranny enveloping America—has instead become the champion of the American police state, absolving government and corporate officials of their crimes while relentlessly punishing the average American for exercising his or her rights. In one month alone in 2013, the justices determined that criminal suspects, who are supposed to be treated as innocent until proven guilty, may have their DNA forcibly extracted from them by police;[6] that staying silent while the police question you may be considered evidence of guilt, despite the Fifth Amendment's protection against self-incrimination and the well-established "right to remain silent";[7] and that it operates in a zone in which First Amendment protections cease to exist, as they have unilaterally barred protests outside the Supreme Court building, countering a federal court decision that determined that activities on the Supreme Court grounds are protected by the First Amendment. These are just three examples of a Court that, like the rest of the government, places profit, security, and convenience above our basic rights.

The military now largely operates as its own branch of the government, controlled less by Congress and the White House than by the profit-driven motives of the corporate state. Indeed, the coup d'état wresting control of our government from civilians and delivering it into the hands of the military industrial complex happened decades ago

President Barack Obama greets Supreme Court Justice Ruth Bader Ginsburg prior to his State of the Union address in front of a joint session of Congress on Tuesday, Jan. 24, 2012, at the Capitol in Washington. (Photography by Associated Press)

while our backs were turned and our minds distracted. Consequently, we now find ourselves in the unenviable position of longing for an elusive peace while trying to rein in a runaway militarized government with a gargantuan and profit-driven appetite for war.[8]

Of course, this quadrumvirate of total control would be completely ineffective without a propaganda machine provided by the world's largest corporations. Besides shoving drivel down our throats at every possible moment, the so-called news agencies, which are supposed to act as bulwarks against government propaganda, have instead become the mouthpieces of the state. One need only look at the media's behavior post-9/11 to understand what I mean. From championing the invasion of Iraq based upon absolute fabrications,[9] to the fanatic support of all government surveillance policies and the demonization of whistle blowers, the pundits who pollute our airwaves are at best court jesters and at worst propagandists for the false reality created by the American government.

In some instances, as legendary journalist Carl Bernstein shows, members of the media have also served as extensions of the surveillance state, with reporters actually carrying out assignments for the CIA. "Reporters shared their notebooks with the CIA," Bernstein writes. "Some of the journalists were Pulitzer Prize winners," with some being "full-time CIA employees masquerading as journalists abroad."[10] Executives with CBS, the *New York Times* and *Time* magazine also worked closely with the CIA to vet the news. Bernstein continues:

> Other organizations which cooperated with the CIA include the American Broadcasting Company, the National Broadcasting Company, the Associated Press, United Press International, Reuters, Hearst Newspapers, Scripps-Howard, *Newsweek* magazine, the Mutual Broadcasting System, the *Miami Herald* and the old *Saturday Evening Post* and *New York Herald-Tribune*.[11]

In other words, the "news" we receive is routinely edited by government surveillance agents.

The Complicity of the Nobodies

Finally, there can be no discounting the role of the American people in bringing about our own ruin. As Nazi concentration camp survivor Hannah Arendt suggests, it is the sheepish masses who mindlessly march in lockstep with the government's dictates—expressing no outrage, demanding no reform, and issuing no challenge to the status quo—who are to blame for the prison walls being erected around us. The author of *The Origins of Totalitarianism*, Arendt warned that "the greatest evil perpetrated is the evil committed by nobodies, that is, by human beings who refuse to be persons."[12]

This is where so-called "free" nations fall to ruin, and bureaucracy and tyranny prevail.

The most superior engine in the world still requires some form of energy to bring it to life and maintain it, and in this particular mechanism, "we the people" serve that vital function. We are the petrol that powers the motor, for good or bad. We now belong to a permanent underclass in America. It doesn't matter what you call us—chattel, slaves, worker bees—it's all the same. What matters is that we are expected to march in lockstep with and submit to the will of the state in all matters, public and private.

Through our complicity in matters large and small, we have allowed an out-of-control corporate-state apparatus to take over every element of American society. Our failure to remain informed about what is taking place in our government, to know and exercise our rights, to vocally protest, to demand accountability on the part of our government representatives, and at a minimum *to care* about the plight of our fellow Americans, has been our downfall. Having allowed ourselves to descend into darkness, refusing to see what is really happening, happily trading the truth for false promises of security and freedom, we have allowed the police state to emerge and to flourish.

Too many of us willingly, knowingly, and deliberately comprise what Arendt refers to as "cogs in the mass-murder machine." These cogs are none other than those of us who have turned a blind eye to the government corruption, or shrugged dismissively at the ongoing injustices, or tuned out the mayhem in favor of entertainment distractions. Just as guilty are those who have traded in their freedoms for a phantom promise of security, not to mention those who feed the machine unquestioningly with their tax dollars and partisan politics.

And then there are those who work for the government, either directly or as contractors for federal, state, or local governments. These government employees—the soldiers, the cops, the technicians, the social workers, etc.—are neither evil nor sadistic. They're simply minions being paid to do a job, whether that job is to arrest you, spy on you, investigate you, crash through your door, etc.[13] However, we would do well to remember that those who worked at the Nazi concentration camps and ferried the victims to the gas chambers were also just "doing their jobs."

A Fearful People

Living in a free society means not having to look over your shoulder to see whether the government is watching or fearing that a government agent might perpetuate violence upon you. Unfortunately, subjected as we are to government surveillance from body scanners, militarized police, roadside strip searches, SWAT team raids, drones, and other trappings of a police state, "we the people" do not live in a free society any longer.

Not only are we no longer a free people but we have become a fearful people, as well, helped along in large part by politicians eager to capitalize on our fears. As Julie Hanus writes for *Utne*: "Since the 1980s, society at large has bolted frantically from one panic to the next. Fear of crime reduced us to wrecks, but before long we were also howling about

A member of the Wichita Falls SWAT team conducts a rifle drill at a law enforcement shooting range March 14, 2013. The exercise was a part of a joint exercise with an Air Force Explosive Ordinance Disposal team from the 366th Training Squadron. (Photography by Jelani Gibson)

deadly diseases, drug abusers, online pedophiles, avian flu, teens gone wild, mad cows, anthrax, immigrants, environmental collapse, and—let us not forget—terrorists."[14]

Now thanks to a militarized police force, a weaponized bureaucracy, a technologically adept surveillance state, and a corporate elite that reigns over all, we've got a few more fears to add to that growing list, and with good reason: fear of the police—local, state, and federal agents—fear of our own government, and fear that we are little more than prisoners in this police state.

A Psychopathic Government

Modern government in general—ranging from the militarized police in SWAT team gear crashing through our doors to the rash of innocent citizens being gunned down by police to the invasive spying on everything we do—is acting illogically, even psychopathically.[15] (Again, the characteristics of a psychopath include a "lack of remorse and empathy, a sense of grandiosity, superficial charm, conning and manipulative behavior, and refusal to take responsibility for one's actions, among others."[16])

When our own government no longer sees us as human beings with dignity and worth but as things to be manipulated, maneuvered, mined for data, manhandled by police, conned into believing it has our best interests at heart, mistreated, jailed if we dare step out of line, and then punished unjustly without remorse—all the while refusing to own up to its failings—we are no longer operating under a constitutional republic. Instead, what we are experiencing is a pathocracy: tyranny at the hands of a psychopathic government, which "operates against the interests of its own people except for favoring certain groups."[17]

Unfortunately, the faceless, nameless, bureaucratic government machine that relentlessly erodes our freedoms through a million laws, statutes, and prohibitions is nearly impossible to shut down once it has been erected and set into motion. Obedience is the precondition to totalitarianism, and the precondition to obedience is fear. Regimes of the past and present understand this. "The very first essential for success," Hitler wrote in *Mein Kampf,* "is a perpetually constant and regular employment of violence."[18]

Slaves in Thrall to the Machine

If there is any glimmer of hope to be found, it will take a citizenry willing to be active at the local level. Clearly we cannot wait for things to get completely out of control. If you wait to act until the SWAT team is crashing through *your* door, until *your* name is placed on a terror watch list, until *you* are reported for such outlawed activities as collecting rainwater or letting your children play outside unsupervised, then it will be too late.

This much I know: we are not faceless numbers. We are not cogs in the machine. We are not slaves. We are people, and free people at that. As the Founders understood, our freedoms do not flow from the government. They were not given to us, to be taken away at the will of the State; they are inherently ours. In the same way, the government's appointed purpose is not to threaten or undermine our freedoms, but to safeguard them.

Until we can get back to this way of thinking, until we can remind our fellow Americans what it really means to *be* a free American, and until we learn to stand our ground in the face of threats to those freedoms and encourage our fellow citizens to stop being cogs in the machine, we will continue to be treated like slaves in thrall to the bureaucratic police state.

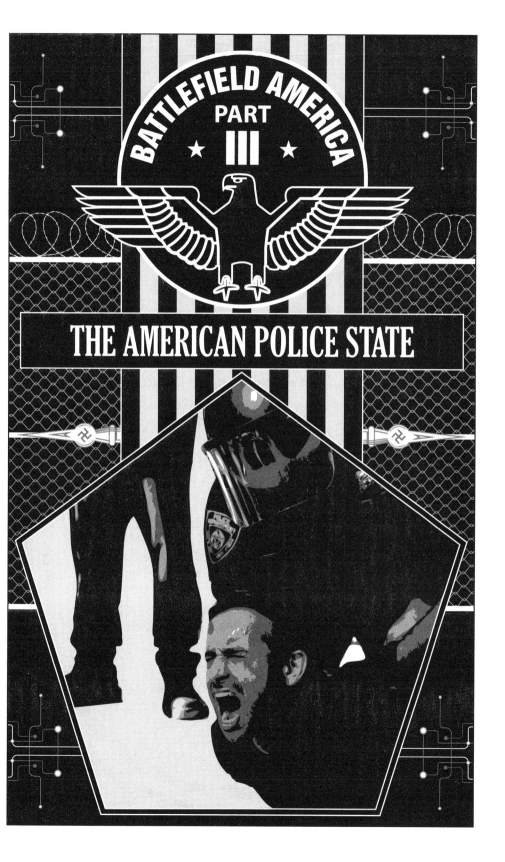

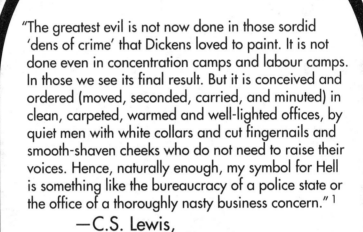

"The greatest evil is not now done in those sordid 'dens of crime' that Dickens loved to paint. It is not done even in concentration camps and labour camps. In those we see its final result. But it is conceived and ordered (moved, seconded, carried, and minuted) in clean, carpeted, warmed and well-lighted offices, by quiet men with white collars and cut fingernails and smooth-shaven cheeks who do not need to raise their voices. Hence, naturally enough, my symbol for Hell is something like the bureaucracy of a police state or the office of a thoroughly nasty business concern." [1]

—C.S. Lewis,
The Screwtape Letters

"There are always risks in challenging excessive police power, but the risks of not challenging it are more dangerous, even fatal." [2]

—Hunter S. Thompson,
Kingdom of Fear: Loathsome Secrets of a Star-Crossed Child in the Final Days of the American Century

"It's an oppressive organization now controlled by one percent of corporate America. Corporate America is using police forces as their mercenaries." [3]

—Ray Lewis,
former Philadelphia police captain

Reality Check

FACT: At least 400 to 500 innocent people are killed by police officers every year.[4] Indeed, Americans are now eight times more likely to die in a police confrontation than they are to be killed by a terrorist.[5] Americans are 110 times more likely to die of foodborne illness than in a terrorist attack.[6]

FACT: There has been a notable buildup in recent years of SWAT teams within non-security-related federal agencies such as the Department of Agriculture, the Railroad Retirement Board, the Tennessee Valley Authority, the Office of Personnel Management, the Consumer Product Safety Commission, the U.S. Fish and Wildlife Service, and the Education Department.[7]

FACT: On an average day in America, over 100 Americans have their homes raided by SWAT teams.[8]

FACT: For the first time in history, Congress is dominated by a majority of millionaires who are, on average, fourteen times wealthier than the average American.[9] According to a scientific study by Princeton researchers, the United States of America is not the democracy that it purports to be, but rather an oligarchy, in which "economic elites and organized groups representing business interests have substantial independent impacts on U.S. government policy."[10]

FACT: Police officers are more likely to be struck by lightning than be made financially liable for their wrongdoing.[11]

CHAPTER 16

A Country at War with Itself

"Soldiers and police are supposed to be different. . . . Police look inward. They're supposed to protect their fellow citizens from criminals, and to maintain order with a minimum of force. It's the difference between Audie Murphy and Andy Griffith. But nowadays, police are looking, and acting, more like soldiers than cops, with bad consequences. And those who suffer the consequences are usually innocent civilians."[1]—Journalist GLENN REYNOLDS

"In case you haven't noticed, America, and Europe, we are presently locked into a permanent state of war, or *war state*. The question is, against who? As the existential enemy becomes ever harder to sell to the public and risks fading into irrelevance, the state is developing an unhealthy fixation—on its own people."[2]—Journalist PATRICK HENNINGSEN

Violence has become our government's calling card.

Indeed, the greatest perpetrator of violence in American society and around the world is none other than the U.S. government. America even exports violence worldwide, with one of this country's most profitable exports being weapons.

From the endless wars waged abroad in the name of fighting terrorism by America's military empire to the more than 80,000 SWAT team raids carried out every year on unsuspecting Americans,[3] the U.S. government has a troubling tendency to use violence as a means to an end. This is true, whether in matters of foreign or domestic policy, when heavily armed agents enforce a myriad of arcane, bureaucratic regulations that impinge on Americans simply going about their business, such as the goat farmers whose homes were raided by SWAT teams with the Food and Drug Administration[4] or those attempting to

Communities across America are finding themselves "gifted" with drones, tanks, grenade launchers and other military equipment better suited to the battlefield. And it's all being done through federal programs that allow the military to "gift" battlefield-appropriate weapons, vehicles and equipment to domestic police departments across the country. Pictured: United States Marshals Service Tools.   (Source: U.S. Marshals)

exercise their constitutional rights, such as the Occupy protesters who were subjected to all manner of violence.[5]

It is no coincidence that the assault weapons used by killer Adam Lanza in the Newtown, Conn., Sandy Hook school shooting in 2012 were military-grade weapons.[6] These weapons, commonly wielded in video games, action movies, and by invading SWAT teams, go hand in hand with the steady diet of violence that permeates everything in our culture. What is more significant, however, is that these weapons are not just the stuff of celluloid fantasy. In the hands of government agents, whether they are members of the military, law enforcement or some other government agency, these weapons have become routine parts of America's day-to-day life, a byproduct of the rapid militarization of government agents over the past several decades.

This is what happens when you turn a nation into a police state: weapons of war become accepted instruments of tyranny, whether in the hands of government agents or in the hands of raging lunatics. We are a country at war with itself.

Militarized Police

It all started back in 1997 when Congress launched the 1033 Program to allow the Department of Defense to transfer surplus military goods to state and local police agencies. Since then, this federal "recycling" program has transferred more than $4.3 *billion* in military equipment to police agencies in all fifty states and U.S. territories.[7] In 2013 alone, local police agencies received more than half a billion dollars' worth of assault rifles, grenade launchers, bayonets, combat knives, night-vision equipment, bomb detonator robots, airplanes, helicopters, and "deception equipment" such as camouflage gear.[8]

The 1033 program allows small towns like Rising Star, Texas, with a population of 835 and only one full-time police officer, to acquire $3.2 million worth of goods and military gear from the federal government.[9] Included among the military equipment sent to local police departments are high-powered weapons, assault vehicles, tactical gear, and Mine-Resistant Ambush Protected (MRAP) armored vehicles that are used in foreign warzones to engage insurgents.[10] Police agencies also receive a variety of other toys and gizmos, including "aircraft,

Military equipment for local police (Source: Dept. of Defense)

boats, Humvees, body armor, weapon scopes, infrared imaging systems and night-vision goggles," not to mention more general items such as "bookcases, hedge trimmers, telescopes, brassieres, golf carts, coffee makers, and television sets."[11]

In addition to equipping police with militarized weapons and equipment, the government has also instituted an incentive program of sorts, the Byrne Formula Grant Program, which awards federal grants based upon "the number of overall arrests, the number of warrants served or the number of drug seizures."[12] A sizable chunk of taxpayer money has kept the program in full swing over the years.[13]

Armed and Ready to Kill

This armory of weaponry designed for war is not limited to local law enforcement agencies. All levels of government, including regulatory

Hollow point bullets, which explode on contact and wreak havoc on the human body, have been held in violation of international law and are banned in some countries. (Photography by Oleg Volk)

agencies within the federal government, are in possession of high-powered weapons, including hollow point bullets. Hollow point bullets, which explode on contact and wreak havoc on the human body, have been held in violation of international law and are banned in some countries.[14]

Well aware of this fact, however, defense contractor ATK agreed to produce 450 million hollow point rounds to be used by the Department of Homeland Security (DHS) and its Immigration and Customs Enforcement office.[15] DHS placed another order for 750 million rounds of various ammunition in August 2012.[16] In August 2012 the Social Security Administration (SSA) placed an order for 174,000 rounds of hollow point ammunition.[17] The SSA distributed ammunition to 41 locations throughout the United States, including major cities such as Los Angeles, Detroit, and Philadelphia, among others.[18]

No wonder many Americans are armed to the hilt. Many feel the need to protect themselves against their own government.

Who Will Protect You from the Police?

What we are faced with is a dangerous paradigm shift in which civilians (often unarmed and defenseless) not only have less rights than militarized police, but also one in which the safety of civilians is treated as a lower priority than the safety of their police counterparts. Moreover, the privacy of civilians is negligible in the face of the government's various missions, and the homes of civilians are no longer the refuge from government intrusion that they once were.

It wasn't always this way, however. There was a time in America when a man's home really was a sanctuary where he and his family could be safe and secure from the threat of invasion by government agents. Those agents were held at bay by the dictates of the Fourth Amendment, which protects American citizens from unreasonable searches and seizures.

The Fourth Amendment was added to the U.S. Constitution by colonists still smarting from the abuses they had been forced to endure while under British rule, among these were home invasions by the military under the guise of writs of assistance. These writs were nothing less than open-ended royal documents which British soldiers used as a justification for barging into the homes of colonists and rifling through their belongings. James Otis, a renowned colonial attorney, "condemned writs of assistance because they were perpetual, universal (addressed to every officer and subject in the realm), and allowed anyone to conduct a search in violation of the essential principle of English liberty that a peaceable man's house is his castle."[19] As Otis noted:

> Now, one of the most essential branches of English liberty is the freedom of one's house. A man's house is his castle; and whilst he is quiet, he is as well guarded as a prince in his castle. This writ, if it should be declared legal, would totally annihilate this privilege. Custom-house officers may enter our houses when they please; we are commanded to permit their entry. Their menial servants may enter, may break locks, bars, and everything in their way; and whether they break through malice or revenge, no man, no court can inquire. Bare suspicion without oath is sufficient.[20]

To our detriment, we have now come full circle, returning to a time before the American Revolution when government agents—with the blessing of the courts—could force their way into a citizen's home with seemingly little concern for lives lost and property damaged in the process.

Actually, we may be worse off today than our colonial ancestors when one considers the extent to which courts have sanctioned the use of no-knock raids by police SWAT teams; the arsenal of lethal weapons available to local police agencies; the ease with which courts now dispense search warrants based often on little more than a suspicion of wrongdoing; and the inability of police to distinguish between reasonable suspicion and the higher standard of probable cause, the latter of which is required by the Constitution before any government official can search an individual or his property.

The Hammer and the Nail

We're entering the final phase of America's transition to authoritarianism, a phase notable for its co-opting of civilian police as military forces. American police forces were never supposed to be a branch of the military, nor were they meant to be private security forces for the reigning political faction. Instead, they were intended to be an aggregate of countless local police units, composed of citizens like you and me that exist for a sole purpose: to serve and protect the citizens of each and every American community.

However, as a result of the increasing militarization of the police in recent years, the police now not only look like the military, but they function like them as well. Thus we no longer have a civilian force of peace officers entrusted with serving and protecting the American people. Instead, today's militarized law enforcement officials have shifted their allegiance from the citizenry to the state, acting preemptively to ward off any possible challenges to the government's power, unrestrained by the boundaries of the Fourth Amendment.

The phenomenon we are experiencing with the police is what philosopher Abraham Kaplan referred to as the law of the instrument,[21] which essentially says that to a hammer, everything looks like a nail. In the scenario that has been playing out in recent years, we the citizenry have become the nails to be hammered by the government's henchmen, a.k.a. its guns for hire, a.k.a. its standing army, a.k.a. the nation's law enforcement agencies. Indeed, there can no longer be any doubt that armed police officers are the end product of a merger between the government (federal, local, and state) and law enforcement agencies. The result is a "standing" or permanent army composed of full-time professional soldiers who do not disband. Yet these permanent armies are exactly what those who drafted the U.S. Constitution and Bill of Rights feared as tools used by despotic governments to wage war against its citizens.[22]

CHAPTER 17

Vigilantes with a Badge

"Police are specialists in violence. They are armed, trained, and authorized to use force. With varying degrees of subtlety, this colors their every action. Like the possibility of arrest, the threat of violence is implicit in every police encounter. Violence, as well as the law, is what they represent."[1] —Author KRISTIAN WILLIAMS

"Well, what is a vigilante man?
Tell me, what is a vigilante man?
Has he got a gun and a club in his hand?
Is that a vigilante man?
Oh, why does a vigilante man,
Why does a vigilante man
Carry that sawed-off shot-gun in his hand?
Would he shoot his brother and sister down?"[2]

—WOODY GUTHRIE, "Vigilante Man"

Here's a recipe for disaster: Take a young man, raise him on a diet of violence, hype him up on the power of the gun in his holster and the superiority of his uniform, render him woefully ignorant of how to handle a situation without resorting to violence, and train him well in military tactics. At the same time, allow him to be illiterate about the Constitution, and never stress to him that he is to be a peacemaker and a peacekeeper, respectful of and subservient to the taxpayers, who are in fact his masters and employers.

Once you have fully indoctrinated this young man (or woman) with the idea that the police belong to a brotherhood of sorts, with its own honor code and rule of law, this person is then placed in situations

A police tactical team moves in to disperse a group of protesters in Ferguson, Mo.
(Photography by Associated Press)

where he will encounter individuals who knowingly or unknowingly challenge his authority, where he may, justifiably or not, feel threatened, and where he will have to decide between firing a weapon or—the more difficult option—adequately investigating a situation in order to better assess the danger and risk posed to himself and others. And then he or she will act on it by defusing the tension or de-escalating the violence.

I'm not talking about a situation so obviously fraught with risk that there is no other option but to shoot, although I am hard pressed to consider what that might be outside of the sensationalized Hollywood hostage crisis scenario. I'm talking about the run-of-the mill encounters between police and citizens that occur daily. In an age when police are increasingly militarized, weaponized, and protected by the courts, these once-routine encounters are now inherently dangerous for any civilian unlucky enough to be in the wrong place at the wrong time.

I'm not the only one concerned, either. Indeed, I've been contacted by many older police officers who are equally alarmed by the attitudes and behaviors of younger police today, the foot soldiers in the police state. Yet this is what happens when you go from a representative democracy in which all members are subject to the rule of law to a hierarchical one in which there is one set of laws for the rulers and another, far more stringent set, for the ruled.

Peace Officers or Vigilantes?

Seldom does a day go by without reports of police officers overstepping the bounds of the Constitution and brutalizing, terrorizing, and killing the citizenry. Indeed, the list of incidents in which unaccountable police abuse their power and leave taxpayers bruised, broken, and/or killed grows longer and more tragic by the day to such an extent that Americans are now *eight* times more likely to die in a police confrontation than they are to be killed by a terrorist.[3]

Making matters worse, when these officers, who have long since ceased to be *peace* officers, violate their oaths by bullying, beating, tasering, shooting, and killing their employers—"we the people," the taxpayers to whom they owe their allegiance—they are rarely given more than a slap on the hands before resuming their patrols.

Ironically, even when the victims are awarded multi-million dollar settlements to compensate for the injuries suffered at the hands of out-of-control police, amped up on the power of the badge and the gun, it's the taxpayer-funded government that pays for their transgressions. All the while, the officers, never held accountable for their actions, continue to collect regular paychecks, benefits, and pensions.

Consider, for example, the sad scenario that played out when police used a battering ram to break into the home of 92-year-old Kathryn Johnson, mistakenly believing the house to be a drug den. Fearing that burglars were entering her home, which was situated in a dangerous neighborhood, Johnson fired a warning shot when the door burst open. Police unleashed a hail of gunfire, hitting Johnson with six bullets.[4] She was killed.

Eighty-year-old Eugene Mallory suffered a similar fate when deputies with the Los Angeles Sheriff's Department, claiming to have smelled chemicals related to the manufacture of methamphetamine, raided the multi-unit property in which Mallory lived. Thinking that his home was being invaded by burglars, Mallory allegedly raised a gun at the intruders, who shot him six times. Mallory died. "The lesson here," observed the spokesman for the sheriff's department, "is don't pull a gun on a deputy."[5]

What exactly are young officers being taught in the police academies when the slightest thing, whether it be a hand in a pocket, a man running towards them, a flashlight on a keychain, or a dehumanizing stare, can ignite a strong enough "fear for their safety" to justify doing whatever is deemed necessary to neutralize the threat, even if it means firing on an unarmed person? (Illustration by Caroline Jonik)

In Fort Worth, Texas, two rookie police officers sent to investigate a possible burglary circled 72-year-old Jerry Waller's house with flashlights shining. Waller, concerned that *his* home was being cased, went to his garage, armed with a gun for self-defense. The two officers snuck up on Waller, who raised his gun on the intruders. When Waller failed to obey orders to lower his gun, the officers shot and killed him. It turned out the officers had gone to the wrong address. They blamed the shooting death on "poor lighting."[6]

During a raid in Ogden, Utah, police dressed in black and carrying assault rifles charged into a darkened home. Upon entering the hallway and encountering a man holding a shiny object that one officer thought was a sword, police opened fire. Three shots later, 45-year-old Todd Blair fell to the floor dead. In his hands was a shiny golf club.[7]

In Sarasota, Florida, after receiving a tip about a child rape suspect, a mixture of federal and local police converged on the apartment complex where Louise Goldsberry lived. Unaware of police activity outside,

Louise was washing dishes in her kitchen when a man wearing what appeared to be a hunting vest pointed a rifle at her through her window. Fearing that she was about to be attacked, Louise retrieved her revolver from her bedroom. Meanwhile, the man began pounding on Louise's front door, saying, "We're the f@#$ing police; open the f@#$ing door."[8] Identifying himself as a police officer, the rifle-wielding man then opened the door, pointed a gun at Goldsberry and her boyfriend, who was also present, and yelled, "Drop the f@#$ing gun or I'll f@#$ing shoot you."[9] Ironically, the officer later justified his behavior on the grounds that he didn't like having a gun pointed at him.[10]

Badly Trained, Illiterate and Ignorant

Before I go any further, let me say this: the problem is not that all police are bad. The problem is that increasing numbers of police officers are badly trained, illiterate when it comes to the Constitution (especially the Fourth Amendment), and, in some cases, willfully ignorant about the fact that they are supposed to be peacekeepers working for us, the taxpayer.

When police officers take advantage of their broad discretion and repeatedly step beyond the bounds of the law, ignoring their responsibility to respect the Bill of Rights, they become little more than vigilantes—albeit vigilantes with a badge, backed by the corporate state. A vigilante is one who may act on behalf of the state but who steps beyond the moral boundaries of acceptable human behavior while terrorizing the citizenry.

Our communities are presently overrun by individuals entrusted with enforcing the law who are allowed to operate above the law and break the laws with impunity. This lawlessness on the part of law enforcement, an unmistakable characteristic of a police state, is made possible in large part by police unions that routinely oppose civilian review boards and resist the placement of names and badge numbers on officer uniforms;[11] police agencies that abide by the Blue Code of Silence, the quiet understanding among police that they should not implicate their colleagues for their crimes and misconduct;[12] prosecutors who treat police offenses with greater leniency than civilian offenses;[13] courts that sanction police wrongdoing in the name of security;[14] and legislatures that enhance the power, reach, and arsenal of the police.

That said, the police officers who make headlines for vigilante-style behavior are not necessarily any different from the rest of the citizenry. Just like you and me, these officers have spouses and children to care for, homes to maintain, bills to pay, and worries that keep them up at night. Like most of us, they strive to do their jobs as best as they know how, but that's where the problems arise. Clearly, they have been poorly trained in how to determine what is a real threat. They have also been indoctrinated into the mindset that they have a right to protect themselves at all cost and are empowered to shoot first and ask questions later with a veritable arsenal of military artillery provided by the federal government.

The Disease Has Spread

Unfortunately, whereas shootings of unarmed individuals by what *Slate* terms "trigger happy"[15] cops once took place primarily in big cities, that militarized, urban-warfare mindset among police has spread to small-town America. No longer is this just a problem for immigrants, or people of color, or lower income communities, or young people who look like hooligans out for trouble. We're all in this together, black and white, rich and poor, urban and suburban, guilty and innocent alike. We're all viewed the same by the powers that be: as potential lawbreakers to be viewed with suspicion and treated like criminals.

CHAPTER 18

When Police Shoot First and Ask Questions Later

"I watched the police break down doors, search houses and question, arrest, or chase people through houses fifty-two times. Nine times, police helicopters circled overhead and beamed searchlights onto local streets. I noted blocks taped off and traffic redirected as police searched for evidence . . . seventeen times. Fourteen times during my first eighteen months of near daily observation, I watched the police punch, choke, kick, stomp on, or beat young men with their night-sticks."[1]—Sociologist ALICE GOFFMAN, *On the Run: Fugitive Life in an American City*

If you don't want to get probed, poked, pinched, tasered, tackled, searched, seized, stripped, manhandled, arrested, shot, or killed, don't say, do, or even suggest anything that even hints of noncompliance. This is the new "thin blue line" which you must not cross in interactions with police if you want to walk away with your life and freedoms intact.

The growing tension inherent in most civilian-police encounters today is due to a transformation in the way police view themselves and their line of duty and, more critically, the use of militarized police to perform relatively routine tasks, resulting in situations fraught with danger to both civilians and police alike.

Whether it's full SWAT teams executing no-knock search warrants on the homes of law-abiding citizens over nothing more than a suspicion that the occupant owns a gun[2] or drivers being shot by police during routine traffic stops merely for reaching for their license and registration,[3] we're dealing with a skewed shoot-to-kill mindset in which police are increasingly responding to challenges to their "authority" by using their weapons.

129

Trained to view themselves as warriors or soldiers in a war, whether it's a war against drugs, terror, or crime, police shoot first and ask questions later in order to get the "bad" guys—i.e., anyone who is a potential target—before the "bad" guys get them. For example, consider what happened when two Cleveland police officers mistook the sounds of a backfiring car for gunfire and immediately began pursuing the car and its two occupants. Within 20 minutes, more than 60 police cars, some unmarked, and 115 officers had joined the pursuit, which ended in a middle school parking lot with more than 140 bullets fired by police in less than 30 seconds. The "suspects"—dead from countless bullet wounds—were unarmed.[4]

In Long Beach, California, police responded with heavy firepower to a perceived threat by a man holding a water hose.[5] The 35-year-old

man had reportedly been watering his neighbor's lawn when police, interpreting his "grip" on the water hose to be consistent with that of someone discharging a firearm, opened fire.[6] The father of two was pronounced dead at the scene.[7]

File photo is from a December 2010 press conference where Long Beach Police Department officers and Chief Jim McDonnell address the media near a photo of the water nozzle held by Douglas Zerby when he was shot and killed. (Source: *Long Beach Post*)

Thirteen-year-old Andy Lopez was shot and killed after two sheriff's deputies, a mere 20 feet away, saw him carrying a toy BB gun in public.[8] Lopez was about 20 feet away from the deputies, his back turned to them, when the officers took cover behind their car and ordered him to drop the "weapon." When Lopez turned around, toy gun in hand, one of the officers—a 24-year veteran of the force—shot him *seven* times. The time span between the deputies calling in a suspicious person sighting and shooting Lopez was a mere *ten* seconds. The young boy died at the scene.[9] Clearly, no attempt was made to use less lethal force.

Rationalizing the shooting incident, Lt. Paul Henry of the Santa Rosa Police Department explained, "The deputy's mindset was that he was fearful that he was going to be shot." Yet as commentator William Norman Grigg points out:

[T]he preoccupation with "officer safety" . . . leads to unnecessary police shootings. A peace officer is paid to assume certain risks, including those necessary to de-escalate a confrontation with someone believed to be a heavily armed suspect in a residential neighborhood. A "veteran" deputy with the mindset of a peace officer would have taken more than a shaved fraction of a split-second to open fire on a small male individual readily identifiable as a junior high school student, who was carrying an object that is easily recognizable as a toy—at least to people who don't see themselves as an army of occupation, and view the public as an undifferentiated mass of menace.[10]

Don't Cross the Thin Blue Line

The following incidents and many more like them serve as chilling reminders that in the American police state, "we the people" are at the mercy of law enforcement officers who have almost absolute discretion to decide who is a threat, what constitutes resistance, and how harshly they can deal with the citizens they were appointed to "serve and protect."[11]

For example, 16-year-old Kimani Grey was fired at eleven times and shot seven times, including three times in the back, after "anti-crime" police officers noticed him adjusting "his waistband in a manner the officers deemed suspicious." Reportedly, the teenager was unarmed and unthreatening.[12]

Police arrested Chaumtoli Huq because she failed to promptly comply when ordered to "move along" while waiting outside a Ruby Tuesday's

Police detain human rights lawyer Chaumtoli Huq.
(Photography by Charles Meacham)

restaurant for her children, who were inside with their father, using the bathroom. NYPD officers grabbed Huq, a lawyer with the New York City Public Advocate's office, flipped her around, pressed her against a wall, handcuffed her, searched her purse, arrested her, and told her to "shut up" when she cried out for help, before detaining her for nine hours.[13] Huq was charged with obstructing governmental administration, resisting arrest, and disorderly conduct.[14]

Oregon resident Fred Marlow was jailed and charged with interfering and resisting arrest after he filmed a SWAT team raid that took place across the street from his apartment and uploaded the footage to the Internet.[15] The footage shows police officers threatening Marlow, who was awoken by the sounds of "multiple bombs blasting and glass breaking" and ran outside to investigate only to be threatened with arrest if he didn't follow orders and return inside.[16]

Eric Garner, 43 years old, asthmatic and unarmed,[17] died after being put in a chokehold by NYPD police, allegedly for resisting arrest over his selling untaxed, loose cigarettes. Video footage of the incident shows little resistance on Garner's part. Indeed, the man was screaming, begging and insisting he couldn't breathe. And what was New York Mayor Bill De Blasio's advice to citizens in order to avoid a similar fate? Don't resist arrest.[18] (Mind you, the NYPD arrests more than 13,000 people every year on charges of resisting arrest, although only a small fraction of those charged ever get prosecuted.[19])

Then there was Marine Brandon Raub, who was questioned at his home by a swarm of DHS, FBI, Secret Service agents, and local police. He was then tackled to the ground, handcuffed, and forcibly transported to a police station. Raub was subsequently detained against his will in a psychiatric ward, without being provided any explanation, having any charges levied against him, or being read his rights— all allegedly because of controversial song lyrics and political views posted on his Facebook page. Incredibly, police insisted that Raub was not in fact under arrest.[20]

Of course, Raub *was* under arrest. When your hands are handcuffed behind you, when armed policemen are tackling you to the ground and transporting you across town in the back of a police car, and then forcibly detaining you against your will, you're not free to walk away.

Neutralizing a Threat

Frankly, it doesn't matter whether it's a casual "show your ID" request on a boardwalk, a stop-and-frisk search on a city street, or a traffic stop for speeding or just to check your insurance: if you feel like you can't walk away from a police encounter of your own volition—and more often than not you can't, especially when you're being confronted by someone armed to the hilt with all manner of militarized weaponry and gear—then for all intents and purposes, you're under arrest from the moment a cop stops you.

So do Americans really have any recourse at all when it comes to obeying an order from a police officer, even if it's just to ask a question or assert one's rights, or should we just "surrender quietly"[21]?

The short answer is that anything short of compliance may get you arrested and jailed. The long answer is a little more complicated, con-voluted and full of legal jargon and dissonance among the courts, but the conclusion is still the same: anything short of compliance is being perceived as "threatening" behavior or resistance to be met by police with extreme force resulting in injury, arrest, or death for the resistor. The key word, of course, is *comply*: meaning to obey, submit, or conform.

If you do attempt to walk away, be warned that the consequences will likely be even worse, as Tremaine McMillian[22] learned the hard way. Miami-Dade police slammed the 14-year-old boy to the ground, putting him in a chokehold and handcuffing him after he allegedly gave them "dehumanizing stares" and walked away from them, which the officers found unacceptable. According to Miami-Dade Police Detective Alvaro Zabaleta, "His body language was that he was stiffening up and pulling away. . . . When you have somebody resistant to them and pulling away and somebody clenching their fists and flailing their arms, that's a threat. Of course we have to neutralize the threat."[23]

This mindset that any challenge to police authority is a threat that needs to be "neutralized" is part of a dangerous nationwide trend that sets law enforcement officers beyond the reach of the Fourth Amendment guarantee against unreasonable search and seizure by government agents. It also serves to chill the First Amendment's assurances of free speech, free assembly, and the right to petition the government for a redress of grievances. Equally problematic is the trend in the courts that acquits officers involved in such shootings.

Safety at All Costs

What exactly are young officers being taught in the police academies when the slightest thing, whether it be a hand in a pocket, a man running towards them, a flashlight on a keychain, or a dehumanizing stare can ignite a strong enough "fear for their safety" to justify doing whatever is deemed necessary to neutralize the threat, even if it means firing on an unarmed person?

This is exactly what Jerome Skolnick and James Fyfe explore in their book *Above the Law: Police and the Excessive Use of Force*:

> [P]olice work is often viewed by those in the force *as an us-versus-them war* rather than a chance for community-oriented engagement and problem solving. The authors also point to a lack of accountability as one of the reasons why police violence persists. They acknowledge that, yes, police officers are placed in dangerous situations that at times require immediate responses. But they maintain that that doesn't excuse using more force than is needed to subdue someone, the lack of professional training that leads to such fear-based responses, or treating citizens as enemy combatants.[24]

Unfortunately, this police preoccupation with ensuring their own safety at all costs—a mindset that many older law enforcement officials find abhorrent in light of the more selfless code on which they were trained—is spreading like a plague among the ranks of police officers across the country with tragic consequences for the innocent civilians unlucky enough to be in the wrong place at the wrong time. Yet the fatality rate of on-duty patrol officers is reportedly far lower than many other professions, including construction, logging, fishing, truck driving, and even trash collection. In fact, police officers have the same rate of dying on the job as do taxi drivers.[25]

Nevertheless, according to the Bureau of Justice Statistics, 400 to 500 innocent people are killed by police officers every year.[26] That does not include the number of unarmed individuals shot and injured by police simply because they felt threatened or feared for their safety. This is the danger of having a standing army (which is what police forces, increasingly made up of individuals with military backgrounds and/or training, have evolved into) that has been trained to view the citizenry as little more than potential suspects, enemy combatants, and insurgents.

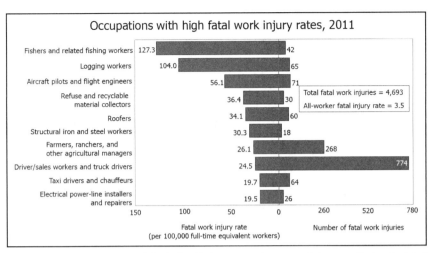

Occupations with high fatal injury rates (Source: U.S. Bureau of Labor Statistics)

What we're dealing with is what author Kristian Williams describes as the dual myths of heroism and danger: "The overblown image of police heroism, and the 'obsession' with officer safety, do not only serve to justify police violence after the fact; by providing such justification, they legitimize violence, and thus make it more likely."[27]

Targets of the Day

Just as troubling as this "shoot first, ask questions later" mindset is what investigative journalist Katie Rucke uncovered about how police are being trained to use force without hesitation and report their shootings in such a way as to legally justify a shooting.[28] Rucke reports the findings of one concerned citizen, "Jack," who went undercover in order to attend 24 hours of law enforcement training classes organized by the private, for-profit law enforcement training organization Calibre Press.[29]

"Jack says it was troubling to witness hundreds of SWAT team officers and supervisors who seemed unfazed by being instructed to not hesitate when it comes to using excessive, and even deadly, force," writes Rucke. "'From my personal experience, these trainers consistently promote more aggression and criticize hesitation to use force,' Jack said. 'They argue that the risk of making a mistake is worth it to absolutely minimize risk to the officer. And they teach officers how to

Police train on a shooting range.

use the law to minimize legal repercussions in almost any scenario. All this is, of course, done behind the scenes, with no oversight from police administrators, much less the public.'"[30]

Rucke continues:

> According to the learning materials, . . . there isn't time for logic and analysis, encouraging officers to fire multiple rounds at subjects because "two shots rarely stops 'em," and outlines seven reasons why "excessive use of force" is a myth. Other lessons Jack learned from the "Anatomy of Force Incidents" training . . . include a need to over-analyze one's environment for deadly threats by using one's imagination to create "targets of the day" who could be "reasonably" shot, to view racial profiling as a legitimate policing technique, even if the person is a child, pregnant woman or elderly person, and to use the law to one's advantage to avoid culpability.[31]

Police have been insulated from accusations of wrongdoing for too long and allowed to operate in an environment in which whatever a cop says, goes. The current practice is to let the police deal with these transgressions internally by suspending the officer involved with administrative pay, dragging out the investigation until the public forgets about the incident, and then eventually declaring the shooting incident justified based on the officer's fear for his safety, and allowing him to go back to work as usual. And if, on the off-chance, a shooting incident goes before the courts, the judiciary defers to police authority in almost all instances. For example, in a 2014 ruling, the U.S. Supreme Court declared that police officers who used deadly force to terminate a car chase were immune from a lawsuit. The officers were accused of needlessly resorting to deadly force by shooting multiple times at a man and his passenger in a stopped car, killing both individuals.[32]

Master or Slave?

There comes a time when law and order are in direct opposition to justice. This tension is at the heart of the issue over police brutality. It is carried out by individuals who may not themselves be evil but are merely following orders, marching in lockstep with a government machine that views us as less than human.

When police officers cease to look and act like civil servants or peace officers but instead look and act like soldiers occupying a hostile territory, it alters their perception of "we the people." Those who founded this country believed that we were the masters and that those to whom we pay salaries from our hard-earned tax dollars are our servants.

If daring to question, challenge, or even hesitate when a cop issues an order can get you charged with resisting arrest or disorderly conduct, you're not the master in a master-servant relationship. In fact, you're not even the servant—you're the slave.

This is not freedom. This is not even a life. This is a battlefield, a war zone, if you will, governed by martial law and disguised as a democracy. No matter how many ways you fancy it up with shopping malls, populist elections, and Monday night football, the fact remains that "we the people" are little more than prisoners in the American police state, and the police are our jailers and wardens.

CHAPTER 19

In the War Zone

"We have historically been a paramilitary organization. And we serve whoever sits in that chair, regardless of race, gender, creed, or political party. I don't know what we would do if we had to go to battle, and we had to make a determination, based on past practices, whether or not we wanted to go into battle. ... I am a soldier in an army."[1]

—Indianapolis Police Chief RICK HITE

Evolution of the police uniform
(Illustration by John Darkow)

It's 3 a.m. You've been asleep for hours when suddenly you hear a loud "Crash! Bang! Boom!" Based on the yelling, shouting and mayhem, it sounds as if someone, or several someones, are breaking through your front door.

With your heart racing and your stomach churning, all you can think about is keeping your family safe from the intruders who have invaded your home. You have mere seconds before the intruders make their way to your bedroom. Desperate to protect your loved ones, you scramble to lay hold of something—anything—that you might use in self-defense. It might be a flashlight, your son's baseball bat, or that still unloaded shotgun you thought you'd never need.

In a matter of seconds, the intruders are at your bedroom door. You brace for the confrontation, a shaky grip on your weapon. In the moments before you go down for the count, shot multiple times by the strangers who have invaded your home, you get a good look at your attackers.

It's the police.

Horror Stories

With every passing week, there are more and more horror stories in which homeowners are injured or killed simply because they mistook a SWAT team raid by police for a home invasion by criminals. Never mind that the unsuspecting homeowner, woken from sleep by the sounds of a violent entry, has no way of distinguishing between a home invasion by a criminal as opposed to a government agent.

Even dogs aren't spared. Family dogs are routinely shot and killed during SWAT team raids,[2] even if the SWAT team is at the wrong address or the dog is in the next yard over.[3]

Too often, the destruction of life and property wrought by the police is no less horrifying than that carried out by criminal invaders. For instance, when an Atlanta SWAT team attempted to execute a no-knock drug warrant in the middle of the night by launching a flashbang grenade into the targeted home, the grenade landed in a crib where a 19-month-old baby lay sleeping. The grenade exploded in the baby's face, burning his face, lacerating his chest, and leaving him paralyzed. He ended up in the hospital in a medically induced coma.[4]

If this were the first instance of police overkill, if it were even the fifth, there might be hope of reforming our system of law enforcement. But what happened to this baby, whose life will never be the same, has become par for the course in a society that glorifies violence, turns a blind eye to government wrongdoing, and sanctions any act by law

SWAT TEAM ATTACKS BABY
GARY FRANCHI REPORTING
NEXT NEWS NETWORK

A Georgia SWAT team launched a flash-bang grenade into the house in which Baby Bou, his three sisters and his parents were staying. The grenade landed in the 2-year-old's crib, burning a hole in his chest and leaving him with scarring that a lifetime of surgeries will not be able to easily undo.

enforcement, no matter how misguided or wrong. Indeed, this state-sponsored violence is a necessary ingredient in any totalitarian regime to ensure a compliant, cowed, and fearful populace.

Where Was the Outrage?

Each time we as a rational, reasoning, free-minded people fail to be outraged by government wrongdoing—whether it's the SWAT team raids that go awry, the senseless shootings of unarmed citizens,[5] the stockpiling of military weapons and ammunition by government agencies (including small-town police),[6] the unapologetic misuse of our taxpayer dollars for graft and pork, the incarceration of our fellow citizens in forced labor prisons[7]—we become accomplices in our own downfall.

There's certainly no shortage of things to be outraged about, starting with this dangerous mindset that has come to dominate police agencies and the courts that protecting the lives and safety of police officers (of all stripes) is more important than the lives and safety of the citizenry. This mindset holds true even if it means that greater numbers of innocent civilians will get hurt or killed (police kill roughly five times more often than they are killed[8]), police will become laws unto themselves, and the Constitution will be sidestepped, or worse disregarded, at every turn.

For example, where was the outrage when a Minnesota SWAT team raided the wrong house in the middle of the night, handcuffed the three young children, held the mother on the floor at gunpoint, shot the family dog, and then "forced the handcuffed children to sit next to the carcass of their dead pet and bloody pet for more than an hour" while they searched the home?[9]

Or what about the SWAT team that drove an armored Lenco Bearcat into Roger Serrato's yard, surrounded his home with paramilitary troops wearing face masks, threw a fire-starting flashbang grenade into the house, then when Serrato appeared at a window, unarmed and wearing only his shorts, held him at bay with rifles? Serrato died of asphyxiation from being trapped in the flame-filled house, and the county was ordered to pay $2.6 million to Serrato's family. It turns out the father of four had done nothing wrong. The SWAT team had misidentified him as someone involved in a shooting.[10] Even so, the police admitted no wrongdoing.[11]

And then there was the police officer who tripped and "accidentally" shot and killed Eurie Stamps, who had been forced to the floor of his home at gunpoint while a SWAT team attempted to execute a search warrant against his stepson.[12] Equally outrageous was the four-hour SWAT team raid on a California high school where students were locked down in classrooms, forced to urinate in overturned desks and generally terrorized by heavily armed, masked gunmen searching for possible weapons that were never found.[13]

The problem with all of these incidents, as one reporter rightly concluded, is "not that life has gotten that much more dangerous, it's that authorities have chosen to respond to even innocent situations as if they were in a warzone."[14]

Waging War on America's Military Veterans

This battlefield mindset takes an even deadlier turn when military veterans are involved, due in large part to government protocols that portray veterans as ticking time bombs in need of intervention. In 2012, for instance, the Justice Department launched a pilot program aimed at training SWAT teams to deal with confrontations involving highly trained combat veterans.[15]

Unfortunately, as we've seen in recent years, the problem with depicting veterans as potential enemy combatants is that any encounter with a military veteran can escalate very quickly into an explosive and deadly situation—at least, on the part of law enforcement.

John Edward Chesney, a 62-year-old Vietnam veteran, was killed in 2014 by a SWAT team allegedly responding to a call that the Army veteran was standing in his San Diego apartment window waving what looked like a semi-automatic rifle. SWAT officers locked down Chesney's street, took up positions around his home, and fired 12 rounds into Chesney's apartment window. It turned out that the gun Chesney reportedly pointed at police from three stories up was a "realistic-looking mock assault rifle."[16]

Police "standoff" with a man holding a toy gun
(Photography by CBS News 8)

Thankfully, Ramon Hooks' encounter with a Houston SWAT team did not end as tragically, but it very easily could have. Hooks, a 25-year-old Iraq war veteran, was using an air rifle gun for target practice outside when a Homeland Security agent, allegedly house shopping in the area, reported him as an active shooter. It wasn't long before the quiet neighborhood was transformed into a war zone, with dozens of cop cars, an armored vehicle and heavily armed police. Hooks was arrested, his air rifle pellets and toy gun confiscated, and charges filed against him for "criminal mischief."[17]

Battlefield Mindset

This battlefield mindset has so corrupted law enforcement agencies that the most routine tasks, such as serving a search warrant—intended to uncover evidence of a suspected crime—becomes a death warrant for the alleged "suspect," his family members and his pets once a SWAT team, trained to kill, is involved.

Unfortunately, SWAT teams are no longer reserved exclusively for deadly situations. Owing to the militarization of the nation's police forces, SWAT teams are now increasingly being deployed for relatively routine police matters, with some local SWAT teams sent out as much as five times a day.[18] For example, police in both Baltimore and Dallas have used SWAT teams to bust up poker games. A Connecticut SWAT team was sent into a bar that was believed to be serving alcohol to underage individuals. In Arizona, a SWAT team was used to break up an alleged cockfighting ring.[19] An Atlanta SWAT team raided a music studio, allegedly out of a concern that it might have been involved in illegal music piracy.[20]

In 1980, there were roughly 3,000 SWAT team-style raids in the US. By 2001, that number had grown to 45,000[21] and has since swelled to more than 80,000 SWAT team raids per year.[22] In fact, there are few communities without a SWAT team on their police force today.[23]

The problem, of course, is that as SWAT teams and SWAT-style tactics are used more frequently to carry out routine law enforcement activities, Americans find themselves in increasingly dangerous and absurd situations.

For example, in late July 2013, a no-kill animal shelter in Kenosha, Wisconsin, was raided by nine Department of Natural Resources

Pulaski County police in Arkansas received an MRAP, part of the military's recycling program. (Photography by KTHV-TV)

(DNR) agents and four deputy sheriffs. The raid was prompted by tips that the shelter was home to a baby deer that had been separated from its mother. The shelter officials had planned to send the deer to a wildlife rehabilitation facility in Illinois. However, the agents, who stormed the property unannounced, demanded that the deer be handed over because citizens are not allowed to possess wildlife. When the thirteen agents entered the property "armed to the teeth," they corralled the employees around a picnic table while they searched for the deer. When they returned, one agent had the deer slung over his shoulder in a body bag, ready to be euthanized.[24]

When asked why they didn't simply ask shelter personnel to hand the deer over instead of conducting an unannounced raid, the DNR Supervisor compared their actions to drug raids, saying "If a sheriff's department is going in to do a search warrant on a drug bust, they don't call them and ask them to voluntarily surrender their marijuana or whatever drug that they have before they show up."[25]

If these raids are becoming increasingly common and widespread, you can chalk it up to the "make-work" philosophy, in which you assign at-times unnecessary jobs to government agents to keep them busy or employed. In this case, however, the make-work principle is being used to justify the use of sophisticated military equipment[26] and, in the process, qualify for federal funding.[27]

Moreover, when it comes to SWAT-style tactics being used in routine policing, the federal government is one of the largest offenders, with multiple agencies touting their own SWAT teams, including the Fish and Wildlife Service, the Consumer Product Safety Commission, NASA, the Department of Education, the Department of Health and Human Services, the National Park Service, and the FDA.[28]

Occupied Territory

Clearly, the government has all but asphyxiated the Fourth Amendment. However, what about the Third Amendment, which has been interpreted to not only prohibit the quartering of soldiers in one's home and martial law but also standing armies?

A vivid example of this took place on July 10, 2011, in Henderson, Nevada, when local police informed homeowner Anthony Mitchell that they wanted to occupy his home in order to gain a "tactical advantage" in dealing with a domestic abuse case in an adjacent home. Mitchell refused the request, but this didn't deter the police, who broke down Mitchell's front door using a battering ram. Five officers pointed weapons at him, ordering him to the ground, where they shot him with pepper-ball projectiles.[29]

The point is this: America today is not much different from the America of the early colonists who had to contend with British soldiers who were allowed to "enter private homes, confiscate what they found, and often keep the bounty for themselves."[30] This practice is echoed today through SWAT team raids and the execution of so-called asset forfeiture laws, "which allow police to seize and keep for their departments cash, cars, luxury goods and even homes, often under only the thinnest allegation of criminality."[31]

It is this intersection of law enforcement and military capability which so worried the founding fathers and which should greatly concern us today. What Americans must decide is what they're going to do about this occupation of our cities and towns by standing armies operating under the guise of keeping the peace.

CHAPTER 20

America's Standing Armies

"The argument for up-armoring is always based on the least likely of terrorist scenarios. Anyone can get a gun and shoot up stuff. No amount of SWAT equipment can stop that."[1]

—MARK RANDOL, former terrorism expert with the Congressional Research Service

Police are increasingly resembling standing armies.
(Photography by Associated Press)

D espite the steady hue and cry by government agencies about the need for more police, more sophisticated weaponry, and the difficulties of preserving the peace and maintaining security in our modern age, the reality is far different. Violent crime in America has been on a steady decline,[2] a clear referendum on the fact that communities would be better served by smaller, demilitarized police forces. Nevertheless, police agencies throughout the country are dramatically increasing in size and scope.

For those who want to credit hefty police forces for declining crime rates, the data just doesn't show a direct correlation. In fact, cities such as Seattle and Dallas actually cut their police forces during this time and still saw crime rates drop.[3]

Small Armies

Some of the nation's larger cities boast police forces the size of small armies, so much so that former New York City Mayor Michael Bloomberg used to brag that the NYPD was his personal army.[4]

The statistics are alarming. For example, the Los Angeles Police Department (LAPD) has reached a total of 10,000 officers.[5] It takes its place alongside other cities boasting increasingly large police forces, including New York (36,000 officers) and Chicago (13,400 officers).[6] When considered in terms of cops per square mile, Los Angeles assigns a whopping 469 officers *per square mile*, followed by New York with 303 officers per square mile, and Chicago with 227 cops per square mile.[7]

Of course, such heavy police presence comes at a price. Los Angeles spends over $2 billion annually on its police force,[8] which consumes over 55 percent of Los Angeles' discretionary budget. Meanwhile, street repair and maintenance spending has declined by 36 percent, and in 2011, one-fifth of the city's fire stations lost units, increasing response times for 911 medical emergencies.[9]

There was a time in our nation's history when Americans would have revolted against the prospect of city police forces the size of small armies, or rampaging SWAT teams tearing through doors and terrorizing families. Today, the need for ramped up, militarized police is largely sold to the American public by way of the media through reality TV shows,[10] and by politicians well-versed in promising greater security in exchange for the government being given greater freedom to operate as it sees fit while running roughshod over the Constitution.

Drones, Tanks, and Grenade Launchers

Why does a police department which hasn't had an officer killed in the line of duty in over 125 years in a town of less than 20,000 people need tactical military vests like those used by soldiers in Afghanistan?[11] For that matter, why does a police department in a city of 35,000 people need a military-grade helicopter? Why are police departments across the country acquiring heavy-duty military equipment and weaponry? For the same reason that perfectly good roads get repaved, perfectly good equipment gets retired and replaced, and perfectly good employees spend their days twiddling their thumbs—and all of it at taxpayer expense.

It's called make-work programs, except in this case, instead of unnecessary busy work to keep people employed, communities across America are finding themselves "gifted" with drones, tanks, grenade launchers, and other military equipment better suited to the battlefield. And it's all being done through federal programs that allow the military to "gift" battlefield-appropriate weapons, vehicles, and equipment to domestic police departments across the country.[12]

It's a Trojan Horse, of course—one that is sold to communities as a benefit; all the while the real purpose is to keep the defense industry churning out profits, bring police departments in line with the military, and establish a standing army. As journalists Andrew Becker and G. W. Schulz report: federal grants provided by the Department of Homeland Security (DHS) have "transformed local police departments into small, army-like forces, and put intimidating equipment into the hands of civilian officers. And this is raising questions about whether the strategy has gone too far, creating a culture and capability that jeopardizes public safety and civil rights while creating an expensive false sense of security."[13] For example, note Becker and Schulz:

> In Montgomery County, Texas, the sheriff's department owns a $300,000 pilotless surveillance drone, like those used to hunt down al Qaeda terrorists in the remote tribal regions of Pakistan and Afghanistan. In Augusta, Maine, with fewer than 20,000 people and where an officer hasn't died from gunfire in the line of duty in more than 125 years, police bought eight $1,500 tactical vests. Police in Des Moines, Iowa, bought two $180,000 bomb-disarming robots, while an Arizona sheriff is now the proud owner of a surplus Army tank.[14]

Small counties and cities throughout the country are now being "gifted" with 20-ton Mine Resistant Ambush Protected (MRAP) vehicles.[15] MRAPs, some costing as much as $733,000, are built to withstand roadside bombs and other explosives, a function which seems unnecessary for any form of domestic policing. Yet police in Jefferson

County, New York, and in Boise and Nampa, Idaho, as well as High Springs, Florida, have all acquired MRAPs.[16] Police in West Lafayette, Indiana, also have an MRAP, valued at half a million dollars.[17]

Universities are also getting in on the action. In September 2013, the Ohio State University Department of Public Safety acquired an MRAP, which a university spokesperson said will be used for "officer rescue, hostage scenarios, bomb evaluation"—situations which are not too common on OSU's campus.[18] In reality, the MRAP will most likely be used for crowd control at football games and other situations where students gather together to exercise their First Amendment rights to free speech.[19]

Coming Soon to a Police Department Near You

While police departments like to frame the acquisition of military surplus as a money-saving method, in a twisted sort of double jeopardy, the taxpayer ends up footing a bigger bill. First, taxpayers are forced to pay millions of dollars for equipment which the Defense Department purchases from megacorporations only to abandon after a few years. Then taxpayers find themselves footing the bill to maintain the costly equipment once it has been acquired by the local police.[20] It didn't take the residents of Tupelo, Mississippi, long to discover that nothing comes free. Although the Tupelo police department was "gifted" with a free military helicopter, residents quickly learned that it required "$100,000 worth of upgrades and $20,000 each year in maintenance."[21]

Police departments are also receiving grants for extensive surveillance systems in order to create microcosms of the extensive surveillance systems put in place by the federal government in the years since 9/11. For example, using a $2.6 million grant from the DHS, police in Seattle purchased and set up a "mesh network" throughout the city capable of tracking every Wi-Fi enabled device within range. Police claim it won't be used for surveillance, but the devices are capable of determining "the IP address, device type, downloaded applications, current location, and historical location of any device that searches for a Wi-Fi signal."[22] Police have already been testing the network.[23]

It doesn't look like this trend towards the militarization of domestic police forces will be slowing down anytime soon, either. In fact, it seems to have opened up a new market for corporate contractors.[24]

In addition to being an astounding waste of taxpayer money, this equipping of police with military-grade equipment and weapons also gives rise to a dangerous mindset in which police feel compelled to put their newly high-power toys and weapons to use. The results are deadly, as can be seen in the growing numbers of unarmed civilians shot by police during relatively routine encounters and in the use of SWAT teams to carry out relatively routine tasks. For example, a team of police in Austin, Texas broke into a home in order to search for stolen koi fish. In Florida, over fifty barbershops were raided by police donning masks and guns in order to enforce barber licensing laws.[25]

Thus, while recycling unused military equipment might sound thrifty and practical, the ramifications are proving to be far more dangerous and deadly. This is what happens when you have police not only acquiring the gear of American soldiers but also the mindset of an army occupying hostile territory. With police playing the part of soldiers on the battlefield and the American citizenry left to play the part of enemy combatants, it's a safe bet that this exercise in the absurd will not have a happy ending.

Time to Demilitarize the Police?

There might be some hope of reform if only the problem of police brutality were not so widespread and endemic, if the citizenry actually had some sway with their representatives, if communities actually had some say over how law enforcement agencies "police" their communities, if police unions did not have such a stranglehold over the oversight process, if the courts were more impartial and less inclined to blindly sanction the actions of the police, and if the federal government itself had not already co-opted state and local police agencies in order to transform them into extensions of the military.

In the absence of any credible scenarios that would hold the police accountable to abiding by the rule of law—our U.S. Constitution—and respecting the citizenry's right to be treated with respect and dignity, the police have become a law unto themselves.

If ever there were a time to de-militarize and de-weaponize local police forces, it's now. The same goes for scaling back on the mindset adopted by cops that they *are* the law and should be revered, feared and obeyed. As for the idea that citizens must be compliant or risk being treated like lawbreakers, that's nothing more than authoritarianism with a badge. The end result of this logic, as we have seen with former regimes, is tyranny.

War on the American Citizenry

It's bad enough that the police now look like the military—with their foreboding uniforms and arsenal of lethal weapons—but when they no longer

act as peace officers entrusted with serving and protecting the American people and keeping the peace, then they have clearly lost sight of their overarching duty: to abide by the dictates of the U.S. Constitution and act as public servants *in service to the taxpayers of this country* rather than commanders directing underlings who must obey without question. Unfortunately, having watered down the Fourth Amendment's

Having watered down the Fourth Amendment's strong prohibitions intended to keep police in check and functioning as peacekeepers, we now find ourselves in the unenviable position of having militarized standing armies enforcing the law.

strong prohibitions intended to keep police in check and functioning as peacekeepers, we now find ourselves in the unenviable position of having militarized standing armies enforcing the law.

What we are witnessing today is nothing less than a war against the American citizenry.

CHAPTER 21

The Complicity of the Courts

"[I]f the individual is no longer to be sovereign, if the police can pick him up whenever they do not like the cut of his jib, if they can "seize" and "search" him in their discretion, we enter a new regime. The decision to enter it should be made only after a full debate by the people of this country."[1]

—U.S. Supreme Court Justice WILLIAM O. DOUGLAS

Despite what some may think, the Constitution is no magical incantation against government wrongdoing. Indeed, it's only as effective as those who abide by it. However, without government officials committed to abiding by the rule of law, courts willing to uphold the Constitution's provisions when government officials disregard them, and a citizenry knowledgeable enough to take action when those provisions are undermined, it provides little to no protection against SWAT team raids, domestic surveillance,[2] police shootings of unarmed citizens,[3] indefinite detentions, and the like.

Unfortunately, the courts and the police have meshed in their thinking to such an extent that anything goes when it's done in the name of

national security, crime fighting and terrorism. Consequently, America no longer operates under a system of justice characterized by due process, an assumption of innocence, probable cause and clear prohibitions on government overreach and police abuse. Instead, our courts of justice have been transformed into courts of

Courts have ruled that driving with stiff posture is now against the law.

order, advocating for the government's interests rather than championing the rights of the citizenry, as enshrined in the Constitution.

The Supreme Court's approach to law and order invariably favors the police.
(Illustration by Dwane Powell)

Kowtowing to the Police State

A review of the Supreme Court's rulings over the past ten-plus years reveals a startling and steady trend towards pro-police state rulings by an institution concerned more with establishing order and protecting government agents than with upholding the rights enshrined in the Constitution:

Police officers can use lethal force in car chases without fear of lawsuits. In *Plumhoff v. Rickard* (2014),[4] the Court declared that police officers who used deadly force to terminate a car chase were immune from a lawsuit. The officers were accused of needlessly resorting to deadly force by shooting multiple times at a man and his passenger in a stopped car, killing both individuals.

Police officers can stop cars based only on "anonymous" tips. In a 5-4 ruling in *Navarette v. California* (2014),[5] the Court declared that police officers can, under the guise of "reasonable suspicion," stop cars and question drivers based solely on anonymous tips, no matter how dubious, and whether or not they themselves witnessed any troubling behavior. This ruling came on the heels of a ruling by the Tenth Circuit Court of Appeals in *U.S. v. Westhoven* that driving too carefully, with a rigid posture, taking a scenic route, and having acne are sufficient reasons for a police officer to suspect you of doing something illegal, detain you, search your car, and arrest you—even if you've done nothing illegal to warrant the stop in the first place.[6]

Secret Service agents are not accountable for their actions, as long as they're done in the name of security. In *Wood v. Moss* (2014),[7] the Court granted "qualified immunity" to Secret Service officials who physically moved and relocated anti-Bush protesters, despite concerns raised that the protesters' First Amendment right to freely speak, assemble, and petition their government leaders had been violated. These decisions, part of a recent trend toward granting government officials "qualified immunity" in lawsuits over alleged constitutional violations (basically insulating them from being held accountable for their actions), merely incentivize government officials to violate constitutional rights without fear of repercussion.

Citizens only have a right to remain silent if they assert it. The Supreme Court ruled in *Salinas v. Texas*[8] (2013) that persons who are not under arrest must specifically invoke their Fifth Amendment privilege against self-incrimination in order to avoid having their refusal to answer police questions used against them in a subsequent criminal trial. What this ruling says, essentially, is that citizens had better know what their rights are and understand when those rights are being violated, because the government is no longer going to be held responsible for informing you of those rights before violating them.

Police have free reign to use drug-sniffing dogs as "search warrants on leashes," justifying any and all police searches of vehicles stopped on the roadside. In *Florida v. Harris* (2013),[9] a unanimous Court determined that police officers may use highly unreliable drug-sniffing dogs to conduct warrantless searches of cars during routine traffic stops.[10] In doing so, the justices sided with police by claiming that all the police need to do to prove probable cause for a search is simply assert that a drug detection dog has received proper training. The ruling turns man's best friend into an extension of the police state.

Police can forcibly take your DNA, whether or not you've been convicted of a crime. In *Maryland v. King* (2013), a divided Court determined that a person arrested for a crime (who is supposed to be presumed innocent until proven guilty) must submit to forcible extraction of their DNA.[11] Once again the Court sided with the guardians of the police state over the defenders of individual liberty in determining that DNA samples may be extracted from people arrested for "serious offenses." While the Court claims to have made its decision based upon concerns of properly identifying criminal suspects upon arrest, what they actually did is open the door for a nationwide dragnet of suspects targeted via DNA sampling.

Police can stop, search, question, and profile individuals. The Supreme Court declared in *Arizona v. United States* (2012) that Arizona police officers have broad authority to stop, search, and question citizens and non-citizens alike.[12] While the law prohibits officers from considering race, color, or national origin, it amounts to little more than a perfunctory nod to discrimination laws on the books, while paving the way for outright racial profiling and destroying the Fourth Amendment.

Police can subject Americans to virtual strip searches no matter the "offense." A divided Supreme Court actually prioritized making life easier for overworked jail officials over the basic right of Americans to

Veiled demonstrators at a march against racially disproportionate policing in New York City (Photography by LongIslandWins)

be free from debasing strip searches. In its 5-4 ruling in *Florence v. Burlington* (2012),[13] the Court declared that any person who is arrested and processed at a jail house, regardless of the severity of his or her offense (i.e., they can be guilty of nothing more than a minor traffic offense), can be subjected to a virtual strip search by police or jail officials, which involves exposing the genitals and the buttocks.

Immunity protections for Secret Service agents trump the free speech rights of Americans. The court issued a unanimous decision in *Reichle v. Howards* (2012), siding with two Secret Service agents who arrested a Colorado man simply for daring to voice critical remarks to Vice President Cheney.[14] However, contrast the Court's affirmation of the "free speech" rights of corporations and wealthy donors in *McCutcheon v. FEC* (2014), which does away with established limits on the number of candidates an entity can support with campaign contributions, and *Citizens United v. FEC* (2010)[15] with its tendency to deny those same rights to average Americans when government interests abound, and you'll find a noticeable disparity.

Police can break into homes without a warrant, even if it's the wrong home. In an 8-1 ruling in *Kentucky v. King* (2011), the Supreme Court placed their trust in the discretion of police officers, rather than in the dictates of the Constitution, when they gave police greater leeway to break into homes or apartments without a warrant. Despite the fact that the police in question ended up pursuing the *wrong* suspect, invaded the *wrong* apartment and violated just about every tenet that stands between us and a police state, the Court sanctioned the warrantless raid, leaving Americans with little real protection in the face of all manner of abuses by police.[16]

Police can interrogate minors without parents present. In a devastating ruling that could very well do away with what little Fourth Amendment protections remain to public school students and their families—the Court threw out a lower court ruling in *Camreta v. Greene* (2011),[17] which required government authorities to secure a warrant, a court order or parental consent before interrogating students at school. The ramifications are far-reaching, rendering public school students as wards of the state.

It's a crime to not identify yourself when a policeman asks your name. In *Hiibel v. Sixth Judicial District Court of the State of Nevada*

(2004), a majority of the high court agreed that refusing to answer when a policeman asks "What's your name?" can rightfully be considered a crime under Nevada's "stop and identify" statute.[18] No longer will Americans, even those not suspected of or charged with any crime, have the right to remain silent when stopped and questioned by a police officer.

Justice Denied

The cases the Supreme Court refuses to hear, allowing lower court judgments to stand, are almost as critical as the ones they rule on. Some of the cases turned away in recent years alone have delivered devastating blows to our freedoms.

Legally owning a firearm is enough to justify a no-knock raid by police. Justices refused to hear *Quinn v. Texas* (2014), the case of a Texas man who was shot by police through his closed bedroom door and whose home was subject to a no-knock, SWAT-team style forceful entry and raid based solely on the suspicion that there were legally-owned firearms in his household.[19]

The military can arrest and detain American citizens. In refusing to hear *Hedges v. Obama* (2014), a legal challenge to the indefinite detention provision of the NDAA, the Supreme Court affirmed that the President and the U.S. military can arrest and indefinitely imprison individuals, including American citizens.[20] In so doing, the high court also passed up an opportunity to overturn its 1944 ruling in *Korematsu v. United States*, which allowed the internment of Japanese-Americans in concentration camps.

Students can be subjected to random lockdowns and mass searches at school. The Court refused to hear *Burlison v. Springfield Public Schools* (2013), a case involving students at a Missouri public school who were subjected to random lockdowns, mass searches, and drug-sniffing dogs by police.[21] In so doing, the Court let stand an appeals court ruling that the searches and lockdowns were reasonable in order to maintain the safety and security of students at the school.

Police officers who don't know their actions violate the law aren't guilty of breaking the law. The Supreme Court let stand a Ninth Circuit Court of Appeals decision in *Brooks v. City of Seattle* (2012)[22] in which police officers, who clearly used excessive force when they repeatedly tasered a pregnant woman until she was unconscious during a routine traffic stop, were granted immunity from prosecution. The Ninth Circuit actually rationalized its ruling by claiming that the officers couldn't have known beyond a reasonable doubt that their actions—tasering a pregnant woman who was not a threat in any way—violated the Fourth Amendment.

Police State Courts?

When all is said and done, what these assorted court rulings add up to is a disconcerting mindset that interprets the Constitution one way for the elite—government entities, the police, corporations and the wealthy—and uses a second measure altogether for the underclasses—that is, you and me.

Keep in mind that in former regimes such as Nazi Germany and the Soviet Union, the complicity of the courts was the final piece to fall into place before the totalitarian beast stepped out of the shadows and into the light. As Professor Robert Gellately writes in his book *Backing Hitler: Consent and Coercion in Nazi Germany*:

> All these courts adopted a simple rule of thumb, as one newspaper story put it: "anyone who offends the community of the people [that is, the state], must fall."[23]

CHAPTER 22

The Mastermind Behind It All

"A standing military force, with an overgrown Executive
will not long be safe companions to liberty."[1]
—JAMES MADISON

"Here [in New Mexico], we are moving more toward a
national police force. Homeland Security is involved with
a lot of little things around town. Somebody in Washington
needs to call a timeout."[2]
—DAN KLEIN, retired Albuquerque Police Department sergeant

While the courts have been complicit in greasing the wheels for the
emergence of the American Police State, it is the Department of
Homeland Security which has masterminded the entire process. The
agency from which all weapons, training, and policies flow and spread
across America has become the police chief to our national police force,
ruthlessly efficient when it comes to building what the Founders feared
most—a standing army on American soil.

Creating a Militarized America

The third largest federal agency behind the Departments of Veterans
Affairs and Defense,[3] the DHS—with its 240,000 full-time workers, $61
billion budget,[4] and sub-agencies that include the Coast Guard, Cus-
toms and Border Protection, Secret Service, Transportation Security
Administration (TSA) and the Federal Emergency Management Agency
(FEMA)[5]—has been aptly dubbed a "runaway train."

In the years since it was established to "prevent terrorist attacks
within the United States," the DHS has grown from a post-9/11, knee-jerk
reaction to a leviathan with tentacles in every aspect of American life.

DHS, America's standing army
(Photography by Douglas J. Hagmann and Canada Free Press)

In fact, the DHS routinely hands out six-figure grants to enable local municipalities to purchase military-style vehicles,[6] as well as a veritable war chest of weaponry, ranging from tactical vests, bomb-disarming robots, assault weapons, and combat uniforms. This rise in military equipment purchases funded by the DHS has, according to analysts Andrew Becker and G.W. Schulz, "paralleled an apparent increase in local SWAT teams."[7] The end result? An explosive growth in the use of SWAT teams for otherwise routine police matters, an increased tendency on the part of police to shoot first and ask questions later, and an overall mindset within police forces that they are at war, and the citizenry are the enemy combatants.

Along with other government agencies, the DHS has also been stockpiling an alarming amount of ammunition in recent years, which only adds to the discomfort of those already leery of the government. As of 2013, DHS had 260 million rounds of ammo in stock, which averages out to between 1,300 to 1,600 rounds per officer. The U.S. Army, in contrast, has roughly 350 rounds per soldier. And, as we have seen, DHS has since requisitioned more than 1.6 billion rounds of ammo, "enough," concludes *Forbes* magazine, "to sustain a hot war for 20+ years."[8]

Adding to the level of concern, DHS funds military-style training drills in cities across the country. These Urban Shield exercises, elaborately staged with their own set of professionally trained Crisis Actors playing the parts of shooters, bystanders and victims, fool law enforcement officials, students, teachers, bystanders, and the media into thinking it's a real crisis.[9]

Erecting an Electronic Concentration Camp

The DHS is also the common denominator behind much of the government's surveillance programs, both those carried out by the agency and

its many sub-agencies, as well as through its distribution of technology and funding to the states to enable them to spy on American citizens. For instance, in 2009 DHS released three infamous reports on Rightwing and Leftwing "Extremism" and another entitled Operation Vigilant Eagle, outlining a surveillance program targeting veterans. The reports collectively and broadly define extremists as individuals and groups "that are mainly antigovernment, rejecting federal authority in favor of state or local authority, or rejecting government authority entirely." And in 2013 it was revealed that the DHS, the FBI, state and

In 2009, the DHS released three infamous reports on Rightwing and Leftwing "Extremism," which used the terms "terrorist" and "extremist" interchangeably.

local law enforcement agencies, and the private sector were working together to conduct nationwide surveillance on protesters' First Amendment activities.

To this end, government employees have been enlisted to spy on their fellow citizens. Terrorism Liaison Officers, for example, are made up of firefighters, police officers, and even corporate employees who have received training to spy on and report back to government entities on the day-to-day activities of their fellow citizens. These individuals are authorized to report "suspicious activity," which can include such innocuous activities as taking pictures with no apparent aesthetic value, making measurements and drawings, taking notes, conversing in code, espousing radical beliefs, and buying items in bulk.[10]

Under the direction of the TSA, American travelers have been subjected to all manner of searches ranging from whole-body scanners[11] and enhanced pat downs at airports to bag searches in train stations. In response to public outrage over what amounted to a virtual strip search, the TSA has begun replacing the scanners with equally costly yet less detailed models. The old scanners will be used by prisons for now. The TSA now searches a variety of government and private databases, including things like car registrations and employment information, in order to track travelers before they ever get near an airport.[12] Other information collected includes "tax identification number, past travel itineraries, property records, physical characteristics, and law enforcement or intelligence information."[13]

Moreover, as Charlie Savage reports for the *Boston Globe,* the DHS has funneled "millions of dollars to local governments nationwide for purchasing high-tech video camera networks, accelerating the rise of a 'surveillance society' in which the sense of freedom that stems from being anonymous in public will be lost."[14] These camera systems are installed on city streets and in parks and transit systems. They operate in conjunction with sophisticated computer systems that boast intelligent video analytics, digital biometric identification, and military-pedigree software for analyzing and predicting crime and facial recognition software, creating a vast surveillance network that can target millions of innocent individuals.[15]

For example, the DHS has already distributed more than $50 million in grants to enable local police agencies to acquire license plate readers, which rely on mobile cameras to photograph and identify cars, match them against a national database, and track their movements.[16] Relying on private contractors to maintain a license plate database allows the DHS and its affiliates to access millions of records without much in the way of oversight.[17] Similarly, Stingray devices enable police to track individuals' cell phones—and their owners—without a court warrant or court order.[18] The amount of information conveyed by these devices about one's activities, whereabouts and interactions is considerable.

As one attorney explained: "Because we carry our cellphones with us virtually everywhere we go, stingrays can paint a precise picture of where we are and who we spend time with, including our location in a lover's house, in a psychologist's office or at a political protest."[19]

The DHS also spearheads widespread spying through the use of fusion centers. Aided by the National Security Agency, these data

Memphis Police Department vehicle with a license plate reader mounted on the roof
(Photography by Thomas R. Machnitzki)

collecting agencies—of which there are at least 78 scattered around the U.S.[20]—constantly monitor our communications, collecting and cataloguing everything from our Internet activity and web searches to text messages, phone calls, and emails. This data is then fed to government agencies that are now interconnected: the CIA to the FBI, the FBI to local police. Despite a budget estimated to be somewhere between $289 million and $1.4 billion,[21] these fusion centers have proven to be exercises in incompetence, often producing irrelevant, useless, or inappropriate intelligence, while spending millions of dollars on "flat-screen televisions, sport utility vehicles, hidden cameras, and other gadgets."[22]

Utilizing drones and other spybots, the DHS has been at the forefront of funding and deploying surveillance robots and drones for land, sea, and air, including robots that resemble fish and tunnel-bots that can travel underground.[23] Despite repeated concerns over the danger surveillance drones used domestically pose to Americans' privacy rights, the DHS has continued to expand its fleet of Predator drones, which come equipped with video cameras, infrared cameras, heat sensors, and radar.[24] DHS also loans its drones out to local, state, and federal law enforcement agencies for a variety of tasks, although the agency refuses to divulge any details as to how, why and in what capacity these drones are being used by police.[25] Incredibly, the DHS has also been handing out millions of dollars in grants to local police agencies to "accelerate the adoption" of drones in their localities.[26]

Laying the Groundwork for Martial Law

As discussed earlier, in 2006 the DHS awarded a $385 million contract to a subsidiary of the megacorporation Halliburton to build detention centers on American soil.[27] The government justified these domestic detention centers as necessary in the event of "natural disasters," to handle "an emergency influx of immigrants," *or to support the "rapid development of new programs."*[28] Viewed in conjunction with the NDAA provision allowing the military to arrest and indefinitely imprison anyone, including American citizens, it would seem the building blocks are already in place for such an eventuality.

The DHS through its various programs has also accustomed the average American to searches of their person and property and roving military patrols. On orders from the DHS, the government's efforts along the border have become little more than an exercise in police state power. This ranges from aggressive checkpoints to the widespread use of drone technology, often used against American citizens traveling within the country. Border patrol operations occur within 100 miles of an international crossing, putting some 200 million Americans within the bounds of aggressive border patrol searches and seizures, as well as increasingly expansive drone surveillance.[29] With 71 checkpoints found along the southwest border of the United States alone, suspicionless search and seizures on the border are rampant. Border patrol agents also search the personal electronic devices of people crossing the border without a warrant.[30]

VIPR task forces, comprised of federal air marshals, surface transportation security inspectors, transportation security officers, behavior detection officers, and explosive detection canine teams, have laid the groundwork for the government's effort to secure so-called "soft" targets such as malls, stadiums, and bridges. Some security experts predict that checkpoints and screening stations will eventually be established at *all* soft targets, including department stores, restaurants,

U.S. Customs and Border Protection officers wielding the H&K UMP
(Photography by James Tourtellotte)

and schools.[31] For example, the DHS' Operation Shield, a program which seeks to check up on security protocols around the country with unannounced visits, conducted a surprise security exercise at the Social Security Administration building in Leesburg, Fla., where they subjected people who went to pick up their checks to random ID checks by federal agents armed with semi-automatic weapons.[32]

A Wasteful, Growing, Fear-Mongering Beast

It's not difficult to see why the DHS has been described as a "wasteful, growing, fear-mongering beast."[33] If it is a beast, however, it is a beast that is accelerating our nation's transformation into a police state through its establishment of a standing army, a.k.a. a national police force.

Is it time to cage the beast? In making the case for shutting down the de facto national police agency, analyst Charles Kenny offers the following six reasons: one, the agency lacks leadership; two, terrorism is far less of a threat than it is made out to be; three, the FBI has actually stopped more alleged terrorist attacks than the DHS; four, the agency wastes exorbitant amounts of money with little to show for it; five, "An overweight DHS gets a free pass to infringe civil liberties without a shred of economic justification"; and six, the agency is just plain bloated.[34]

To Kenny's list, I will add the following: The menace of a national police force, a literal standing army, vested with massive power cannot be overstated, nor can its danger be ignored. Indeed, just about every nefarious deed, tactic, or thuggish policy advanced by the government today can be traced back to the DHS, its police state mindset, and the billions of dollars it distributes to police agencies in the form of grants.[35]

A Totalitarian Regime?

Historically, the establishment of a national police force has served as a fundamental building block for every totalitarian regime that has ever wreaked havoc on humanity, from Hitler's all-too-real Nazi Germany to George Orwell's fictional Oceania. Whether fictional or historical, however, the calling cards of these national police agencies remain the same: brutality, inhumanity, corruption, intolerance, rigidity, and bureaucracy—in other words, evil.

The Banality of Evil

"In a system like Nazi Germany, where social acceptance was the reward for evil, the socially normal individual sees evil as good. Doing evil becomes nothing more than healthy self-interest, and the horrifying irony is that the person committing unimaginable cruelty comes across in other social contexts as a perfectly "normal," uninteresting individual, no more conspicuous than the rumpled businessman sitting next to you on the train."[1]

—Journalist MCLEAN GORDON

Adolph Eichmann epitomized the "banality of evil" in his explanation that he was just "following orders" when administrating Hitler's death camps. (Photo courtesy of Israel Government Press Office)

Adolph Eichmann, the Nazi bureaucrat who supposedly signed off on the Holocaust and helped organize Hitler's death camps, was not necessarily a blood-hungry monster. To look at, he was an average looking guy with thinning hair, a pencil pusher.

"Except for an extraordinary diligence in looking out for his personal advancement, he had no motives at all," Hannah Arendt, a survivor of the Nazi concentration camps, wrote in her searing account of Eichmann's 1962 war crimes trial: Eichmann was, as he tried to explain at his trial, "just following orders."[2]

Arendt denounced Eichmann not because he was evil per se. It was because he was a bureaucrat who unquestioningly carried out orders—through the mechanized, bureaucratic process—that were immoral, inhumane and evil. This, Arendt concluded, was "the banality of evil," where the so-called ordinary person engages in wrongdoing or turns a blind eye to it without taking any responsibility for their actions or inactions.[3]

The truly efficient bureaucratic system—especially if it happens to be a government wielding power—can and has turned average citizens—perhaps the guy next door—into ogres without consciences while preserving the mask of humanity. As George Orwell recognized during World War II:

As I write, highly civilized human beings are flying overhead, trying to kill me. They do not feel any enmity against me as an individual, nor I against them. They are only "doing their duty," as the saying goes. Most of them, I have no doubt, are kind-hearted law abiding men who would never dream of committing murder in private life. On the other hand, if one of them succeeds in blowing me to pieces with a well-placed bomb, he will never sleep any the worse for it.[4]

The Psychology of Compliance

Shortly before Eichmann's trial, in 1961, Stanley Milgram conducted an experiment at Yale University in which subjects were asked to administer an increasingly intense shock punishment to a friend or acquaintance in another room whenever he or she answered a question wrong.[5] The test subjects believed they were causing another human being great harm, even though in reality they were not. Despite the fact that many subjects were visibly uncomfortable (nervously laughing, etc.) with giving painful shocks to another human being, twenty-six out of forty participants continued shocking people up to the highest (450-volt) level, labeled "XXX," on the machine. No subject stopped before giving a 300-volt shock, labeled "Intense Shock" despite the fact that the person in the next room expressed severe agony and health concerns.[6] All of the subjects were voluntary participants. When a participant expressed an unwillingness to administer the next shock, experimenters prodded them to do so by asking them to "Please continue" or stating: "The experiment requires that you continue."[7]

A decade later, researchers conducting the Stanford Prison Experiment[8] randomly assigned college-aged participants to be either guards or prisoners in an intricate role-play. With only the instruction to "maintain order" in the simulated prison, the "guards" began harassing and intimidating prisoners. "Prisoners" did attempt to rebel, but always returned to compliance quickly after an outburst, despite the fact that they were mere volunteers. Due to the extreme aggression of guards, the experiment was terminated after only five days (the original design would have held students for two weeks).

In the decades following these shocking studies, psychologists have asked, why do people (those in power or those subordinate to power) act aggressively? Organizations like the military or police forces have been widely studied to answer this question. Today, theories of learned obedience are generally accepted.

For example, a SWAT member who believes a raid is unconstitutional will likely not defy orders from his superior because compliance was engendered in him during the training process. Norm Stamper, a former police chief, believes that the current "rank-and-file" organization of police departments results in "bureaucratic regulations [being emphasized] over conduct on the streets."[9] In war zones, soldiers are trained as subordinates to fulfill their superior's commands.

Milgram's participants felt they were under the employ of the researchers and took the orders issued to them. Stamper argues that utilizing similar rigid power hierarchies in police departments leads to blind obedience. Researcher Eungkyoon Lee backs up Stamper's musings with empirical research. Lee found that trait compliance is highest in contexts that feature a well-defined authority figure and when the subject in question has a clearly inferior role.[10]

We-Ness

"The essence of obedience," Milgram agreed, "consists in the fact that a person comes to view himself as the instrument for carrying out another person's wishes, and he therefore no longer regards himself as responsible for his actions."[11] However, a recent academic study by several psychology professors seems to suggest that blind obedience is not necessarily the norm and people don't just simply do what they are told. There are, as the study concludes, other factors:

> At root, the fundamental point is that tyranny does not flourish because perpetuators are helpless and ignorant of their actions. It flourishes because they actively identify with those who promote vicious acts as virtuous.[12]

The conclusion is that people don't simply line up and salute. After all, we're not robots—not yet anyway. It is through one's own personal identification with a given leader, party, or social order that they become agents of good or evil.

What this means is that we the citizenry—whether we are the police, politicians, or average Americans just trying to make a living—must be very careful that we are not manipulated into marching in lockstep with an oppressive regime. As this study seems to indicate, any resistance to such regimes depends on the strength of opinions in the minds of those who choose to fight back. Much depends on how leaders "cultivate a sense of identification with their followers," says Professor Alex Haslam. "I mean one pretty obvious thing is that leaders talk about 'we' rather than 'I,' and actually what leadership is about is cultivating this sense of shared identity about 'we-ness' and then getting people to want to act in terms of that 'we-ness,' to promote our collective interests. ... [We] is the single word that has increased in the inaugural addresses over the last century . . . and the other one is 'America.'"[13]

The goal of the modern corporate state is obvious: to promote, cultivate, and embed a sense of shared identification among its citizens. That's what modern leadership has become. However, this doesn't mean that "we" should blindly follow the regime. Flag waving, political slogans such as "change" and "hope," militarized SWAT team raids, or citizens gathering to attack or demean protesters—all of this is not done blindly. If people identify with the leaders and follow government policy or aggression, they respond enthusiastically, creatively, and with fervor.

Moreover, when people act on such a shared identity, often they are not simply doing what they are told. "I think that's obviously critical when you try to explain the behavior of people like Eichmann and other kinds of Nazis," said Haslam. "They were never just following orders: they were responding in an engaged fashion to what they perceived to be the requirements of the situation and the requirements of a leadership with which they identified."[14]

Is Brutality Part of the Job?

An unprovoked "stop and frisk" encounter with police officers left one man hospitalized with a ruptured testicle. A mother was violently dragged out of her car and aggressively arrested in front of her young children for allegedly "trespassing" at her own apartment complex. A Georgia toddler's face was badly burned when police threw a flashbang grenade in his playpen during a SWAT team raid. And an elderly man was left in need of facial reconstructive surgery after police entered his home without a warrant to sort out a dispute about a trailer.[15] Meanwhile, there are more than 1,100 people shot to death by police in America each year (that's a 9/11 death toll every three years). According to the FBI, approximately 400 of these deaths are "justifiable."[16] Compare that to Germany, a nation of 80 million, where police killed all of eight people. In Britain and Japan, with a combined population of 191 million, the police didn't kill anyone.[17]

Why the rise in police brutality in America? As we've seen, maybe a police officer who violently engages a nonviolent citizen isn't just following orders. Could it be that police brutality—cracking skulls, not keeping the peace—is systemic or inherently part and parcel of the job of modern policing?

Unfortunately, the emergence of the militarized police, combined with training in the police academies that teaches a combat philosophy in regard to we "civilians," ensures that police are no longer peace officers. Indeed, as journalist Bernie Suarez argues: "Police are more trained to think in a way that is very dangerous to all Americans. Whether it's a man reaching for his cell phone only to get shot and killed because the officer sees a gun, or whether it's the person simply running away from the police. The person running away doesn't realize that the police officer sees things dramatically different from how civilians see it."[18]

Systemic violence against people, as any psychiatrist will tell you, is a diseased state of mind. However, as Suarez recognizes:

Imagine what it's like to be trained into thinking that anyone in your country can be a suspect, a criminal or a threat to your life. Under any other circumstances, this would be considered a clinical disorder of paranoia. But what about when your job requires you to be paranoid? What if you are an officer and you genuinely believe that man's cell phone to be a gun? Who is responsible for this paranoia which has led to the murder of Americans on almost a daily basis nationwide? Did anyone confront the Nazis about their potential mental disorders? Would anyone have listened? This police violence phenomenon has put police nationwide into a position which can now be arguably described as a position which involuntarily, systematically, and gradually is turning otherwise good men and women into mentally deranged zombies exclusively operating to protect and enforce an inhuman, immoral and robotic legal system that enforces laws and rules which have no moral, logical, or reasonable justification.[19]

Does this sound like the Eichmann syndrome? Just following orders?

Making matters worse is the lack of accountability for police misconduct. The statistics nationwide are staggering. "Only *one out of every three* accused cops are convicted nationwide, while the conviction rate for civilians is *literally double that,*" writes journalist Bonnie Kristian. "On a national level, *upwards of 95 percent* of police misconduct cases referred for federal prosecution are declined by prosecutors because, as reported in *USA Today,* juries are conditioned to believe cops, and victims credibility is often challenged. Failure to remedy this police/civilian double standard cultivates an abuse-friendly legal environment."[20] A U.S. Department of Justice study reveals that "84 percent of police officers report that they've seen colleagues use excessive force on civilians, and 61 percent admit they don't always report 'even serious criminal violations that involve abuse of authority by fellow officers.'"[21]

The lesson here is that police minds are wired into a logic—which is upheld by a code blue camaraderie (we-ness)—that is entirely disconnected from the world in which the average citizen lives. Moreover, while they may just be doing their jobs—jobs steeped in violence—there are personal consequences as well. In fact: "Two studies have found that *at least 40 percent* of all police officer families experience domestic violence, in contrast to 10 percent of families in the general population.

A third study of older and more experienced officers found a rate of 24 percent, indicating that domestic violence is two to four times more common among police families than American families in general."[22]

In other words, what the police practice on the streets often follow them home and with disastrous consequences.

Monsters Are Us?

Yes, quite a few of us humans do some pretty bad things. Much too often, it is those among us who are called government agents. Clearly, it's time to begin the battle to take back what has been stolen from us. If not, the banality of evil will soon engulf us.

Freedom is a choice. You are defined by your choices. What will you choose?

Will you sit by as evil eats away at your freedoms? Will you, in effect, become one of them? If so, then maybe, just maybe, filmmaker John Carpenter was right when he remarked:

> Monsters in movies are us, always us, one way or the other. They're us with hats on. The zombies in George Romero's movies are us. They're hungry. Monsters are us, the dangerous parts of us. The part that wants to destroy. The part of us with the reptile brain. The part of us that's vicious and cruel. We express these in our stories as the monsters out there.[23]

Let us join together and stop the fictional monsters from becoming our reality. The time to act is now.

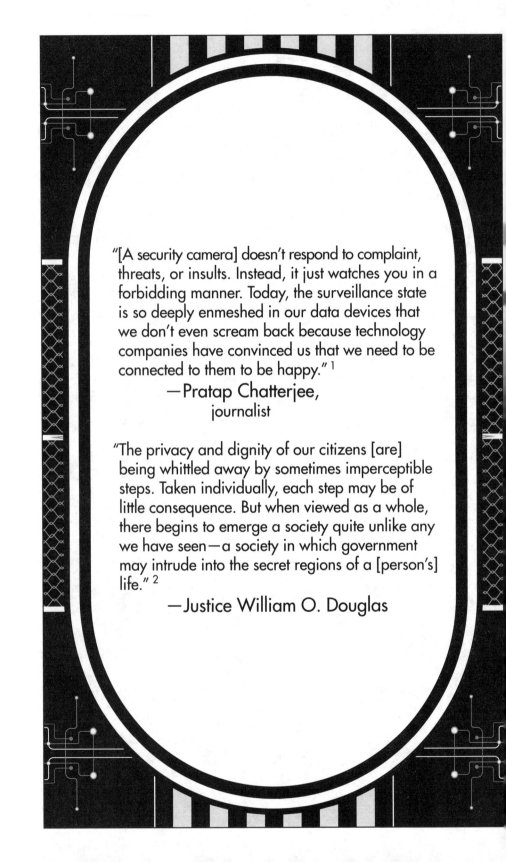

"[A security camera] doesn't respond to complaint, threats, or insults. Instead, it just watches you in a forbidding manner. Today, the surveillance state is so deeply enmeshed in our data devices that we don't even scream back because technology companies have convinced us that we need to be connected to them to be happy." [1]

—Pratap Chatterjee,
journalist

"The privacy and dignity of our citizens [are] being whittled away by sometimes imperceptible steps. Taken individually, each step may be of little consequence. But when viewed as a whole, there begins to emerge a society quite unlike any we have seen—a society in which government may intrude into the secret regions of a [person's] life." [2]

—Justice William O. Douglas

Reality Check

FACT: In 2015 mega-food corporations will begin rolling out high-tech shelving outfitted with cameras in order to track the shopping behavior of customers, as well as information like the age and sex of shoppers.[3]

FACT: The FBI's Next Generation Identification (NGI) facial recognition system, which is set to hold data on millions of Americans, will include a variety of biometric data, including palm prints, iris scans, and face recognition data.[4] The FBI hopes to have 52 million images by 2015. NGI will be capable of uploading 55,000 images a day, and conducting tens of thousands of photo searches a day.[5]

FACT: Comprising an $80 billion industry,[6] at least 30,000 drones are expected to occupy U.S. airspace by 2020.[7]

FACT: Devices are now being developed that would allow police to stop a car remotely, ostensibly to end police chases.[8]

FACT: Everything we do will eventually be connected to the Internet. By 2030 it is estimated there will be 100 trillion sensor devices connecting human electronic devices (cell phones, laptops, etc.) to the Internet.[9] Much, if not all, of our electronic devices will be connected to Google.

CHAPTER 24

The Watchers

"If, as it seems, we are in the process of becoming a totalitarian society in which the state apparatus is all-powerful, the ethics most important for the survival of the true, free, human individual would be: cheat, lie, evade, fake it, be elsewhere, forge documents, build improved electronic gadgets in your garage that'll outwit the gadgets used by the authorities."[1]—PHILIP K. DICK

"The only person who is still private in Germany is somebody who is asleep."[2]—ROBERT LEY, Nazi leader

In the totalitarian future at our doorsteps, the futuristic technologies once reserved for movie blockbusters such as drones, tasers, and biometric scanners will be used by the government to track, target, and control the populace, especially dissidents. Mind you, these technologies are already in use today and being hailed for their safety "advantages" and their potentially life-saving, cost-saving, time-saving benefits. However, it won't be long before the drawbacks to having a government equipped with technology that makes it all-seeing, all-knowing, and all-powerful will far outdistance the benefits.

Consider that on any given day, the average American going about his daily business will be monitored, surveilled, spied on, and tracked in more than twenty different ways by both government and corporate eyes and ears.[3]

A byproduct of this new age in which we live, whether you're walking through a store, driving your car, checking email, or talking to friends and family on the phone, you can be sure that some government agency, whether it's the NSA, FBI, or some other entity, is listening in and tracking your behavior. This doesn't even begin to touch on the corporate trackers that monitor your purchases, web browsing, Facebook posts, and other activities taking place in the cyber sphere.

Thus, the news that the NSA is routinely operating outside of the law and overstepping its legal authority by carrying out surveillance on American citizens is not really much of a surprise. This is what happens when you give the government broad powers and allow government agencies to routinely sidestep the Constitution. Indeed, the privacy violations carried out by the NSA and revealed by various whistleblowers only scrape the surface in revealing the lengths to which government agencies and their corporate allies will go to conduct mass surveillance on all communications and transactions within the United States.

The Many Ways That You're Being Tracked, Catalogued and Controlled

Any hope of holding onto even a shred of privacy is rapidly dwindling. Indeed, the life of the average American is an open book for government agents. As the following will show, the electronic concentration camp, as I have dubbed the surveillance state, is perhaps the most insidious of the police state's many tentacles. This impacts almost every aspect of our lives and makes it that much easier for the government to encroach on our most vital freedoms, ranging from free speech, assembly, and the press to due process, privacy, and property, by eavesdropping on our communications, tracking our every movement, and spying on our activities.

Already, the government can track you based on what you say and do on your phone, your computer, and in your car. Combined with facial recognition technology, our cell phones have become a tell-all about our personal lives. Cell phones serve as a "combination phone bug, listening device, location tracker and hidden camera."[4] Indeed, it's incredibly easy to activate a cell phone's GPS and microphone capabilities remotely. For example, the FBI uses the "roving bug" technique, which allows agents to remotely activate the microphone on a cell phone and use it as a listening device.[5]

Federal agents now employ a number of hacking methods in order to gain access to your computer activities and "see" whatever you're

Tracking plates for parking tickets

Cal State Fullerton has invested in a camera system to identify parking violators who have more than 5 infractions.

Infrared camera captures image of license plate.

In-car processor matches plate to a "hotlist".

Officer is alerted if there is a match with types of infractions.

Officers can update the "hotlist" from the field.

Parking enforcement

CSF

ABC1234

Source: ELSAG North America Law Enforcement Systems

Molly Zisk/ The Register

License plate readers—which collect upwards of 1,800 images per hour—can identify the owner of any car that comes within its sights. (Illustration by Molly Zisk, courtesy of *The Register*)

seeing on your monitor. Malicious hacking software, installed via a number of inconspicuous methods, can be used to search through files stored on a hard drive, log keystrokes, or take real time screenshots of whatever a person is looking at on their computer, whether personal files, web pages, or email messages. It can also be used to remotely activate cameras and microphones, offering another glimpse into the personal business of a target.[6]

License plate readers—which collect upwards of 1,800 images per hour—can identify the owner of any car that comes within its sights and, as you might imagine, are growing in popularity among police agencies.[7] Affixed to overpasses or cop cars, these devices give police a clear idea of where your car was at a specific date and time, whether at the doctor's office, a bar, a church, synagogue or mosque, or at a political rally. License plate readers work by recognizing a passing license plate, photographing it, and running the information against a predetermined database that lets police know if they've got a "hit"—a person of interest, though not necessarily a suspected criminal. All of the data points collected by license plate readers can be traced and mapped so that a picture of a vehicle's past movements can be re-constructed.[8] The implications for privacy are dire.

There are reportedly tens of thousands of these license plate readers now in operation throughout the country. The data collected from these devices is also being shared between police agencies, as well as with fusion centers and private companies.[9] Over 99 percent of the people being unnecessarily surveilled are entirely innocent.[10]

To cap it off, private companies are also getting into the data collection game, as data collected on innocent drivers is being shared with government agencies and corporations alike. One such business, Final Notice, offers the information they gather to police agencies and intends to start selling the information to other groups, including bail bondsmen, private investigators and insurers.[11] Another company, MVTrac, claims to have data on "a large majority" of vehicles in the United States, and the Digital Recognition Network has more than 550 affiliates that feed over 50 million plate reads into a national database containing "over 700 million data points on where American drivers have been."[12]

Thanks to a torrent of federal grants, police departments across the country are able to fund surveillance systems that turn the most basic human behaviors into suspicious situations to be studied and analyzed. Police all across the country are also now engaging in big data mining operations, often with the help of private companies, in order to develop city-wide nets of surveillance.[13] The surveillance system operated by the New York Police Department "links 3,000 surveillance cameras with license plate readers, radiation sensors, criminal databases and terror suspect lists."[14]

Using Your Face, Mannerisms, Social Media and You-ness Against You

You can be tracked based on what you buy, where you go, what you do in public, and how you do what you do.

Facial recognition software promises to create a society in which every individual who steps out into public is tracked and recorded as they go about their daily business. The goal is for government agents to be able to scan a crowd of people and instantaneously identify all of the individuals present. Facial recognition programs are being rolled out in states all across the country.[15] In fact, as we shall see, the FBI is developing a $1 billion program, Next Generation Identification, which involves creating a massive database of mug shots for police all across the country.[16] One Russian marking company, Synqera, "uses facial recognition technology to tailor marketing messages to customers according to their gender, age, and mood." As one company representative noted, "if you are an angry man of 30, and it is Friday evening, [the Synqera software] may offer you a bottle of whiskey."[17]

As we have seen, fusion centers are federal-state law enforcement partnerships which attempt to aggregate a variety of data on so-called "suspicious persons." They have actually collected reports on people buying pallets of bottled water, photographing government buildings, and applying for a pilot's license as "suspicious activity."[18]

Moreover, retailers are getting in on the surveillance game as well. Large corporations such as Target have been tracking and assessing the behavior of their customers, particularly their purchasing patterns, for years.[19] Mega-food corporations plan to roll out high-tech shelving outfitted with cameras in order to track the shopping behavior of customers, as well as information like the age and sex of shoppers.[20]

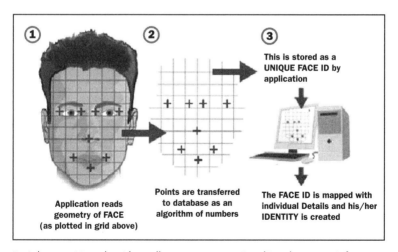

Facial recognition algorithms allow computers to "read" and map one's features.

Sensing a booming industry, private corporations are jumping on the surveillance state bandwagon, negotiating lucrative contracts with police agencies throughout the country in order to create a web of surveillance that encompasses all major urban centers. Companies such as NICE and Bright Planet are selling equipment and services to police departments with the promise of monitoring large groups of people seamlessly, as in the case of protests and rallies. They are also engaging in extensive online surveillance, looking for any hints of "large public events, social unrest, gang communications, and criminally predicated individuals."[21] Defense contractors are attempting to take a bite out of this lucrative market as well. Raytheon has developed a software package known as Riot, which promises to predict the future behavior of an individual based upon his social media posts.[22]

With private corporations also taking advantage of this technology, the outlook is decidedly grim. In an attempt to mimic the tracking capabilities of online retailers, brick-and-mortar stores now utilize WIFI-enabled devices to track the movements of their customers by tracking their phones as they move throughout the store. The data gathered by these devices include "'capture rate' (how successful window displays are at pulling people into the store); number of customers inside the store; customer visit duration and frequency; customer location within the store; people who walk by the store without coming in; and the amount of foot traffic around the store."[23]

The obsession with social media as a form of surveillance will have some frightening consequences in coming years. As Helen A.S. Popkin, writing for *NBC News*, has astutely observed:

> We may very well face a future where algorithms bust people en masse for referencing illegal "Game of Thrones" downloads, or run sweeps for insurance companies seeking non-smokers confessing to lapsing back into the habit. Instead of that one guy getting busted for a lame joke misinterpreted as a real threat, the new software has the potential to roll, Terminator-style, targeting every social media user with a shameful confession or questionable sense of humor.[24]

The Point of No Return

To put it bluntly, we are living in an electronic concentration camp. We're on the losing end of a technological revolution that has already taken hostage our computers, our phones, our finances, our entertainment, our shopping, our appliances, and our cars.

Through a series of imperceptible steps, we have willingly allowed ourselves to become enmeshed in a system that knows the most intimate details of our lives, analyzes them, and treats us accordingly. Whether via fear of terrorism, narcissistic pleasure or lazy materialism, we have slowly handed over our information to all sorts of entities, corporate and governmental, public and private, who are now using that information to cow and control us for their profit.

So it is that we now find ourselves operating in a strange paradigm where the government not only views the citizenry as suspects but treats them as suspects, as well. By sifting through the detritus of your once-private life, the government will come to its own conclusions about who you are, where you fit in, and how best to deal with you should the need arise. Indeed, we are all becoming data collected in government files. Whether or not the surveillance is undertaken for "innocent" reasons, surveillance of all citizens, even the innocent sort, gradually poisons the soul of a nation. Surveillance limits personal options—denies freedom of choice—and increases the powers of those who are in a position to enjoy the fruits of this activity.

If this is the new "normal" in the United States, it is not friendly to freedom. Frankly, we are long past the point where we should be merely alarmed. These are no longer experiments on our freedoms. These are acts of aggression.

We have just about reached the point of no return. "If we do not seize this unique moment in our constitutional history to reform our surveillance laws and practices, we are all going to live to regret it," warned Senator Ron Wyden in 2013. "The combination of increasingly advanced technology with a breakdown in the checks and balances that limit government action could lead us to a surveillance state that cannot be reversed."[25]

Short of living in a cave, cut off from all communications and commerce, anyone living in the concentration camp that is America today must cede his privacy and liberty to a government agency, a corporation or both in order to access information via the Internet, communicate with friends and family, shop for food and clothing, or travel to work. As George Orwell warned, "You had to live—did live, from habit that became instinct—in the assumption that every sound you made was overheard, and, except in darkness, every movement scrutinized."[26]

CHAPTER 25

The Abyss of No Return

"The National Security Agency's capability at any time could be turned around on the American people, and no American would have any privacy left, such is the capability to monitor everything: telephone conversations, telegrams, it doesn't matter. There would be no place to hide. If a dictator ever took over, the N.S.A. could enable it to impose total tyranny, and there would be no way to fight back."[1]
—Senator FRANK CHURCH (1975)

"[T]he powers claimed by presidents in national security have become the controlling wheel of government, driving everything else. Secrecy then makes it possible for the president to pose as the sole competent judge of what will best protect our security. Secrecy permits the White House to control what others know. How many times have we heard a president say, "If you only knew what I know, you would understand why I'm doing what I'm doing." But it's a self-defeating situation. As Lord Acton said, "Everything secret degenerates, even the administration of justice." So in the bunker of the White House, the men who serve the president put loyalty above analysis. Judgment yields to obedience. Just salute and follow orders."[2]
—Journalist BILL MOYERS, who served as White House Press Secretary during the Johnson administration

Senator Frank Church (D-Ida.), who served as the chairman of the Select Committee on Intelligence that investigated the National Security Agency in the 1970s, understood only too well the dangers inherent in allowing the government to overstep its authority in the name of national security. Church recognized that such surveillance

Frank Church speaking at a Senate Foreign Relations Committee hearing (Photograph courtesy of the Frank Church Papers, Boise State University Library, Special Collections and Archives)

powers "at any time could be turned around on the American people, and no American would have any privacy left."[3]

Noting that the NSA could enable a dictator "to impose total tyranny" upon an utterly defenseless American public, Church declared that he did not "want to see this country ever go across the bridge" of constitutional protection, congressional oversight and the necessity for privacy. He avowed that "we," implicating both Congress and its constituency in this duty, "must see to it that this agency and all agencies that possess this technology operate within the law and under proper supervision, so that we never cross over that abyss. That is the abyss from which there is no return."[4]

Unfortunately, we have long since crossed over into that abyss, first under George W. Bush, who, among other things, authorized the NSA to listen in on the domestic phone calls of American citizens in the wake of the 9/11 attacks, and then under President Obama, whose administration did more to undermine the Fourth Amendment's guarantee of privacy and bodily integrity than any prior administration. Whether he intended it or not, it well may be that Barack Obama is remembered as the president who put the final chains in place to imprison us in an electronic concentration camp from which there is no escape.

Secret Courts, Secret Laws and Total Surveillance

In a bizarre and ludicrous attempt at "transparency," the Obama administration announced in late July 2013 that it had asked a *secret* court to
approve a *secret* order to allow the government to *secretly* keep spying
on millions of Americans, and the secret court granted its request.[5] In so
doing, the government doubled down on the numerous spying programs
aimed at the American people, some of which were exposed by whistleblower Edward Snowden, who temporarily pulled back the veil on the
government's gigantic spying apparatus.

As Senator Ron Wyden, a longtime critic of the American surveillance state, points out, government agencies operate based upon a secret
interpretation of the Patriot Act, which allows them to extract massive
amounts of data from third party agencies, enabling them to collect
information on "bulk medical, financial, credit card and gun-ownership
records or lists of 'readers of books and magazines deemed subversive.'"[6]

This is the bizarre logic which now defines American governance:
it doesn't matter if we spy on you without your consent, so long as you
know that we're doing it, and so long as we give the impression that
there is a process by which a court reviews the order.

Ironically, the seeds for this brave new world were planted in an
attempt to reform the ludicrous mantra of the Nixon administration
that "if the president does it, it's not illegal." In the aftermath of the
Watergate incident, the Senate held meetings in order to determine
exactly what sorts of illicit activities the American intelligence apparatus was engaged in under the direction of Nixon, and how future violations of the law could be stopped. The result was the passage of the
Foreign Intelligence Surveillance Acts (FISA) and the creation of the
Foreign Intelligence Surveillance Court, which was supposed to over-
see and correct how intelligence information is collated.

Fast-forward to the present day, and what we see is that the alleged
solution to the problem of government entities engaging in unjustified
and illegal surveillance has instead become the main perpetrator of such
activities. The FISA Court, which meets in secret, holds secret hearings,
and issues secret rulings,[7] has a history of rubberstamping the NSA's
surveillance programs. In fact, out of a mind-boggling 34,000 requests
for surveillance, the FISA court has denied only 11 such requests.[8]

When Secrecy and Surveillance Trump the Rule of Law

The constitutional accountability clause found in Article 1, section 9, clause 7 of the Constitution demands that government agencies function within the bounds of the Constitution. It does so by empowering the people's representatives in Congress to know what governmental agencies are actually doing by way of an accounting of their spending and also requiring full disclosure of their activities. However, because agencies such as the NSA operate with "black ops" (or secret) budgets, they are not accountable to Congress.

In his book *Body of Secrets*, author James Bamford describes the NSA as "a strange and invisible city unlike any on earth" that lies beyond a specially constructed and perpetually guarded exit ramp off the Baltimore-Washington Parkway. "It contains what is probably the largest body of secrets ever created."[9]

Bamford's use of the word "probably" is significant since the size of the NSA's staff, budget, and buildings is kept secret from the public. Intelligence experts estimate that the agency employs around 38,000 people, with a starting salary of $50,000 for its entry-level mathematicians, computer scientists, and engineers.[10] Its role in the intelligence enterprise and its massive budget dwarf those of its better-known counterpart, the Central Intelligence Agency (CIA). The NSA's website provides its own benchmarks:

> Neither the number of employees nor the size of the Agency's budget can be publicly disclosed. However, if the NSA/CSS were considered a corporation in terms of dollars spent, floor space occupied, and personnel employed, it would rank in the top 10 percent of the Fortune 500 companies.[11]

The NSA

If the NSA's size seems daunting, its scope is disconcerting, especially as it pertains to surveillance activities domestically. The NSA is collecting some 5 billion records on cell phone location data every single day.[12] The NSA also has a surveillance program by which they penetrate digital devices not connected to the Internet by means of radio waves. This program has been active since at least 2008, and the NSA has penetrated almost 100,000 computers through this method.[13] And then there's

XKeyscore, a surveillance program which "intercepts 1.7 billion emails, phone calls and other types of communications *each day*" and "allows the government to enter a person's name or other question into the program and sift through oceans of data to produce everything there is on the Internet by or about that person or other search term."[14]

The Utah Data Center (UDC),[15] the central hub of the NSA's vast spying infrastructure, serves as a clearinghouse and a depository for every imaginable kind of information—whether innocent or not, private or public—including communications, transactions, and the like. In fact, anything and everything you've ever said or done, from the trivial to the damning—phone calls, Facebook posts, Twitter tweets, Google searches, emails, bookstore and grocery purchases, bank statements, commuter toll records, etc.—are tracked, collected, catalogued, and analyzed by the UDC's supercomputers and teams of government agents. This massive $2 billion facility handles yottabytes of metadata (equivalent to one septillion bytes—imagine a one followed by 24 zeroes) on American communications.[16]

Metadata is an incredibly invasive set of data to have on a person. Indeed, with access to one's metadata, one can "identify people's friends and associates, detect where they were at a certain time, acquire clues to religious or political affiliations, and pick up sensitive information like regular calls to a psychiatrist's office, late-night messages

The news that the NSA is routinely operating outside of the law and overstepping its legal authority by carrying out surveillance on American citizens is not really much of a surprise. This is what happens when you give the government broad powers and allow government agencies to routinely sidestep the Constitution.

(Illustration by EFF designer Hugh D'Andrade)

to an extramarital partner or exchanges with a fellow plotter."[17] The NSA is particularly interested in metadata, compiling information on Americans' social connections "that can identify their associates, their locations at certain times, their traveling companions and other personal information."[18] As Sara Watson wrote in *The Atlantic*, "Today, simply googling a parenting question will lump you in with that demographic, regardless of whether you are or want to be identified as part of it."[19]

Mainway, the NSA tool used to connect the dots on Americans' social connections, collected 700 million phone records *per day* in 2011. That number increased by 1.1 billion in August 2011.[20] The NSA is now working on creating "a metadata repository capable of taking in 20 billion 'record events' daily and making them available to NSA analysts within 60 minutes."[21]

Not to be overlooked are the NSA's many nasty and nefarious methods of carrying out surveillance, including infecting target computers with malware by way of spam emails and Facebook in order to give NSA hackers access to the data stored on those devices, and recording audio or video from a computer's microphone and webcam.[22] This program, dubbed TURBINE, which has already infected up to 100,000 computers, can record conversations with computer microphones, snap photos with a webcam, record Internet browsing history, record login/password information, log keystrokes, and take data off of flash drives plugged into the computer.[23]

Another NSA program, MYSTIC, allows NSA agents to retrieve and listen to up to 30 days' worth of *all* phone calls abroad, including those of American citizens traveling abroad or placing calls outside the country. Clips of millions of those phone calls are then processed and kept for long-term storage.[24]

Violating the Spirit of the Law

Unfortunately, with so much of the public attention focused on the NSA's misdeeds, there is a tendency to forget that the NSA is merely one of a growing number of clandestine intelligence agencies tasked with spying on the American people. In fact, the CIA, FBI, DHS, and DEA, among others, routinely step outside the bounds of the law in order to spy on and control the citizenry.

This violates not only the letter of the law but the spirit of the law, as well. By law, I am referring to the only law that truly matters—the U.S. Constitution—the only law that truly safeguards us against government abuse, overreach, expansion, and secrecy. For these very reasons, the Constitution continues to be trampled upon, shoved aside, disregarded, whittled down, choked to death, and generally castrated by the president, Congress and the courts, who without fail march in lockstep to the bidding of the military-security industrial complex, law enforcement officials, corporations and the like.

Thus, if our nation is riddled with all manner of problems, it's *because* we have government officials in the executive branch, Congress, and the courts incapable of abiding by the Constitution. These people have proven time and again that they cannot be trusted to do what they say, and they certainly can't be trusted to abide by their oaths of office to uphold and defend the Constitution.

Why Should You Care?

I often hear many Americans ask, if I'm not doing anything wrong, why should I care if the government wants to spy me?

You should care for this reason: once you allow the government to start breaking the law, no matter how seemingly justifiable the reason, you relinquish the contract between you and the government which establishes that the government works for and obeys you, the citizen—the employer—the master. And once the government starts operating outside the law, answerable to no one but itself, there's no way to rein it back in, short of revolution.

As for those who are not worried about the government filming you when you drive, listening to your phone calls, using satellites to track your movements, and drones to further spy on you, you'd better start worrying. At a time when the average American breaks at least three laws a day *without knowing it*—all thanks to the glut of laws being added to the books every year[25]—there's a pretty good chance that if the government chose to target you as a lawbreaker, they'd be able to come up with something without much effort.

Kafka's Nightmare

The runaround and circular logic of the courts, Congress, the intelligence agencies, and the White House calls to mind Franz Kafka's various depictions of bureaucracy gone mad and the shortcomings of a government which is only accountable to itself.

One of Franz Kafka's most famous novels, *The Trial*, tells the story of Josef K., an ordinary middle manager who one morning awakes to

find himself accused of a terrible crime, a crime which is too awful for his accusers to speak of. *The Trial* is ultimately a frightening depiction of what it means to live under a regime which operates on a circular logic that prevents outsiders, including those subject to its rule, from understanding—let alone challenging—the rules of the game and who is making them.

Josef K.'s plight, one of bureaucratic lunacy and an inability to discover the identity of his accusers, is increasingly an American reality. We now live in a society in which a person can be accused of any number of crimes without knowing what exactly he has done. He might be apprehended in the middle of the night by a roving band of SWAT police. He might find himself on a no-fly list, unable to

As Bertolt Brecht wrote, "Kafka described with wonderful imaginative power the future concentration camps, the future instability of the law, the future absolutism of the state Apparat."

travel for reasons undisclosed. He might have his phones or Internet connection tapped based upon a secret order handed down by a secret court, with no recourse to discover why he was targeted. Indeed, this is Kafka's nightmare, and it is slowly becoming America's reality.

CHAPTER 26

Orwell's Nightmare: Big Brother Meets Big Business

"The Google services and apps that we interact with on a daily basis aren't the company's main product: They are the harvesting machines that dig up and process the stuff that Google really sells: for-profit intelligence."[1]

—Journalist YASHA LEVINE

"We know where you are. We know where you've been. We can more or less know what you're thinking about."[2]

—Former Google CEO ERIC SCHMIDT

What would happen if the most powerful technology company in the world and the largest clandestine spying agency in the world joined forces?

No need to wonder. Just look around you. It's happened already. Thanks to an insidious partnership between Google and the NSA that grows more invasive and more subtle with every passing day,[3] "we the people" have become little more than data consumer commodities to be bought, sold, and paid for over and over again.[4]

With every smartphone we buy, every GPS device we install, every Twitter, Facebook, and Google account we open, every frequent buyer card we use for purchases—whether at the grocery, the yogurt shop, the airlines, or the department store—and every credit and debit card we use to pay for our transactions, we're helping Corporate America build a dossier for its government counterparts on who we know, what we think, how we spend our money, and how we spend our time.

What's worse, this for-profit surveillance scheme, far larger than anything the NSA could capture just by tapping into our phone calls,[5] is made possible by our consumer dollars and our cooperation. All those

Former Google CEO Eric Schmidt in Buenos Aires, Argentina, during his visit in April, 2007 (Photography by Gisela Giardino)

disclaimers you scroll though without reading them, the ones written in minute font, only to quickly click on the "Agree" button at the end so you can get to the next step—downloading software, opening up a social media account, adding a new app to your phone or computer: those signify your written consent to having your activities monitored, recorded, and shared.

It's not just the surveillance you *consent* to that's being shared with the government, however. It's the very technology you happily and unquestioningly use which is being hardwired to give the government easy access to your activities.

The government's motives aren't too difficult to understand, but what do corporate giants like Google, Amazon, and Apple stand to gain from colluding with Big Brother? Money, power, control. As privacy and security expert Bruce Schneier observed, "The main focus of massive Internet companies and government agencies both still largely align: to keep us all under constant surveillance. When they bicker, it's mostly role-playing designed to keep us blasé about what's really going on."[6]

While one billion people use Google every day,[7] none of them pay to utilize Google's services. However, there's a good reason why Google doesn't charge for its services, and it has nothing to do with magnanimity, generosity, altruism, or munificence. If as the old adage warns, there's no such thing as a free lunch, then what does Google get out of the relationship? Simple: Google gets us.

We Are Soylent Green

It turns out that *we* are Soylent Green. The 1973 film of the same name, starring Charlton Heston and Edward G. Robinson, is set in 2022 in an overpopulated, polluted, starving New York City whose inhabitants depend on synthetic foods manufactured by the Soylent Corporation for survival. Heston plays a policeman investigating a murder, who then discovers the grisly truth about what the wafer, soylent green—the principal source of nourishment for a starved population—is really made of. "It's people. Soylent Green is made out of people," declares Heston's character. "They're making our food out of people. Next thing they'll be breeding us like cattle for food."

Oh, how right he was. Soylent Green is indeed people, or in our case, Soylent Green is our own personal data, repossessed, repackaged, and

In *Soylent Green*, the world is ruled by ruthless corporations whose only goal is greed and profit.

used by corporations and the government to entrap us. In this way, we're being bred like cattle but not for food—rather, we're being bred for our data. That's the secret to Corporate America's success.

Indeed, collaboration between the biggest Silicon Valley firms and U.S. intelligence agencies has become commonplace. For example, Amazon launched a multi-million dollar computing cloud that serves all 17 intelligence agencies. The program stems from a deal struck between Amazon and the CIA.[8] Google has long enjoyed a relationship with clandestine agencies such as the CIA and NSA, which use Google's search-technology for scanning and sharing various intelligence.[9] The technology leviathan turns a profit by processing, trading, and marketing products based upon our personal information, including our relationships, daily activities, personal beliefs, and personalities. Thus, behind the pleasant glow of the computer screen lies a leviathan menace, an intricate system of data collection which transforms all Americans into a string of data, to be added, manipulated, or deleted based upon the whims of those in control.

Take, for example, Google's Street View program, which gives a fully immersive street level view of towns across the world. The program was constructed by Google Street View cars outfitted with 360 degree cameras, which seemed a neat idea to many people, most of whom didn't realize that the cars were not only taking pictures of all residential and commercial districts which they drove through, but were also "siphoning loads of personally identifiable data from people's Wi-Fi connections all across the world," including emails, medical records, and any other electronic documents that were not encrypted.[10]

Even the most seemingly benign Google program, Gmail, has been one of the most astoundingly successful surveillance programs ever concocted by a state or corporate entity. Journalist Yasha Levine explains:

> All communication was subject to deep linguistic analysis; conversations were parsed for keywords, meaning, and even tone; individuals were matched to real identities using contact information stored in a user's Gmail address book; attached documents were scraped for intel—that info was then cross-referenced with previous email interactions and combined with stuff gleaned from other Google services, as well as third-party sources . . .[11]

Google then creates profiles on Gmail users, based upon:

Concepts and topics discussed in email, as well as email attachments

The content of websites that users have visited

Demographic information—including income, sex, race, marital status

Geographic information

Psychographic information—personality type, values, attitudes, interests, and lifestyle interests

Previous searches users have made

Information about documents a user viewed and or edited by the users

Browsing activity

Previous purchases[12]

Even if one isn't using Gmail themselves, but merely contacting a Gmail user, that person is subject to this mass collection and analysis of personal data. Google has gone so far as to disingenuously argue that "people who used Internet services for communication had 'no legitimate expectation of privacy'—and thus anyone who emailed with Gmail users had given 'implied consent' for Google to intercept and analyze their email exchange."[13]

The Age of Infopolitics

What Google's vast acquisition and analysis of information indicates is that we are entering what some have called an age of infopolitics, in which the human person is broken down into data sets to be collated, analyzed, and used for a variety of purposes, including marketing, propaganda, and the squelching of dissent.[14] As philosopher Colin Koopman notes, we may soon find ourselves in a more efficient version of the McCarthy era, in which one's personal beliefs or associations become fodder for the rising corporate surveillance state.[15]

Email, social media, and GPS are just the tip of the iceberg, however. Google has added to its payroll the best and brightest minds in the

Atomic bombing of Nagasaki on August 9, 1945 (Photo taken by Charles Levy from one of the B-29 Superfortresses used in the attack.)

fields of military defense,[16] robotics (including humanoid robotics),[17] surveillance, machine learning,[18] artificial intelligence,[19] web-controlled household appliances (such as Nest thermostats),[20] and self-driving cars.[21] As journalist Carole Cadwalladr predicts, "The future, in ways we can't even begin to imagine, will be Google's."[22]

Towards this end, Google has been working to bring about what one investor called "a Manhattan project of AI [artificial intelligence]."[23] For those who remember their history, the Manhattan Project was a top-secret, multi-agency, multi-billion-dollar, military-driven government project aimed at building the first atom bombs. The project not only spawned the nuclear bombs used at Hiroshima and Nagasaki, but it also ushered in a nuclear arms race that, to this day, puts humanity on the brink of annihilation.[24]

As we shall see, no less powerful and potentially destructive to the human race are modern-day surveillance and robotic technologies, manufactured by corporations working in tandem with government agencies. These are the building blocks of the global electronic concentration camp encircling us all, and Google, in conjunction with the NSA, has set itself up as a formidable warden.

Looking Back on the Past with Longing

The question, when all is said and done, is where will all this technology take us?

It won't be long before we find ourselves, much like Edward G. Robinson's character in *Soylent Green*, looking back on the past with longing, back to an age where we could speak to whom we wanted, buy what we wanted, and think what we wanted without those thoughts, words and activities being tracked, processed, and stored by corporate giants such as Google, sold to government agencies such as the NSA and CIA, and used against us by militarized police with their army of futuristic technologies.

CHAPTER 27

The Twilight Zone Awaits Us

"It's a future where you don't forget anything. . . . In this new future you're never lost . . . We will know your position down to the foot and down to the inch over time. . . . Your car will drive itself, it's a bug that cars were invented before comput-ers . . . you're never lonely . . . you're never bored . . . you're never out of ideas. . . We can suggest where you go next, who to meet, what to read. . . What's interesting about this future is that it's for the average person, not just the elites."[1]

—former Google CEO ERIC SCHMIDT on his vision of the future

We're about to enter a Twilight Zone of sorts, one marked by drones,[2] smart phones,[3] GPS devices, smart TVs,[4] social media, smart meters,[5] surveillance cameras, facial recognition software,[6] online banking, license plate readers,[7] and driverless cars.[8] These devices are all part of the interconnected technological spider web that is life in the American police state, and every new gadget pulls us that much deeper into the sticky snare.

In the ominous world awaiting us, there will be no communication not spied upon, no movement untracked, no thought unheard. In other words, there will be nowhere to run and nowhere to hide.

The Double-Edged Sword

Technology has always been a double-edged sword. Delighted with tech-nology's conveniences, its ability to make our lives easier by performing an endless array of tasks faster and more efficiently, we have given it free rein in our lives, with little thought to the legal or moral ramifications of allowing surveillance technology to uncover nearly every intimate detail of our lives. Once it outstrips our ability as humans to control it, it inevi-tably becomes something akin to Frankenstein's monster. So it was with

205

GPS devices, which quickly became a method by which the government could track our movements, and with online banking and other transactions, which also gave the government the ability to track our purchases and activities. So it shall be with the entire arsenal of technological gadgets and gizmos being unleashed on an unsuspecting public.

V2V Transmitters and Black Boxes

As if the government wasn't already able to track our movements on the nation's highways and byways by way of satellites, GPS devices, license plate readers, and real-time traffic cameras, all new vehicles will soon come installed with black box recorders and vehicle-to-vehicle (V2V) communications,[9] ostensibly to help prevent crashes.[10] Yet strip away the glib Orwellian doublespeak, and what you will find is that these black boxes and V2V transmitters—which will not only track a variety of data, including speed, direction, location, the number of miles traveled, and seatbelt use, but will also *transmit* this data to other drivers, *including the police*—are little more than Trojan Horses, stealth attacks on our last shreds of privacy, sold to us as safety measures for the sake of the greater good,[11] all the while poised to wreak havoc on our lives.

Black boxes and V2V transmitters are just the tip of the iceberg, though. The 2015 Corvette Stingray comes with a performance data recorder, which "uses a camera mounted on the windshield and a global positioning receiver to record speed, gear selection, and brake force," but also provides a recording of the driver's point of view as well as recording noises made inside the car.[12] As journalist Jaclyn Trop reports for the *New York Times*, "Drivers can barely make a left turn, put on their seatbelts or push 80 miles an hour without their actions somehow, somewhere being tracked or recorded."[13]

Indeed, as Jim Farley, Vice President of Marketing and Sales for Ford Motor Company, all but admitted, corporations and government officials already have a pretty good sense of where you are at all times: "We know everyone who breaks the law, we know when you're doing it. We have GPS in your car, so we know what you're doing."[14]

Now that the government and its corporate partners-in-crime know *where* you're going and how *fast* you're going when in your car, the next big hurdle will be to know how many passengers are in your car, what contraband might be in your car (and that will largely depend on whatever is outlawed at the moment, which could be anything from Sudafed cold medicine to goat cheese), what you're saying and exactly what you're doing within the fiberglass and steel walls of your vehicle.

Big Brother Behind the Wheel?

By the time you add self-driving cars into the futuristic mix, equipped with computers that know where you want to go before you do, you'll be so far down the road to Steven Spielberg's vision of the future as depicted in *Minority Report* that privacy and autonomy will be little more than distant mirages in your rearview mirror. The film, set in 2054 and based on a short story by Philip K. Dick, offered movie audiences a special effect-laden techno-vision of a futuristic world in which the government is all-seeing, all-knowing, and all-powerful. And if you dare to step out of line, dark-clad police SWAT teams will bring you under control.

Mind you, while critics were dazzled by the technological wonders displayed in *Minority Report*, few dared to consider the consequences of a world in which Big Brother is literally and figuratively in the driver's seat. Even the driverless cars in *Minority Report* answer to the government's (and its corporate cohorts') bidding.

Google driverless car operating on a testing path
(Photography by Steve Jurvetso)

Likewise, we are no longer autonomous in our own cars. Rather, we are captive passengers being chauffeured about by a robotic mind that answers to the government and its corporate henchmen. Soon it won't even matter whether we are seated behind the wheel of our own vehicles, because it will be advertisers and government agents calling the shots.

Case in point: devices are now being developed for European cars that would allow police to stop a car remotely, ostensibly to end police chases.[15] Google is partnering with car manufacturers in order to integrate apps and other smartphone-like technology into vehicles in order to alert drivers to deals and offers at nearby businesses.[16] As Patrick Lin, professor of Stanford's School of Engineering, warns: in a world where third-party advertisers and data collectors control a good deal of the content we see on a daily basis, we may one day literally be driven to businesses not because we wanted to go there, but because someone paid for us to be taken there.[17]

In other words, the term "driverless cars" is a misnomer. Someone or something will be driving these futuristic vehicles. The question is who or what will be behind the wheel?

The Coming Drone Invasion

By the time drones—unmanned aerial vehicles—take to the skies, there will literally be nowhere that government agencies and private companies cannot track your movements. Once used exclusively by the military to carry out aerial surveillance and attacks on enemy insurgents abroad, these remotely piloted, semi-autonomous robots were authorized by Congress and President Obama for widespread use in American airspace starting in 2015.[18]

It is estimated that at least 30,000 drones will be airborne by 2020,[19] all part of an $80 billion industry that is already creating a buzz in the atmosphere. These gadgets, ranging from the colossal to the miniature, can do everything from conducting surveillance and delivering pizza to detonating explosive charges, seeing through the walls of your home,[20] and tracking your every movement. Indeed, with government agencies authorized to use drones for everything from border control and aerial surveillance to traffic enforcement, crowd control, and fighting forest fires, drones are about to become a permanent fixture in the American landscape.[21] The FBI, Drug Enforcement Agency, and Border Patrol are already using drone technology for surveillance operations.[22]

Many drones will come equipped with cameras that provide a live video feed, as well as heat sensors and radar. Some will be capable of peering at figures from 20,000 feet up and 25 miles away and can keep track of 65 persons of interest at once.[23] Some drones are already capable of hijacking Wi-Fi networks and intercepting electronic communications such as text messages.[24]

The military has developed drones with facial recognition software,[25] as well as drones that can complete a target-and-kill mission without any human instruction or interaction.[26] Police departments throughout the country are already acquiring drones equipped with lethal weapons such as grenade launchers and shotguns. There will also be drones armed with "less-lethal" weapons of compliance, such as tear gas,[27] rubber buckshot,[28] bean bag guns and tasers, flying over political demonstrations, sporting events, and concert arenas conducting surveillance for police and sweeps in advance of major "security" events.

The Nano Hummingbird surveillance and reconnaissance aircraft developed by AeroVironment, Inc. under contract with the United States Government's Defense Advanced Research Projects Agency

(Photography by DARPA)

While the government's use of drone technology poses the gravest threats to our privacy rights, it's the commercial drones used for deliveries, to capture news footage, to film theatrical events and feature films, or just for sport, that will really "sell" this technology to the American people. The online retailer Amazon has designed its own pilotless delivery drones, octocopters, which will be used to deliver products under five pounds within a ten-mile range and with a thirty-minute turnaround.[29] The Domino's pizza chain is considering unmanned drones as a way to give it an edge on its competitors. The "DomiCopter" is being developed to deliver two Domino's pizzas in the company's Heatwave bags.[30] Not to be outdone, there's also a Taco-Copter drone—for delivering tacos—in the works.[31]

Unfortunately, while the legislation opening American skies to drones was steamrollered into place after intense corporate lobbying by corporate drone makers and potential customers,[32] no safeguards were put in place on either the federal or state level to establish effective safeguards for Americans' civil liberties and privacy rights. Without a doubt, drones will give rise to a whole new dialogue in the courts about where to draw the line when it comes to the government's ability to monitor one's public versus private lives.

Whatever you can imagine, it will not be long before there is a drone suited to every purpose under the sun. One thing you can be sure of: whether you make a wrong move, or appear to be doing something suspicious (even if you don't actually do anything suspicious), the information of your whereabouts, including what stores and offices you visit, what political rallies you attend, and what people you meet—all of this information will be tracked, recorded, and streamed to a government command center where it will be saved and easily accessed at a later date.

The New Citizenry

Rod Serling, creator of the sci-fi series *Twilight Zone* and one of the most insightful commentators on human nature, once observed, "We're developing a new citizenry. One that will be very selective about cereals and automobiles, but won't be able to think."[33]

Indeed, not only is the corporate state developing a new citizenry incapable of thinking for themselves, they're also instilling in them a complete and utter reliance on the government and its corporate partners to do everything for them: tell them what to eat, what to wear, how to think, what to believe, how long to sleep, who to vote for, whom to associate with, and on and on.

In this way, we have created a welfare state, a nanny state, a police state, and now a surveillance state; in other words, we live in an electronic concentration camp. Call it what you will, the meaning is the same: in our quest for less personal responsibility, a greater sense of security, and no burdensome obligations to each other or to future generations, we have created a society in which we have no true freedom.

Pandora's Box has been opened and there's no way to close it. As Rod Serling warned in a Commencement Address at the University of Southern California in March 17, 1970:

> It's simply a national acknowledgement that in any kind of priority, the needs of human beings must come first. Poverty is here and now. Hunger is here and now. Racial tension is here and now. Pollution is here and now. These are the things that scream for a response. And if we don't listen to that scream—and if we don't respond to it—we may well wind up sitting amidst our own rubble, looking for the truck that hit us—or the bomb that pulverized us. Get the license number of whatever it was that destroyed the dream. And I think we will find that the vehicle was registered in our own name.[34]

The warning signs of any fascistic regime are there to those who are alert. They are hinted at on television programs, the Internet and various so-called news resources. This includes those fiction writers and filmmakers who have been warning us for years that we are on the verge of a totalitarian regime. One such writer was Rod Serling, the creator and writer of the celebrated *Twilight Zone* television series.

You can add the following to that list of needs requiring an urgent response: Police abuse is here and now. Surveillance is here and now. Imperial government is here and now. Yet while the vehicle bearing down upon us is, in fact, registered in our own name, we've allowed Big Brother to get behind the wheel, and there's no way to put the brakes on this runaway car. Indeed, we're hurtling down this one-way road at mind-boggling speeds, the terrain is getting more treacherous by the minute, and we've passed all the exit ramps. From this point forward, there is no turning back.

CHAPTER 28

The FBI: America's Thought Police

"Whether he went on with the diary, or whether he did not go on with it, made no difference. The Thought Police would get him just the same. He had committed—would still have committed, even if he had never set pen to paper—the essential crime that contained all others in itself. Thoughtcrime, they called it. Thoughtcrime was not a thing that could be concealed forever. You might dodge successfully for a while, even for years, but sooner or later they were bound to get you."[1]

—GEORGE ORWELL, *1984*

The nation's entire law enforcement system seems to be headed towards a pre-crime detection system aimed at detecting and pursuing those who "might" commit a crime before they have an inkling, let alone an opportunity, to do so. (Illustration by Brian Farrington)

Orwell's prophecy of the emergence of a Thought Police in Western society, meant to regulate the ideas people discussed, wrote about, or even contemplated within their own heads, has become a stark reality in American society. From the emergence of so-called "trigger warnings" at universities throughout the country,[2] intended to shield students from ideas which may be stressful or traumatic, to the authors of parody Twitter accounts being raided by police in SWAT team raids,[3] there is no shortage of evidence that speaking your mind is becoming increasingly dangerous.

Unbeknownst to most, however, there has been a federal agency, which since its very inception, has concerned itself not with actual crimes being committed by the American people, but rather with their thoughts, beliefs, and associations. It is an organization, which by all accounts fits the exact description of the Thought Police, but is better known as the Federal Bureau of Investigation (FBI).

Like Orwell's Thought Police, the FBI commandeers its authority from an omnipresent surveillance of the identities, associations, and beliefs of as many Americans as possible. While the NSA has captured the spotlight over its far-reaching surveillance, the FBI's clandestine activities have not been as closely scrutinized, despite the fact that it engages in much of the same kinds of surveillance.

The FBI, whose crimes against dissidents and minority groups stretch back to the founding of the organization, works closely with the NSA in order to help foster their intelligence gathering capabilities. It is an often-overlooked fact that it was the FBI, not the NSA, which was tasked with collecting data from telecoms under the NSA's Prism system. The FBI picked that data out of private servers, then turned around and handed it over to the NSA.[4]

The NSA returned the favor, as declassified documents from the FISA Court, the secret court tasked with regulating the NSA's activities, have revealed. In fact, the NSA was (and may still be) sharing information gleaned from their surveillance efforts with the FBI. The documents claim that two to three tips were shared every day, going back to the year 2006.[5]

Never Forgetting a Face

The incestuous collusion between the NSA and the FBI demonstrates a desire by the federal government to have a catalog of every thought, image, word, and action that occurs within the United States, whether or not they pose any real threat to the country. Simply put, it's a program designed to institute total control over the population.

In addition to helping out the NSA, the FBI conducts its own signals intelligence program, which focuses on collecting emails and other Internet data from American companies. The main core of this operation is the Data Intercept Technology Unit (DITU), whose motto is "Vigilance Through Technology." One of the DITU's many responsibilities is making software that private companies install onto their networks in order to allow government agents ready access to personal information, whether emails or Internet traffic. This surveillance is generally conducted without a warrant, as the FBI asserts the authority to collect metadata under the Patriot Act.[6]

All of this vacuuming up of our personal correspondence is bad enough, but the FBI isn't stopping there. As previously noted, the FBI's Next Generation Identification (NGI) facial recognition system, capable of uploading 55,000 images a day, and conducting tens of thousands of photo searches a day,[7] builds off the FBI's current database of over 100 million fingerprints and will include a variety of biometric data, including palm prints, iris scans, and facial recognition data.[8]

The database connects the identifying information with biographical information such as name, home address, ID number, immigration status, age, and race. This information is shared with other federal agencies and over 18,000 local and state law enforcement agencies.[9] Perhaps most concerning, the database contains facial images of convicted criminals alongside non-criminals. These are collected from photographs supposedly taken during job background checks.[10]

Capturing facial images doesn't stop with the photos from background checks, Facebook posts, or driver's licenses, however. Digital photos of your face are also captured from the numerous surveillance cameras popping up everywhere, all without a search warrant, of course. According to Stephen Morris, director of the FBI's Criminal Justice Services Division, the ability to use facial images from surveillance cameras and other digital devices will be key to developing a massive facial recognition government database.[11]

Not everyone is as enthusiastic about the rise of facial recognition technology. Dr. Joseph J. Atick, a pioneering researcher and entrepreneur in biometrics and facial recognition systems, is particularly wary of facial recognition technology's potential for abuse. Atick envisions a future where powerful corporations and government agencies use facial recognition to create a mass surveillance society, "basically robbing everyone of their anonymity" and inhibiting people's normal behavior outside their homes.[12]

Mapping Your Body

As if grabbing your fingerprints or facial images weren't bad enough, the FBI's Combined DNA Index System (CODIS) will keep your DNA on file.[13] CODIS catalogues genetic profiles at the local, state, and national levels, and the FBI shares the data with police and government agents across the country.

Of course, the FBI's biometric agenda has some powerful assistance from the courts. In fact, in a 2013 ruling, the U.S. Supreme Court held in *Maryland v. King* that it is not a violation of the Fourth Amendment for police to forcibly take DNA samples from people who are "arrested" (not convicted) of so-called serious crimes. This is done by using a Q-tip to take cheek swabs from suspects. As Justice Antonin Scalia, who dissented in the case, warns: "Make no mistake about it: As an entirely predictable consequence of today's decision, your DNA can be taken and entered into a national DNA database if you are ever arrested, rightly or wrongly, and for whatever reason."[14] If, for example, you are arrested for having a dog off the leash in a park, you could be forced to give a sample of your DNA.

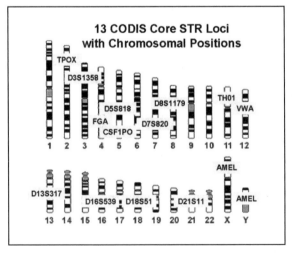

CODIS 13-point profile

Indeed, while states and the federal government already collect DNA samples from people arrested for "serious" crimes, a move is afoot to begin collecting DNA from anyone even charged with a misdemeanor. The FBI already has nearly twelve million DNA profiles on record. Eventually, it is envisioned that the FBI's DNA database will be a huge storage vat of human genetic information, especially since federal law now provides millions of dollars in funding for states to collect DNA.[15]

DNA, it must be emphasized, is a complicated human mapping system. In fact, human DNA is a biological Internet which stores an amazing amount of information—so much so that some scientists now say they will eventually be able to create accurate police mugshots using only DNA.[16]

Your DNA even shows who's related to whom—something that fingerprints or facial images do not reveal. Putting that science to their advantage, states such as California, Colorado, Virginia, and Texas are employing a technique called "familial search,"[17] which allows one's family tree to be detected. That's why "[l]aw enforcement agencies turn to familial search when a crime scene sample only contains a partial match," explains *PBS* journalist Valerie Ross. "That partial match may point investigators to that person's father, brother, son, or another close relative" in attempting to nail a suspect.[18]

Bear in mind that if the FBI, along with local police, can dig deep enough into your genetic history, they may also unearth some troubling or notorious ancestors. In the future, that may be enough to place you under surveillance as a preventive measure. After all, the entire law enforcement system seems to be headed towards a pre-crime detection system aimed at detecting and pursuing those who "might" commit a crime before they have an inkling, let alone an opportunity, to do so.

Inventing Terrorists

A study released by a coalition of prisoners' rights and legal advocacy groups called "Inventing Terrorists: The Lawfare of Preemptive Prosecution" shows that almost 95 percent of the people whom the Justice Department convicted of terrorism between 2001 and 2010 were pursued under the policy of preemptive prosecution, in which individuals or organizations are targeted and prosecuted based upon their "beliefs, ideology, or religious affiliations."[19]

The arrests which the federal government has touted as proof that they've been tracking and preventing terrorist attacks within the United States in general involve (1) the FBI foiling terrorist plots that it concocts itself, before entrapping unsuspecting people into the criminal arrangements, (2) the government charging people with "material support for terrorism" for innocent activities such as free speech, free association, and advocating for peace in the Middle East, and (3) inflating "minor or technical incidents" into incidences of terrorism, including things like incorrectly filling out immigration applications.[20]

Under these schemes, a variety of innocuous activities, including "donating to charity, witnessing a loan, visiting a foreign country, storing a bag of clothes, or posting information on the Internet" have been labeled terrorist activities.[21] Other methods include using conspiracy laws to treat innocent friendships and associations as terrorist conspiracies, and using *agents provocateur* to coerce and entrap targets into criminal plots which the government manufactures and controls, and which the person would have otherwise not engaged in.[22]

In cases where defendants are charged as being part of a conspiracy, they may have absolutely no knowledge of a terrorist plot.[23] In one case, a government informant admitted that three of the so-called "conspirators" had no knowledge of a government-concocted plot to attack Fort Dix, but they were all sentenced to life in prison.[24]

As lawyer Martin Stolar, who represented an individual caught in such a scheme, stated, "The problem with the cases we're talking about is that defendants would not have done anything if not kicked in the ass by government agents. They're creating crimes to solve crimes so they can claim a victory in the war on terror."[25] Put simply, this means that the federal government, particularly the FBI, has been systematically targeting members of certain ideological groups (in this case, Muslims) and either entrapping them into performing illegal activities or inflating minor criminal activities into terrorism charges.

COINTELPRO

This is the latest in a long line of abuses committed by the FBI since its inception, starting with the Palmer Raids in the 1920s, up through blacklisting Communists in the 1950s, to COINTELPRO during the 1960s and 70s.[26] The common thread of all these programs is that the groups targeted were targeted not for any particular attempt to commit a crime but due to their ideological or religious beliefs.

COINTELPRO, which was officially conducted between 1956 and 1971, targeted a number of non-violent political groups, including the National Lawyers Guild and the Southern Christian Leadership Conference.[27] It was an attempt to infiltrate and disrupt political groups, most of whom were nonviolent, and charge them with various sundry crimes so as to protect the federal government from criticism and clamp down on all forms of dissent.

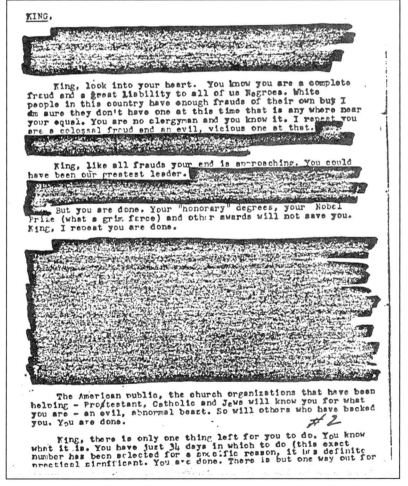

Anonymous letter sent from the Federal Bureau of Investigation to Martin Luther King, Jr., urging the civil rights leader to kill himself

Among those most closely watched by the FBI during that time period was Martin Luther King Jr., a man labeled by the FBI as the "most dangerous and effective Negro leader in the country."[28] With wiretaps and electronic bugs planted in his home and office, King was kept under constant surveillance by the FBI from 1958 until his death in 1968, all with the aim of "neutralizing King as an effective Negro leader."[29] King even received letters written by FBI agents suggesting that either he commit suicide or the details of his private life would be revealed to the public.[30] The FBI file on King is estimated to contain 17,000 pages of materials documenting his day-to-day activities. Incredibly, nearly fifty years later, the FBI maintains a stranglehold on information relating to this "covert" operation. Per a court order, information relating to the FBI wiretaps on King will not be released until 2027.

What we are seeing today is a reboot of COINTELPRO. Non-violent but politically active groups are being targeted for surveillance and arrest by the FBI. This includes not only Muslims, but Occupy Wall Street activists,[31] so-called "Right Wing Extremists," and veterans returning from Iraq and Afghanistan. Indeed, if you seem to be beyond the pale in any way, the federal government most likely has an eye on what you're doing in your daily life.

Targeting Dissent

Ultimately, it comes down to control. If the government knows every little aspect of your life, whether it's your job, relationships, religious beliefs, or political beliefs, and has an arsenal of laws and a criminal justice system at their disposal which can be turned against anyone at any time, it will be that much easier for them to muzzle dissent before it starts.

CHAPTER 29

The Brave New World

"Television results in a kind of zombification—not a great thing for a genuinely democratic society."[1]

—BRUCE LEVINE, clinical psychologist

"Keep you doped with sex and religion and TV. You think you're so clever and classless and free."[2]

—JOHN LENNON

"Through clever and constant application of propaganda, people can be made to see paradise as hell, and the other way around to consider the most wretched sort of life."[3]

—ADOLF HITLER, *Mein Kampf*

We have become a society that believes it has to be constantly connected to some sort of virtual unreality.

Often, as I walk along the streets, I watch those around me. On busy streets, people used to look straight ahead—sometimes moving as if they were on conveyor belts—but somewhat aware of their surroundings. Now, most everyone has their heads down while staring zombie-like into an electronic screen, even when they're crossing the street.

221

Families sit in restaurants with their heads down, separated by their screen devices and unaware of what's going on around them. Young people especially seem dominated by the devices they hold in their hands, oblivious to the fact that they can simply push a button, turn the thing off, and walk away.

Unfortunately, we have become a society that believes it has to be constantly connected to some sort of virtual unreality. "I think citizens actually love the fact that somebody is watching and listening to them," filmmaker Terry Gilliam remarked. "Everybody lives for their selfies and their tweets—to actually exist, something has to be talking to you or listening in on you."4

Strangely enough, this was the scenario presented in author Aldous Huxley's vision of the future in *Brave New World*. Huxley warned that modern culture was becoming so consumed and distracted by entertainment (and/or technological gadgets) that the citizenry would not realize they were trapped in prison until it was too late.

Mob Mentality

For Adolf Hitler, marching was a technique to mobilize people in groups by immobilizing them. Hitler and his regime leaders discovered that when people gather in groups and do the same thing—such as marching or cheering at an entertainment or sporting event—they became passive, non-thinking non-individuals. As political advisor Bertram Gross recognized, by replacing "marching" with electronic screen devices, we have the equivalent of Hitler's method of population control:

> As a technique of immobilizing people, marching requires organization and, apart from the outlay costs involved, organized groups are a potential danger. They might march to a different drum or in the wrong direction.... TV is more effective. It captures many more people than would ever fill the streets by marching—and without interfering with automobile traffic.5

Equally disturbing is a university study which indicates that we become less aware of our individual selves and moral identity in a group.6 In the study, university students were asked to play a game in which a series of personalized messages popped up on the screen in front of them. Some were related to social media that dealt with moral issues such as "I have stolen food from shared refrigerators." The game was a distraction. The researchers' goal was to monitor the activity of the pre-frontal cortex, which is that part of the brain linked to self-reflection—that is, analyzing whether a certain action is right or wrong based upon a sense of morality. For example, should I or should I not steal another's food? Should I or should I not purposely injure another human being? The findings were a bit startling. As journalist Kadhim Shubber notes:

> When participants were told they were playing in a team, there was mark-edly less activity in this part of the brain when moral messages appeared on screen as opposed to when participants were told they were playing solo.[7]

The study's findings strongly suggest that when we act in groups, we tend to consider our moral behavior less while moving in lockstep with the group. Thus, what the group believes or does, be it violence or inhumanity, does not seem to lessen the need to be a part of a group, whether it be a mob or pizza party.

Pacified Zombies

There is no larger group activity than that connected with those who watch screens—meaning viewing television, lap tops, personal comput-ers, cell phones, and so on. In fact, a Nielsen study reports that American screen viewing is at an all-time high. For example, the average American watches approximately 151 hours of television per month.[8]

The question, of course, is what effect does such screen consump-tion have on one's mind? Historically, television has been used by those in authority to quiet discontent and pacify disruptive people. "Faced with severe overcrowding and limited budgets for rehabilita-tion and counseling, more and more prison officials are using TV to keep inmates quiet," according to *Newsweek*.[9] Joe Corpier, a convicted murderer, when interviewed said, "If there's a good movie, it's usually pretty quiet through the whole institution."[10] In other words, television and other screen viewing helps to subdue people.

Not surprisingly, the United States is one of the highest TV-viewing nations in the world. Moreover, the majority of what Americans watch on television is provided through channels controlled by six megacor-porations.[11] This lends support to the view that what we watch is now controlled by a corporate elite and, if that elite needs to foster a particu-lar viewpoint or pacify its viewers, it can do so on a large scale.

Historically, television has been used by those in authority to quiet discontent and pacify disruptive people. (Illustration by Kevin Tuma, courtesy of CNS News)

If what we see and what we are told through the entertainment industrial complex—which includes so-called "news" shows—is what those in power deem to be in their best interests, then endless screen viewing is not a great thing for a citizenry who believe they possess choice and freedom. As Bertram Gross observed:

> No totalitarian regime is possible without censorship. But in the age of the modern information complex, there is much less of a role for the old-fashioned censor as an outsider who clamps down on the mass and elite media against their will. Today, far more information is available than can be possibly used by the mass media in their present form. The filtering-out process by itself represents suppression on a mammoth scale. ... In a certain sense, events exist only if they are recorded or reported by the media.[12]

Supposedly why television—and increasingly movies—are so effective in subduing and pacifying us is that viewers are mesmerized by what TV-insiders call "technical events." These, according to clinical psychologist Bruce Levine, are "quick cuts, zoom-ins, zoom-outs, rolls, pans, animation, music, graphics, and voice-overs, all of which lure viewers to continue watching even though they have no interest in the content."[13] Such technical events, which many action films now incorporate, spellbind people to continue watching.

Moreover, two researches have concluded that technical events have addictive responses in viewers. Psychologically it is similar to drug addiction. They found that "almost immediately after turning on the TV, subjects reported feeling more relaxed, and because this occurs so quickly and the tension returns so rapidly after the TV is turned off, people are conditioned to associate TV viewing with a lack of tension."[14] Research also shows that regardless of the programming, viewers' brain waves slow down, thus transforming them into a more passive, nonresistant state, much like research concerning the lessening of brain activity in the prefrontal cortices. After all, television viewing is a group activity as millions sit motionless watching the same program.

A Dream Come True

According to Levine, authoritarian-based programming is more technically interesting to viewers than democracy-based programming.[15] War and violence, for example, may be rather unpleasant in real life. However, peace and cooperation make for "boring television."[16] And charismatic authority figures—popular politicians—are more interesting on television than are ordinary citizens intent on debating issues of importance.

In fact, any successful candidate for political office—especially the president—must come off well on TV. Television has the lure of involvement. A politically adept president can actually make you believe you are involved in the office of the presidency. The effective president, then, is essentially a television performer. As the renowned media analyst Marshall McLuhan recognized concerning television: "Potentially, it can transform the presidency into a monarchist dynasty."[17] Combine the presidency with the handful of corporations that feed us programming, and you have all the makings for authoritarian control with somewhat of a smile. As Levine writes:

> Television is a "dream come true" for an authoritarian society. Those with the most money own most of what people see. Fear-based TV programming makes people more afraid and distrustful of one another, which is good for an authoritarian society depending on a "divide and conquer" strategy. Television isolates people so they are not joining together to govern themselves.

Viewing television puts one in a brain state that makes it difficult to think critically, and it quiets and subdues a population. And spending one's free time isolated and watching TV interferes with the connection to one's own humanity, and thus makes it easier to accept an authority's version of society and life.[18]

Culture Death

When I was a young man, around the time that television was emerging as a dominant force, it was common for people to refer to television sets as the "boob tube" or the "idiot box." Obviously, there was at least a subconscious awareness that sitting for hours a day watching a screen could have some detrimental effects.

As we have seen, television and other screen devices can be used by those who run the system to manipulate and even indoctrinate us. In fact, television may be the one instrument more than any other that now forms public opinion. Yet wedded to the corporate state as it is, television more than forms public opinion; it can alter the consciousness and worldview of entire populations.

The content most suitable for television is entertainment. Whether it's news, reality shows, or a comedy, television is always presented in a fast moving, sound bite format. Thus, the direction of the future, then, may be towards a *Brave New World* scenario where the populace is constantly distracted by entertainment, hooked on prescription drugs and controlled by a technological elite. As professor Neil Postman observed:

> What Huxley teaches is in the age of advanced technology, spiritual devastation is more likely to come from an enemy with a smiling face than from one whose countenance exudes suspicion and hate. In the Huxleyan prophecy, Big Brother does not watch us, by his choice. We watch him, by ours. There is no need for wardens or gates or Ministries of Truth. When a population becomes distracted by trivia, when cultural life is redefined as a perpetual round of entertainments, when serious public conversation becomes a form of baby-talk, when, in short, a people become an audience and their public business a vaudeville act, then a nation finds itself at risk; a culture-death is a clear possibility.[19]

Are You Smiling?

If the average American is indeed watching over 150 hours of television a week, then there may be little hope for the future of freedom. Freedom, as I say, is an action word. It means turning off your screen devices—or at least greatly reducing your viewing time—and getting active to take to stave off the emerging authoritarian government.

Aldous Huxley, George Orwell, and the countless science fiction writers and commentators have warned that we are in a race between getting actively involved in the world around us or facing disaster. If we're watching, we're not doing. As television journalist Edward R. Murrow warned in a 1958 speech:

> We have currently a built-in allergy to unpleasant or disturbing information. Our mass media reflect this. But unless we get up off our fat surpluses and recognize that television in the main is being used to distract, delude, amuse, and insulate us, then television and those who finance it, those who look at it, and those who work at it, may see a totally different picture too late.[20]

In the end, as Postman concludes, Huxley "was trying to tell us that what afflicted people in *Brave New World* was not that they were laughing instead of thinking, but that they did not know what they were laughing about and why they had stopped thinking."[21] Nevertheless, they kept smiling.

CHAPTER 30

The Matrix

"*Morpheus:* The Matrix is everywhere, it is all around us. It is the world that has been pulled over your eyes to blind you from the truth.

Neo: What truth?

Morpheus: That you are a slave. Neo, like everyone else you were born into bondage, born into a prison that you cannot smell or taste or touch; a prison for your mind."[1] — *The Matrix*

"The twenty-first century...will be the era of World Controllers.... The older dictators fell because they could never supply their subjects with enough bread, enough circuses, enough miracles and mysteries. Nor did they possess a really effective system of mind-manipulation. In the past, free-thinkers and revolutionaries were often the products of the most piously orthodox education. This is not surprising. The methods employed by orthodox educators were and still are extremely inefficient. Under a scientific dictator education will really work — with the result that most men and women will grow up to love their servitude and will never dream of revolution. There seems to be no good reason why a thoroughly scientific dictatorship should ever be overthrown."[2]

— ALDOUS HUXLEY, *Brave New World Revisited*

"Man's conquest of Nature, if the dreams of some scientific planners are realized, means the rule of a few hundreds of men over billions upon billions of men."— C. S. LEWIS, *The Abolition of Man*[3]

"The development of full artificial intelligence could spell the end of the human race."[4]— STEPHEN HAWKING, theoretical physicist

For those interested in maintaining any semblance of freedom—that is, those who are awake—it's important to understand what we are up against and who or what is running the show. Real power is always hidden, lurking in the shadows like a demon, calculating its next move.

The world, it must be remembered, has not been terrorized by despots advertising themselves as devils. Instead, totalitarian regimes—a collective synergy of governmental and corporate interests—have come to power while citing platitudes of liberty, equality, and prosperity. They do what they do, as we are told, to keep us safe, secure, and to promote our happiness.

Indeed, while most of us were moving through life trying to earn a living and attempting to enjoy our existence, megacorporations joined forces with the government while erecting an electronic concentration camp around us.

Singularity

Look around you. Somebody or something is either watching you, listening to you, or reading and/or analyzing what you're typing into your electronic device. "Whatever happened to privacy?" you ask. There is no such thing as privacy anymore.

Yes, those who operate the "Matrix" probably know you better than, say, your best friends. *The Matrix*? So-called science fiction is no longer fiction, if it ever was.

In the 1999 film *The Matrix*, computer programmer Thomas A. Anderson, a hacker known as "Neo," is intrigued by the cryptic references to the "Matrix" that appears from time to time on his computer. Eventually, Neo learns that intelligent computer systems created in the 21st century are acting autonomously and have taken control of all life on earth and now watch and control everyone. These computer systems are parasitical. They harvest the bio-electrical energy of humans. Indeed, humans (or batteries, in this case) are grown in vast nurseries and live out their lives in vats while attached to tubes that supply food and remove waste. Their brains are hardwired to a neuro-interactive simulation of reality. The simulation, called the "Matrix," keeps humans inactive and docile while robotic androids gather the electricity their bodies generate.

Movie poster for *The Matrix*

In order for the machines who run the Matrix to maintain control, they impose what appears to be a perfect world for humans to keep them distracted, content, and submissive. (Translation: the elaborate entertainment industrial complex that surrounds the human race.) Some humans are not so content with the way things appear to be, and when Neo joins a resistance group, he soon finds out that the android police are more than willing to crack skulls to keep dissidents in line with the status quo.

Neo's Matrix is not so far removed from our own technologically cocooned worlds, especially if Google and other corporate giants continue to get their way. As journalist Ben Thompson tells us:

> Think about it: what is more valuable? [Facebook's] Inane chatter, memes, and baby photos, or every single activity you do online (and increasingly offline)? Google+ is about unifying all of Google's services under a single log-in which can be tracked across the Internet on every site that serves Google ads, uses Google sign-in, or utilizes Google analytics. Every feature of Google+—or of YouTube, or Maps, or GMail, or any other service—is a flytrap meant to ensure you are logged in and being logged by Google at all times.[5]

Everything we do will eventually be connected to the Internet. For example, in 2007, there were an estimated 10 million sensor devices connecting human utilized electronic devices (cell phones, laptops, etc.) to the Internet. By 2013, it had increased to 3.5 billion. By 2030, it is estimated to reach 100 trillion.[6] Much, if not all, of our electronic devices will be connected to Google.

But that's not all. Now Google has partnered with the NSA, the Pentagon, and the "Matrix" of surveillance agencies to develop a new "human" species, so to speak. As William Binney, one of the highest-level whistleblowers to ever emerge from the NSA, said, "The ultimate goal of the NSA is total population control."[7]

Let me explain.

Google has resources beyond anything the world has ever seen. This includes the huge data sets that result from one billion people using Google every single day and the Google knowledge graph "which consists of 800 million concepts and billions of relationships between them."[8] In other words, Google is a neural network that approximates a massive global brain, which it is fusing with the human mind. In fact, Google hired transhumanist scientist Ray Kurzweil to do just that.

The plan is a marriage of sorts between machine and human beings, a phenomenon that is dubbed *singularity*—the moment when artificial intelligence and the human brain will merge to form a super-human mind. Google will know the answer to your question before you have asked it. Kurzweil said, "It will have read every email you've ever written, every document, every idle thought you've ever tapped into a search-engine box. It will know you better than your intimate partner does. Better, perhaps, than even yourself."[9]

The term "singularity"—that is, computers simulating human life itself—was coined years ago by mathematical geniuses Stanislaw Ulam and John von Neumann. "The ever accelerating progress of technology," warned von Neumann, "gives the appearance of approaching some essential singularity in the history of the race beyond which human affairs, as we know them, could not continue."[10]

The plan is to develop a computer network that will exhibit intelligent behavior equivalent to, or indistinguishable from that of human beings by 2029.[11] And this goal is to have computers that will be "a billion times more powerful than all of the human brains on earth."[12]

Robo Brain

But why stop with fusing the human mind with the Internet? Why not fuse an over-arching artificial mind with robotic creatures? To this end, Google has purchased "almost every machine-learning and robotics company" in existence—including firms that build "terrifying life-like military robots."[13] As one university professor warns:

> I don't see any end point here. At some point humans aren't going to be fast enough. So what you do is that you make ... autonomous [robots]. And where does that end? *Terminator*?[14]

Terminator, director James Cameron's 1984 film, predicted a future world ruled by overpowering, vicious androids bent on destroying anyone or anything that got in their way.

Again, science fiction has become reality. After all, how does an elite oligarchy that has erected an electronic concentration camp put down an occasional rebellious human resistance movement? It builds android cops. In fact, the government is already developing robot technology that can mimic human behavior. ATLAS, an android developed by the Department of Defense, is 6 feet tall, weighs 330 pounds, and moves, walks and runs like a human.[15] While still in the testing stages, it's not too far-fetched to imagine a time in the near future when artificial intelligence robots are responsible for policing citizens. Considering how difficult it is to exercise one's constitutional rights in our present age when confronted by SWAT-team attired police with little regard for the Constitution, imagine trying to assert your rights when confronted with autonomous machines programmed to maintain order at all costs.

Add to this the fact that Regina Dugan, who now works for Google, once headed the Defense Advanced Research Projects Agency (DARPA), the secretive military agency that also specializes in robotics.[16] Dugan has created a number of controversial programs, including Mind's Eye, a computer-vision system that is so powerful it can monitor the pulse rate of specific individuals in a crowd.[17] And DARPA's Cortical Processor Program will mimic your neocortex—that part of the brain that analyzes and makes moral decisions—by developing a human-machine interface.[18] Much like its partner Google, DARPA · wants to make sure its robotic androids can work together, for whatever

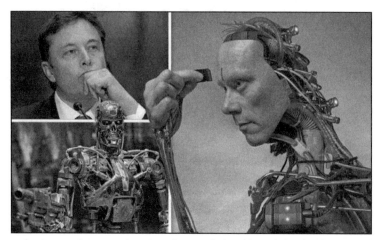

Tesla CEO and SpaceX founder, Elon Musk, has likened the development of artificial intelligence to "summoning the devil." (Source: Eengenious)

reason. That's why it's funding the multi-million dollar "Swarm Challenge," which will ensure that unmanned drones can work in unison.[19] This will include human-like androids. In fact, scientists are creating a robot brain that will rule and/or allow the androids to rule over us. It's called the "Robo Brain." According to *Computerworld*:

> With Robo Brain, individual robots, whether it's a robotic arm working on a factory floor, an autonomous car or a robot assistant helping an elderly person at home, can draw on this store of information and learn from what other robots have already learned.[20]

In other words, robotic androids, whether ones created to harvest vegetables, or to act as "terminator" types, will connect to the various intelligence clouds. Thus, they will be so far superior to any human being so as to view us humans as ant-like threats. Add to this heavily armed robotic drones flying overhead, and you've got hell-on-earth in the making.

Hive Mind

All of this raises rather important questions: How do those in power view us? As human beings with great worth and dignity? If so, why are they spending billions building robots and fusing us with machines and erecting technological webs that will know everything we do and be able to know everything we are thinking? Is this to benefit us or is it to control us?

Despite what the controllers may say, "the trend," writes journalist Kamil Muzyka, "is moving towards eliminating the human factor to the required minimum, thus a single central operation control room could remotely operate and supervise" the electronic concentration camp.[21] The computer intelligence system that Google, DARPA, and its co-conspirators are developing—everything from the car you drive to the phone you use to the laptop you type on to the smart house (with its listening devices and surveillance cameras)—will be controlled by the electronic mind. Even your smart TV will log where, when, how and for how long you use your set. Not only that but these TVs are also coming equipped with voice and facial recognition features—all of which can and will be monitored by corporate and government agents.[22] This "Internet of Things," as it is called, will be a Big Brother watching over us all. As Muzyka recognizes: "This is a large threat of your 'things' starting to 'tell on you' to the proper authorities, due to either illegal data, improper hardware or odd activities."[23]

As part of the "hive mind," you will be studied and watched at all times. In fact, "one of the transhuman tendencies is to intertwine multiple entities, cybernetically interconnecting these like plants, wearable computer devices, and brain computer interfaces. . . . One could be viewed then as a dispersed entity, for one will be connected with the surrounding machines, including vehicles."[24]

Does this not sound somewhat like a Borg-like society as depicted in the *Star Trek* films? As professor John Danaher explains:

> In the world of *Star Trek*, the Borg are a superorganism, much like an ant or termite colony, with an underclass of workers/drones, headed by a "queen." The colony works by "assimilating" new individuals, races and species into a collective mind. Every newly-assimilated drone has their mind and identity fused into the colony's collective consciousness. They consequently are losing any sense of individuality and autonomy: their thoughts are no longer their own; they think and act solely for the benefit of the group. The queen may be the one exception to this.[25]

Of course, concerns have been raised about the loss of individuality and the freedom to disagree or be different in such a society. There is no escape from the fact that in the near future all of our thoughts and actions will be policed. "By constantly monitoring and policing our behavior (and maybe even our thoughts)," writes Danaher, "these technologies could reduce diversity and create an increasingly homogenised set of social actors."[26]

But it doesn't stop there. Again, this will have military combat and police applications as well. Armed human androids (robocops) and drones working in tandem are coming, which raises the possibility of lethal autonomy wherein a network of machines could eventually act independently to neutralize, maim or kill people or destroy their property.

Behavior/Mood Sensors

Advances in neuroscience indicate that future behavior can be predicted based upon activity in certain portions of the brain, potentially creating a nightmare scenario in which government officials select certain segments of the population for more invasive surveillance or quarantine based solely upon their brain chemistry. Case in point: researchers at the Mind Research Center scanned the brains of thousands of prison inmates in order to track their brain chemistry and their behavior after release. In one experiment, researchers determined that inmates with lower levels of activity in the area of the brain associated with error processing allegedly had a higher likelihood of committing a crime within four years of being released from prison.[27] While researchers have cautioned against using the results of their research as a method of predicting future crime, it will undoubtedly become a focus of study for government officials.

Brain to Machine Interface

There's no limit to what can be accomplished—for good or ill—using brain-computer interfaces. Scientists have already created machines that allow people to manipulate robotic arms using just their thoughts.[28] In the near future, we may see scientists observing human thought using "smart dust"—nanomachines the size of dust—which can be placed in the brain to observe neural behavior.[29] Furthermore, hackers have already been able to "steal" information from human brains using extant brain-computer interfaces which read brain waves and are commercially available for $200-300.[30]

Terminator, director James Cameron's 1984 film, predicted a future world ruled by overpowering, vicious androids bent on destroying anyone or anything that got in their way. (Photography by Marcin Wichary)

Researchers at Duke University Medical Center have created a brain-to-brain interface between lab rats, which allows them to transfer information directly between brains. In one particular experiment, researchers trained a rat to perform a task where it would hit a lever when lit. The trained rat then had its brain connected to an untrained rat's brain via electrodes. The untrained rat was then able to learn the trained rat's behavior via electrical stimulation. This even worked over great distances using the Internet, with a lab rat in North Carolina guiding the actions of a lab rat in Brazil.[31]

Metallic Jaws

No matter what we may want to call our electronic devices—our machines—or what personalities we attempt to imprint on them, they are yet machines. This is true even if they resemble humans in language and in form.

Machines, we must remember, when working properly, operate with a fierce regularity. We set a punch press into motion, and it mangles the hand of a worker who gets close to it. The very regularity of the machine is its most fearsome property. We put it to its task and it performs, regularly to be sure, but blindly as well. The punch press processes its material, whether its jaws grasp pieces of metal or a worker's hand.

When we create autonomous machines, we run the risk that before long we will find ourselves in their metallic jaws. It seems to be a perilous path to walk, but a path nevertheless that modern society is traveling.

CHAPTER 31

Welcome to the Posthuman Era

"Don't believe what you see; it's an enthralling—[and] destructive, evil snare. *Under* it is a totally different world, even placed differently along the linear axis [and] your memories are faked to jibe with the fake (inner [and] outer congruency)."[1]—PHILIP K. DICK

"We are now linked to multiple electronic devices which in turn link us to huge amounts of data which in turn link us to those who control the data. Any of us can connect by our cellular devices and by video to people across the planet. And with finger vein scanning devices and other biometric identifiers, every transaction will be recorded and uploaded into corporate computer clouds accessible by government agents— we humans are now data bits."[2]—Journalist JIM EDWARDS

Clearly, transhumanism—the fusing of machines and people—is here to stay and it will continue to grow. "Technological devices," writes journalist Marcelo Gleiser, "will be implanted in our heads and bodies, or used peripherally, like Google Glass, extending our senses and cognitive abilities."[3]

We are rapidly moving into the "posthuman era," one in which humans will become a new type of being. However, as Bill Joy, a cofounder of Sun Microsystems, warns us: humans could become an endangered species. "I think it is no exaggeration to say we are on the cusp of the further perfection of evil, an evil whose possibility spreads well beyond that which weapons of mass destruction bequeathed to the nation-states, onto a surprising and terrible empowerment of extreme individuals."[4]

In fact, as science and technology continue to advance, the ability to control humans will only increase. In 2014, for example, it was revealed

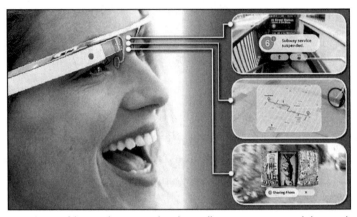

Smart wearables, such as Google Glass, allow users to expand the reach of their technology into the world around them. (Source: Techmaza)

that scientists have discovered how to deactivate that part of our brains that controls whether we are conscious or not. When researchers at George Washington University sent high frequency electrical signals to the claustrum—that thin sheet of neurons running between the left and right sides of the brain—their patients lost consciousness. Indeed, one patient started speaking more slowly until she became silent and still. When she regained consciousness, she had no memory of the event.[5]

Add to this the fact that increasingly humans will be implanted with microchips for such benign purposes as tracking children or as medical devices to assist with our health. Such devices "point to an uber-surveillance society that is Big Brother on the inside looking out," warns Dr. Katina Michael. "Governments or large corporations would have the ability to track people's actions and movements, categorize them into different socio-economic, political, racial, or consumer groups and ultimately even control them."[6]

Big Data, Big Government

Control is the issue. In fact, Facebook and the Department of Defense are working to manipulate our behavior. If it sounds Orwellian, that's because it is.

In a 2012 study, Facebook tracked the emotional states of over 600,000 of its users.[7] The goal of the study was to see if the emotions of

With every smartphone we buy, every GPS device we install, and every Twitter, Facebook, and Google account we open, we're helping Corporate America build a dossier for its government counterparts on who we know, what we think, how we spend our money, and how we spend our time.

users could be manipulated based upon whether they were fed positive or negative information in their news feeds. The conclusion of the study was that "emotional states can be transferred to others via emotional contagion, leading people to experience the same emotions without their awareness."[8]

It indicates the new path forward for large corporations and government entities that want to achieve absolute social control. Instead of relying solely on marauding SWAT teams and full-fledged surveillance apparatuses, they will work to manipulate our emotions to keep us in lock step with the American police state.

Indeed, the Facebook study, which was allegedly funded by the federal government,[9] only scratches the surface of the multitude of methods that the corporate-state has unleashed to keep us in check. It is connected to a Department of Defense (DOD) program called the Minerva Initiative, a broad series of studies being conducted with the help of academics in order to discover what "dynamics, risks and tipping points"[10] can lead to social unrest.[11]

These studies rely primarily on parsing through social media and determining what sort of rhetoric and discussions occur before and during periods of civil unrest. The DOD is also interested in tracking the behavior and beliefs of non-violent protesters in order to determine what separates them from their violent counterparts with the same ideological beliefs.[12]

Total Population Control

It's not just social media that is being tracked by the federal government and its corporate partners. The NSA holds on to a variety of personal information that is wholly irrelevant to their investigations. Documents retained in NSA databases include "stories of love and heartbreak, illicit sexual liaisons, mental-health crises, political and religious conversions, financial anxieties, and disappointed hopes. The daily lives of more than 10,000 account holders who were not targeted are catalogued and recorded nevertheless."[13]

Derived from documents provided by Edward Snowden, the information about the NSA program indicates that the purpose is not any sort of counterterrorism, but simply to disrupt the online activities of perceived enemies. As journalist Glenn Greenwald notes, the people targeted have never been charged with a crime, nor are they linked to any sort of national security threat.[14]

Indeed, one no longer needs to actually declare himself an enemy of the state to be treated like one. Simply having certain political opinions, a certain occupation, or a certain religious belief can get you put on a watch list or lumped in with terrorists.

In short, we're in the midst of a worldwide propaganda and disinformation campaign aimed at innocent political activists, operated in secret by the government and its allies, and aided and abetted by the corporations which foster our daily communications. As Leah Lievrouw, professor of information studies at the University of California at Los Angeles, noted, "There are too many institutional players interested in restricting, controlling, and directing 'ordinary' people's ability to make, access, and share knowledge and creative works online."[15]

Meat Machines

Years ago, an M.I.T. professor described the human brain as a "meat machine."[16] At the time, I thought the label was an aberration. This is no longer true. More and more, we are being viewed by the governmental-scientific complex as simply hardware—beings in meat suits.

The forces of science, technology, and history have ushered in a new era of how we view ourselves. Once we saw ourselves as one step below a supernatural creator. Next in the sequence, we saw ourselves at least as partially rational animals lunging forward in the parade of Darwinian evolution. Now, it seems that those who control the Matrix are purposely evolving us into some form of hybrid machines.

But are we humans really machines? There are some things humans know simply by knowing their own bodies. We experience life's intangibles—love, compassion, hatred—and we know that these, for the present, are not mere machine functions.

Then there is the reverse question: could machines eventually assume human attributes and emotions such as love, fear, or even hate? That was the dilemma posed in director Ridley Scott's 1982 futuristic film *Blade Runner* where artificial humans, called replicants, were created to do hazardous, mundane work in off-world colonies. These replicants possessed far greater strength and intelligence than human beings and, as such, they posed an obvious potential danger to human society. When and if they escaped and returned to Earth—an offense that called for the death penalty—they were systemically retired (but not "killed" since they are inhuman) by special police detectives known as "Blade Runners."

Defining who is human provides most of *Blade Runner's* philosophical focus.

As the story develops, however, it becomes clear that these replicants do have feelings and emotions. This brings us to the question: at what point are humans like machines? And at what point are machines like humans?

Blade Runner Rick Deckard begins to see that maybe, just maybe, Roy Batty, the replicants' leader he is supposed to "retire" is more than a collection of wires and circuits. Defining who is human provides most of *Blade Runner*'s philosophical focus. This is increasingly the dilemma faced by contemporary society—that is, the most vital question confronting us is how to maintain our humanity in the face of overwhelming technologies that may eventually dehumanize us.

Philip K. Dick promulgated a "sheep" metaphor in his novel *Do Androids Dream of Electric Sheep?* (1968), upon which the film *Blade Runner* is based. "Sheep stemmed from my basic interest in the problem of differentiating the authentic human being from the reflexive machine, which I call an android. In my mind android is a metaphor for the people

Blade Runner was based on Philip K. Dick's novel *Do Androids Dream of Electric Sheep?*

who are psychologically human but behaving in a nonhuman way." During research for an earlier book, Dick discovered diaries by Nazi SS men stationed in Poland. One sentence in particular had a profound effect on him: "We are kept awake at night by the cries of starving children." As Dick explained, "There is obviously something wrong with the man who wrote that. I later realized that, with the Nazis, what we were essentially dealing with was a defective group mind, a mind so emotionally defective that the word 'human' could not be applied to them." More importantly for us, Dick observed, "I felt that this was not necessarily a sole German trait. This deficiency had been exported into the world after World War II and could be picked up by people anywhere, at any time."[17]

The dilemma is even more acute than when Dick was penning *Electric Sheep*, for we have moved deeper into the methodological terrain of a new world, one more than ever dominated by the machine. As a consequence, we are being reconstructed in the image of the machine. The question is how much of what it means to be human will be carried over into the machine?

Blade Runner postulates the theorem that what has feelings is human. Thus, *Blade Runner* is as much about Deckard's recovery of empathetic response as it is about the replicants' development of such a response. The irritated Nazis kept awake by the children's cries with their inability to empathize were less than human. "What raises the android Roy Batty to human status in *Blade Runner*," writes author Norman Spinard, "is that, on the brink of his own death, he is able to empathize with Deckard. What makes true beings is that ultimately, on one level or another, whatever reality mazes they may be caught in, they realize that the true base reality is not absolute or perceptual, but moral and empathetic."[18]

The ultimate relevance of *Blade Runner*, therefore, lies in its challenge of what it must mean to be human. It raises the eternal gnawing doubt as to our own humanity or lack of it. These are the same issues raised by the great religions and philosophies of the past, and it speaks to how we respond to the pain of those around us. Do we reach for the one downed by the crushing perplexity of modernity or do we merely pass by, forgetting about that grizzled human lying on the sidewalk who is drowning in the gutter?

The Big Question

Clearly, fusing human conscious with computers and the Internet and eventually creating robotic androids that think creates a dilemma. Mary Shelley recognized that when she had Frankenstein's monster ponder its ill-defined role: "I live, I breathe, I walk, I see—but what am I, man or monster?"[19]

Indeed, as Philip K. Dick realized, we know what it's like to be a monster. They've been wreaking havoc on humanity since the beginning of time. They're called human beings.

However, will a fusion of machines and people by the transhumanists create something even worse? Computer scientist Jaron Lanier, named by *Time* magazine as one of the most influential people in 2010, is concerned that such a transhumanist fusion may create a frightening future. "If that happens," Lanier said, "the ideology of cybernetic totalist intellectuals will be amplified from novelty into a force that could cause suffering for millions of people."[20] Or as Professor Arthur Kroker puts it: "They're creating again and again the exterminism of human memory, the exterminism of human sensibility, the exterminism of individuated human intelligence, the exterminism of human morality itself."[21]

Thus, if all goes according to plan for the transhumanists, we can imagine and expect a "metallic" future. It might be something like this: In a lonely outpost in the distant future where everything—humans, androids, and other robotic entities—are linked together, some foreboding human servant asks, "Is there a God?" Striking the questioner down for his imprudence, his android companion replies, "Now there is."

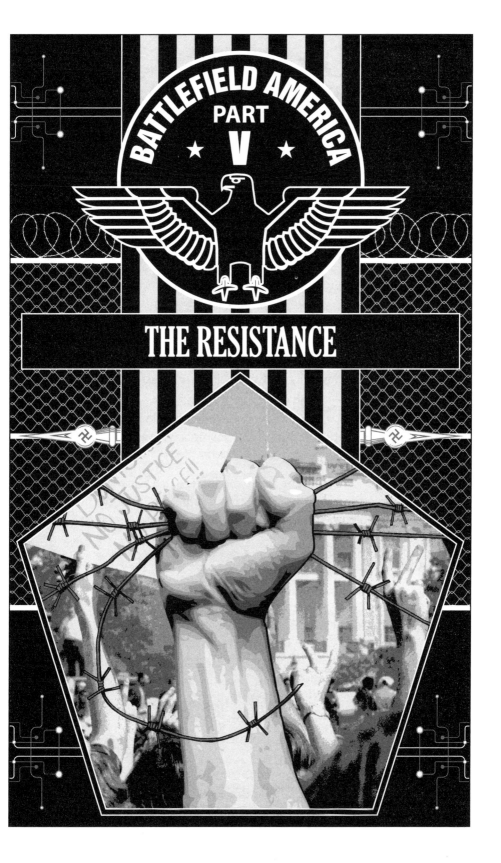

BATTLEFIELD AMERICA
PART V

THE RESISTANCE

"We have been silent witnesses of evil deeds: we have been drenched by many storms; we have learnt the arts of equivocation and pretence; experience has made us suspicious of others and kept us from being truthful and open; intolerable conflicts have worn us down and even made us cynical. Are we still of any use? What we shall need is not geniuses, or cynics, or misanthropes, or clever tacticians, but plain, honest, straightforward men. Will our inward power of resistance be strong enough, and our honesty with ourselves remorseless enough, for us to find our way back to simplicity and straightforwardness?" [1]

—Dietrich Bonhoeffer,
a German-Lutheran pastor and
part of the Resistance movement
against Nazism

"We can be educated for freedom—much better educated for it than we are at present. But freedom...is threatened from many directions, and these threats are of many different kinds—demographic, social, political, psychological. Our disease has a multiplicity of co-operating causes and is not to be cured except by a multiplicity of co-operating remedies. In coping with any complex human situation, we must take account of all the relevant factors, not merely of a single factor. Nothing short of everything is ever really enough. Freedom is menaced, and education for freedom is urgently needed." [2]

—Aldous Huxley,
Brave New World Revisited

Reality Check

FACT: The United States is one of the highest TV viewing nations.[3] According to a Nielsen report, the average American over the age of two "spends more than thirty-four hours a week watching live television . . . plus another three to six hours watching taped programs."[4]

FACT: Only six out of every one hundred Americans know that they actually have a constitutional right to hold the government accountable for wrongdoing, as guaranteed by the right to petition clause of the First Amendment.[5]

FACT: If knowledge is power, it's no wonder Americans are in hot water. According to a study by the National Constitution Center, 41 percent of Americans "are not aware that there are three branches of government, and 62 percent couldn't name them; 33 percent couldn't even name one."[6]

FACT: According to a Gallup poll, Americans place greater faith in the military and the police than in any of the three branches of government.[7]

FACT: When asked to name the greatest problem facing the nation, Americans of all political stripes ranked the government as the number one concern.[8] In fact, almost eight out of ten Americans believe that government corruption is widespread.[9]

CHAPTER 32

Are You a Slave or Rebel?

You say you'll change the Constitution.
Well, you know
We all want to change your head.
You tell me it's the institution.
Well, you know
You'd better free your mind instead.[1]

—JOHN LENNON

"[S]ome of us believe that, without freedom, human beings cannot become fully human and that freedom is therefore supremely valuable. Perhaps the forces that now menace freedom are too strong to be resisted for very long. It is still our duty to do whatever we can to resist them."[2]

—ALDOUS HUXLEY, *Brave New World Revisited*

"Until they become conscious, they will never rebel, and until after they have rebelled, they cannot become conscious."[3]

—GEORGE ORWELL

Freedom, or what's left of it, is threatened from every direction. The threats are of many kinds: political, cultural, educational, media, and psychological. However, as history shows us, freedom is not, on the whole, wrested from a citizenry. It is all too often given over voluntarily and for such a cheap price: safety, security, bread, and circuses.

This is part and parcel of the propaganda churned out by the government machine. That said, what we face today—mind manipulation and systemic violence—is not new. What is different are the techniques used and the large scale control of mass humankind. As we have seen with the erection of the electronic concentration camp, there is virtually no escaping the invisible prison surrounding us. Once upon a time,

Occupy Wall Street protesters in Anonymous masks (Photography by Lee Hassl)

one could run and hide or duck into a cave, but that is no longer feasible as caves are quite scarce, and those running the camp have their eyes watching everything.

Moreover, we are presented with the illusion that we act of our own volition when most of the time we are being watched, prodded, and controlled. "The nature of psychological compulsion is such that those who act under constraint remain under the impression that they are acting on their own initiative," Aldous Huxley stated. "The victim of mind-manipulation does not know that he is a victim. To him, the walls of his prison are invisible."[4]

In fact, with the merger of the Internet and the corporate state, unless you are alert and aware, it will be increasingly difficult to discern the difference between freedom and enslavement. With the methods of mind manipulation available to the corporate state, the very nature of democratic government has been changed. Again, as Aldous Huxley writes:

> [T]he quaint old forms—elections, parliaments, Supreme Courts and all the rest will remain. The underlying substance will be a new kind of nonviolent totalitarianism. All the traditional names, all the hallowed slogans will

remain exactly what they were in the good old days. Democracy and freedom will be the theme of every broadcast and editorial . . . Meanwhile the ruling oligarchy and its highly trained elite of soldiers, policemen, thought-manufacturers and mind-manipulators will quietly run the show as they see fit.[5]

To many, the situation seems hopeless. But is it?

Free Your Mind

If you really want change—one that will restore some semblance of freedom—I suggest taking John Lennon's advice in his song "Revolution": Free your mind and realize that virtually everything surrounding you is not something you entered into by way of free will.

In fact, from the day you're born until the day you die, the choices you exercise are very limited. You don't choose to be born or choose

John Lennon takes part in a protest march.
(Photography by Rowland Scherman)

what sex you are or who your parents are or where you live. When you are a child, you are told what to do, and when you enter school, you sit plastered to a desk and are taught what others demand you should know. Yes, the indoctrinating process begins on day one.

Then there are the rules, the endless rules. If you say the wrong word, write the wrong story or wear the wrong clothes, you can get thrown out of school or even arrested. You live where you are told and eat what others think you should eat. As you grow older, this list expands into employment, marriage, and so on. In other words, your so-called reality is socially constructed. It is predetermined for you, and if you step out of line and disagree with what the current society deems proper, you will be ostracized. If you speak your mind to the governing authorities, you might find yourself behind bars.

The point is that in order to develop a compliant citizenry, people must be forced to live in a mental matrix of words, ideas, ideologies, and teachings that are designed to make us conform. "As the Matrix in the movie was used to facilitate the exploitation of humans," writes author

Henry H. Lindner, "so the current ideological Matrix was created for, and serves to exploit us, turning us into unthinking workers and consumers—slaves of the ruling elite who themselves are trapped in the Matrix." In fact, "few of us are able to escape the Matrix. We do not even know it exists."[6]

Ten Basic Principles

For there to be any hope of real change, you'll have to change how you think about yourself, your fellow human beings, freedom, society, and the government. This means freeing your mind, realizing the truth, and unlearning all the myths you have been indoctrinated with since the day you were able to comprehend language. Unfortunately, the truth, although painful and depressing, can and should be liberating. Thus, the following are a few basic principles that may help any budding freedom fighters in the struggle to liberate themselves and our society.

First, we must come to grips with the reality that the present system does not foster freedom. It denies freedom and must be altered. "Our authoritarian system is based on cruelty and control—it increasingly drives natural love and feelings from our society and produces violence and greed," Lindner recognizes. "Our society is deteriorating morally and intellectually. This system cannot be reformed."[7]

To start with, we must recognize that the government's primary purpose is maintaining power and control. It's an oligarchy composed of corporate giants wedded to government officials who benefit from the relationship. In other words, it is motivated by greed and exists to perpetuate itself. As George Orwell writes:

> We know that no one ever seizes power with the intention of relinquishing it. Power is not a means; it is an end. One does not establish a dictatorship in order to safeguard a revolution; one makes a revolution in order to establish a dictatorship.... The object of power is power.[8]

Second, voting is practically worthless. "In principle, it is a great privilege," Aldous Huxley recognized. "In practice, as recent history has repeatedly shown, the right to vote, by itself, is no guarantee of liberty."[9]

We live in a secretive surveillance state that has virtually no accountability, transparency, or checks and balances of any kind. As

Jordan Michael Smith, writing for the *Boston Globe,* concludes about the American government:

> There's the one we elect, and then there's the one behind it, steering huge swaths of policy almost unchecked. Elected officials end up serving as mere cover for the real decisions made by the bureaucracy.[10]

How many times have the various politicians, when running for office, lied about all they were going to do to bring hope and change to America? Once they get elected, what do they do? They do whatever the corporate powers want. Yes, the old boss is the same as the new boss. The maxim: power follows money.

Moreover, voting is a way to keep the citizenry pacified. However, many Americans intuitively recognize that something is wrong with the way the electoral process works and have withdrawn from the process. That's why the government places so much emphasis on the reassurance ritual of voting. *It provides the illusion of participation.*

Voting provides the illusion of participation.
(Illustration by Caroline Jonik)

Third, question everything. Don't assume anything government does is for the good of the citizenry. Again, that is not the purpose of modern government. It exists to perpetuate a regime. Remember the words of James Madison, considered the father of the U.S. Constitution: "All men having power ought to be distrusted to a certain degree."[11] Power corrupts. And as the maxim goes, absolute power corrupts absolutely.

Fourth, materialism is a death knell to freedom. While it may be true that Americans are better off than citizens of other nations—we have jobs, food, entertainment, shopping malls, etc.—these are the trappings meant to anesthetize and distract us.

Like the dodo, any "bird that has learned how to grub up a good living without being compelled to use its wings will soon renounce the privilege of flight and remain forever grounded," Huxley warned. "Same thing is true of human beings. If bread is supplied regularly and capaciously three times a day, many of them will be perfectly content to live by bread alone—or at least by bread and circuses alone."[12] Free as a bird, some say, but only if you're willing to free your mind and sacrifice all for a dangerous concept—freedom.

In other words, the hope is that the cry of "'give me television and hamburgers, but don't bother me with the responsibilities of liberty,' may give place, under altered circumstances, to the cry of 'give me liberty or give me death.'"[13] This is indeed dangerous freedom.

Fifth, there is little hope for any true resistance if you are mindlessly connected to the electronic concentration camp. Remember, what you're being electronically fed by those in power is meant to pacify, distract, and control you. You can avoid mind manipulations to a large degree by greatly limiting your reliance on electronic devices—cell phones, laptops, televisions, and so on.

Sixth, an armed revolt will not work. Although we may have returned to a 1776 situation where we need to take drastic actions to restore freedom, this is not colonial America with its muskets and people's armies. Local police departments have enough militarized firepower to do away with even a large-scale armed revolt. Even attempting to repel a SWAT team raid on your home is futile. You'll get blown away.

Seventh, be wise and realize that there is power in numbers. Networks, coalitions, and movements can accomplish much—especially if their objectives are focused and practical—and they are very much feared by government authorities. That's why the government is armed to the teeth and prepared to put down even small nonviolent protests.

Eighth, act locally but think nationally. The greatest impact can be had at local governing bodies such as city councils. Join together with friends and neighbors and start a Civil Liberties Oversight Committee. Regularly attend council meetings and demand that government corruption be brought under control and that police activities be brought under the scrutiny of local governing bodies and, thus, the citizenry.

In Albuquerque, New Mexico, for example, police were involved in 39 shootings dating back to 2010. After a 2014 police shooting of an unarmed homeless man camped out in a public park, residents engaged in nonviolent acts of civil disobedience to disrupt the normal functioning of the city government and demand that the police department be brought under control. Community activists actually went so far as to storm a city council meeting and announce that they would be performing a citizens' arrest of the police chief, charging him with "harboring fugitives from justice at the Albuquerque police department" and "crimes against humanity."[14]

Hundreds gather to protest a police shooting of a 38-year-old homeless man in Albuquerque, N.M. (Photography by Luke Montavon)

In Davis County, California, in August 2014, after a public uproar over the growing militarization of local police, council members ordered the police to find a way of getting rid of the department's newly acquired MRAP tank. One man at the council meeting was quoted as saying: "I would like to say I do not suggest you take this vehicle and send it out of Davis, I *demand* it."[15]

Ninth, local towns, cities and states can nullify or say "no" to federal laws that violate the rights and freedoms of the citizenry. In fact, several states have passed laws stating that they will not comply with the NDAA which allows for the military to indefinitely detain (imprison) American citizens.[16] Again, when and if you see such federal laws passed, gather your coalition of citizens and demand that your local town council nullify such laws. If enough towns and cities across the country would speak truth to power in this way, we might see some positive movement from the federal governmental machine.

Tenth, understand what freedom is all about. "Who were the first persons to get the unusual idea that being free was not only a value to be cherished but the most important thing that someone can possess?" asks Professor Orlando Patterson. "The answer in a word: slaves."[17]

Freedom arose from the hearts and minds of those who realized that they were slaves. It became a primary passion of those who were victims of slavery.

Some Americans are beginning to realize that they are slaves and that if they don't act soon, they will find themselves imprisoned in the electronic concentration camp. Mind you, there may not be any chains hanging from the dungeon walls, but it is a prison nonetheless, and we are, without a doubt, inmates serving life sentences.

What Does It Mean To Be a Slave?

"If a man can only obey and not disobey, he is a slave," declared Erich Fromm, but what does it mean to be a slave?[18]

> Obedience to a person, institution or power (heteronomous obedience) is submission; it implies the abdication of my autonomy and the acceptance of a foreign will or judgment in place of my own. Obedience to my own reason or conviction (autonomous obedience) is not an act of submission but one of affirmation.[19]

The choice is clear: are you going to be a slave and march in lockstep with the government regime or are you going to speak out, disagree or even challenge the governmental policies that are destroying freedom? Unfortunately, as Fromm recognized, "an increasing number of people are afraid of the responsibility of freedom, and prefer the slavery of the well-fed robot; they have no faith in democracy and are happy to leave it to the political experts to make the decisions."[20] And, as we have seen, the "political experts" are all too happy to have obedient slaves as they increase their power, control, and profits.

CHAPTER 33

Militant Nonviolent Resistance

Incident at 133rd Street and Seventh Avenue during the Harlem Riots of 1964 (Photography by staff photographer of the *New York World Telegraph & Sun*)

"We know from painful experience that freedom is never voluntarily given by the oppressor; it must be demanded by the oppressed."[1]

—MARTIN LUTHER KING, JR., Letter From Birmingham City Jail

"All martyrs of religious faiths, of freedom and of science have had to disobey those who wanted to muzzle them in order to obey their own consciences, the laws of humanity and of reason. . . . At this point in history, the capacity to doubt, to criticize and to disobey may be all that stands between a future for mankind and the end of the civilization."[2]

—ERICH FROMM, author and psychologist

"To think of disobedient minorities as rebels and traitors is against the letter and spirit of the Constitution whose framers were especially sensitive to the dangers of unbridled majority rule."[3]

—HANNAH ARENDT

A free person or a slave? This was the dilemma faced by Martin Luther King, Jr. and those who fought segregation in America in the 1950s and 60s. They knew that if they didn't act to end injustice in their day, it would continue to spread.

The fateful day was May 2, 1963. The place was Birmingham, Alabama—one of the most racially segregated cities in the country. And the time was ripe for protests. This is how *Time* magazine summed up the Birmingham protests:

> It all began when Rev. Martin Luther King, Jr. decided to throw schoolchildren into the Negro battle line. Police Commissioner Eugene ("Bull") Connor, arch-segregationist, viciously retaliated with club-swinging cops, police dogs and blasts of water from fire hoses. . . . Using school kids—most of them teenagers, but some no more than six years old—the Negro minister sent wave after wave of sign carriers . . . to march on downtown Birmingham. . . . The youngsters clapped and sang excitedly, when Connor's men arrested them, they scampered almost merrily into patrol wagons. About 800 youthful Negroes wound up in Birmingham jails that day. . . . A troop of new marchers left King's church command post next day intoning: "We want freedom. . . ." Black booted firemen turned on their hoses. The kids fell back from the crushing streams. The water pressure increased. Children fell, and lay there bleeding.[4]

King received much criticism for his tactics in Birmingham. Politicians, the media, and even the clergy coalesced into a chorus of criticism for King the lawbreaker, rebel rouser, and troublemaker. However, King's tactics in Birmingham led to nationwide coverage and brought the issue—the struggle for freedom—to the forefront.

The Letter From Jail

Although King rarely bothered to defend himself against his opponents, he put pen to paper when eight prominent "liberal" Alabama clergymen, all white, published an open letter castigating him for inciting civil disturbances through nonviolent resistance. The ministers called on King to let the local and federal courts deal with the question of integration.

King understood, however, that if justice and freedom were to prevail, African-Americans could no longer afford to be long-suffering. At the time, King was in jail serving a sentence for participating in demonstrations. His response, titled "Letter From Birmingham Jail," is a scathing indictment of all those who sit by the sidelines waiting for the "right" time and the "right" place to challenge injustice.

"We are caught in an inescapable network of mutuality, tied in a single garment of destiny," King wrote. "Whatever affects one directly affects all indirectly. Never again can we afford to live with the narrow, provincial 'outside agitator' idea. Anyone who lives in the United States can never be considered an outsider anywhere in this country."[5]

The clergymen, concerned that King advocated civil disobedience, took issue with King for advocating that African-Americans break some laws and violate others: "The answer is found in the fact that there are two types of laws: there are *just* and there are *unjust* laws," King explained. "I would agree with Saint Augustine that 'An unjust law is no law at all.'"[6] And: "Any law that uplifts human personality is just. Any law that degrades human personality is unjust."[7]

However, if you decide to commit civil disobedience and break the law, you must, according to King, accept the penalty. "I submit that an individual who breaks a law that conscience tells him is unjust, and willingly accepts the penalty by staying in jail to arouse the conscience of the community over its injustice, is in reality expressing the very highest respect for the law."[8]

Photograph shows marchers carrying banner "We march with Selma!" on street in Harlem, New York City (March 15, 1965). (Photography by Stanley Wolfson, *New York World Telegram & Sun*)

Governments, we must remember, have from time immemorial erected regimes with oppressive laws that were upheld by the police and courts as legal. "We can never forget that everything Hitler did in Germany was 'legal,'" King warned. "It was 'illegal' to aid and comfort a Jew in Hitler's Germany. But I'm sure that if I had lived in Germany during that time, I would have aided and comforted my Jewish brothers even though it was illegal."[9]

For embracing a doctrine of civil disobedience against unjust laws, King was labeled an "extremist." At first, he was "disappointed" at being categorized as such. "But as I continued to think about the matter, I gradually gained a bit of satisfaction from being considered an extremist." Indeed, reasoned King:

> Was not Jesus an extremist in love—"Love your enemies, bless them that curse you, pray for them that despitefully use you.". . . Was not Abraham Lincoln an extremist—"This nation cannot survive half slave and half free." Was not Thomas Jefferson an extremist—"We hold these truths to be self-evident, that all men are created equal."[10]

An extremist, as King came to realize, is anyone who takes a stand against any law that "degrades" human beings and denies their equality before the law and/or violates their rights: "So the question is not whether we will be extremist but what kind of extremist will we be. Will we be extremists for hate or will we be extremists for love?"[11]

Extremists For Love

How can we become extremists for "love" in such a society? The answer: We must change how we view people and how we view the world around us.

More and more, "we the people" are seen as data bits—things—by the government. In this day and age, "the hierarchically organized bureaucracies in government administer things *and* men as one," Erich Fromm writes. "The individual becomes a number, transforms himself into a thing. But just because there is no overt authority, because he is not 'forced' to obey, the individual is under the illusion that he acts voluntarily, that he follows only 'rational' authority. Who can disobey the 'reasonable'? Who can disobey the computer bureaucracy?"[12] Indeed:

> In spite of all the slogans to the contrary, we are quickly approaching a society governed by bureaucrats who administer a mass-man, well fed, well taken care of, dehumanized and depressed. We produce machines that are like men and men who are like machines.[13]

In other words, if we are going to see any positive change for freedom, then we must change our view of what it means to be human and regain a sense of what it means to love one another. This was a recurring theme for Martin Luther King, Jr. On April 4, 1967, one year to the day before he was assassinated, King summed up the needed perspective:

> [W]e as a nation must undergo a radical revolution of values. We must rapidly begin the shift from a "thing-oriented" society to a "person-oriented" society. When machines and computers, profit motives and property rights are considered more important than people, the giant triplets of racism, materialism, and militarism are all incapable of being conquered.[14]

Indeed, American institutions no longer teach the golden rule—that is, we should do to others what we want done to us. Or, in the reverse, we shouldn't do to others what we don't want done to us. In fact, if this was a basic maxim of police units, we would not see the senseless violence that surrounds and is engulfing American culture.

Viktor Frankl labored in four different Nazi concentration camps and managed to survive with some semblance of hope and valuable lessons learned. In his book *Man's Search For Meaning*, Frankl details the horror and dehumanization of the Nazi prison system. As he recognized:

> [B]eing human always points, and is directed, to something, or someone, other than oneself—be it a meaning to fulfill or another human being to encounter. The more one forgets himself—by giving himself to a cause to serve or another person to love—the more human he is and the more he actualizes himself.[15]

Can you commit yourself to such noble causes? The choice is yours, of course, but it's a pivotal choice. As Frankl writes:

> We who lived in concentration camps can remember the men who walked through the huts comforting others, giving away their last piece of bread. They may have been few in number, but they offer sufficient proof that every-thing can be taken away from a man but one thing: the last of the human freedoms—to choose one's attitude in any given set of circumstances, to choose one's own way.[16]

What will you choose? The path of least resistance? One steeped in materialism while being lost in your electronic devices? Or will you choose to be an extremist for love and justice and, if need be, confront those destroying the country?

Militant Nonviolent Resistance

It's time for those who believe their freedoms are being gutted by an unconstitutional government to be extremists for justice.

Once a government assumes power—unconstitutional or not—it does not relinquish it. The militarized police are not going to stand down. The NSA will continue to collect electronic files on everything we do. More and more Americans are going to face jail time for offenses that prior generations did not concern themselves with.

The government—at all levels—could crack down on virtually anyone at any time. Again, Martin Luther King saw it coming. "Police,

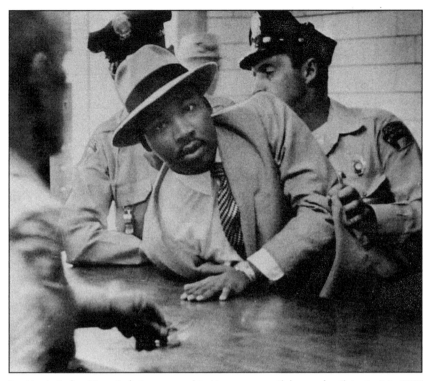

Dr. Martin Luther King, Jr. being arrested in Montgomery, Alabama, for "loitering" in 1958
(Photography by Charles Moore)

national guard and other armed bodies are feverishly preparing for repression," King wrote shortly before he was assassinated. "They can be curbed not by unorganized resort to force . . . but only by a massive wave of militant nonviolence. . . . It also may be the instrument of our national salvation."[17]

What King understood so well like few before him or since is that the government is a bloated, lazy beast that is extremely reluctant to move in any positive way that benefits the people. Thus, the way you impact government the most is to force it to expend energy in dealing with issues.

"A nationwide nonviolent movement is very important," King wrote. "We know from past experience that Congress and the President won't do anything until you develop a movement around which people of goodwill can find a way to put pressure on them."[18]

> This really means making the movement powerful enough, dramatic
> enough, morally appealing enough, so that people of goodwill, the churches,
> laborers, liberals, intellectuals, students, poor people themselves begin to
> put pressure on congressmen to the point that they can no longer elude our
> demands.[19]

"It must be militant, massive nonviolence,"[20] King emphasized. In
other words, besides marches and protests, there would be civil disobedience. Civil disobedience forces the government to expend energy in
many directions—especially if it is nonviolent, organized and is conducted on a massive scale.

This is, as King knew, the only way to move the beast. And it is the
way to effect change without resorting to violence.

What King recognized at the time—and what we face today—"is
a kind of spontaneous explosion of anger by various citizen groups."[21]
Senseless violence, however, can be headed off by planned and directed
"militant, massive nonviolence" while effectuating change.

Although King was murdered on April 4, 1968, he had planned to
conduct an organized protest in Washington, DC, on a massive scale
that spring and summer. It was meticulously planned:

> My staff and I have worked three months on the planning. . . . It will be more
> than a one-day protest—it can persist for two or three months. . . . We plan
> to build a shanty town in Washington. . . . For the past six weeks, we've had
> workshops on nonviolence. . . . [After] two or three weeks, when we will
> begin to call larger numbers in, they will be the marshals, the ones who will
> control and discipline all of the demonstrations.[22]

We have indeed come to a crossroads. Things have greatly wors-
ened since King's era. Either we gather together now and attempt to
restore freedom or all will be lost. As King cautioned, "everywhere,
'time is winding up,' in the words of one of our spirituals, corruption in
the land, people take your stand; time is winding up."[23]

CHAPTER 34

Prisons Without Walls

"It is perfectly possible for a man to be out of prison and yet not free—to be under no physical constraint and yet be a psychological captive, compelled to think, feel and act as the representatives of the national state, or of some private interest within the nation wants him to think, feel and act. . . . To him the walls of his prison are invisible and he believes himself to be free."[1]
—ALDOUS HUXLEY, *A Brave New World Revisited*

"Sometimes people hold a core belief that is very strong. When they are presented with evidence that works against that belief, the new evidence cannot be accepted. It would create a feeling that is extremely uncomfortable, called cognitive dissonance. And because it is so important to protect the core belief, they will rationalize, ignore and even deny anything that doesn't fit in with the core belief."[2]
—Author FRANTZ FANON

"Living is easy with eyes closed, misunderstanding all you see."[3]
—JOHN LENNON

"**F**ree worlders" is prison slang for those who are not incarcerated behind prison walls. Supposedly, those fortunate souls live in the "free world." However, appearances can be deceiving. "As I got closer to retiring from the Federal Bureau of Prisons," writes former prison employee Marlon Brock, "it began to dawn on me that the security practices we used in the prison system were being implemented outside those walls."[4] In fact, if Brock is right, then we "free worlders" do live in a prison—albeit, one without visible walls.

Free Worlders?

In federal prisons, cameras are everywhere in order to maintain "security" and keep track of the prisoners.[5] Likewise, the "free world" is populated with video surveillance and tracking devices. From surveillance cameras in stores and street corners to license plate readers (with the ability to log some 1,800 license plates per hour[6]) on police cars, our movements are being tracked virtually everywhere. With the increasing use of iris scanners and facial recognition software—which drones are equipped with—there would seem to be nowhere to hide.

Detection and confiscation of weapons (or whatever the warden deems "dangerous") in prison is routine. The inmates must be disarmed. Pat downs, checkpoints, and random searches are second nature in ferreting out contraband.

Sound familiar? Metal detectors are now in virtually all government buildings. There are the TSA scanning devices and metal detectors we all have to go through in airports. Police road blocks and checkpoints are used to perform warrantless searches for contraband. Those searched at road blocks can be searched for contraband regardless of their objections—just like in prison. And there are federal road blocks on American

Prison guard tower
(Photography by Rennett Stowe)

roads in the southwestern United States. Many of them are permanent and located up to one hundred miles from the border.[7]

Stop and frisk searches are taking place daily across the country. Some of them even involve anal and/or vaginal searches.[8] In fact, the U.S. Supreme Court has approved strip searches even if you are arrested for a misdemeanor—such as a traffic stop.[9] Just like a prison inmate.

Prison officials open, search and read every piece of mail sent to inmates. This is true of those who reside outside prison walls, as well. In fact, "the United States Postal Service uses a 'Mail Isolation Control and Tracking Program' to create a permanent record of who is corresponding with each other via snail mail."[10] Believe it or not, each piece of physical mail received by the Postal Service is photographed and stored in a database. Approximately 160 billion pieces of mail are recorded each year and the police and other government agents have access to this information.[11]

Prison officials also monitor outgoing phone calls made by inmates.[12] This is similar to what the NSA, telecommunications corporations, and various government agencies do continually to American citizens. The NSA also downloads our text messages, emails, Facebook posts, and so on while watching everything we do.

Then there are the crowd control tactics: helmets, face shields, batons, knee guards, tear gas, wedge formations, half steps, full steps, pinning tactics, armored vehicles, and assault weapons. Most of these phrases are associated with prison crowd control because they were perfected by prisons.[13]

Finally, when a prison has its daily operations disturbed, often times it results in a lockdown.[14] What we saw with the "free world" lockdowns following the 2013 Boston Marathon bombing and the melee in Ferguson, Missouri, in August 2014, mirrors a federal prison lockdown.

These are just some of the similarities between the worlds inhabited by locked-up inmates and those of us who roam about in the so-called "free world." Is there any real difference?

They Live, We Sleep

To those of us who see the prison that's being erected around us, it's a bit easier to realize what's coming up ahead, and it's not pretty. However, and this must be emphasized, what most Americans perceive as life in the

United States of America is a far cry from reality. Real agendas and real power are always hidden.

This is the essential plot of John Carpenter's 1988 film *They Live*, where a group of down-and-out homeless men discover that people have been, in effect, so hypnotized by media distractions that they do not see their prison environment and the real nature of those who control them—that is, an oligarchic elite. Caught up in subliminal messages such as "obey" and "conform," among others, beamed out of television and various electronic devices, billboards, and the like, people are unaware of the elite controlling their lives. As such, they exist, as media analyst Marshall McLuhan once wrote, in "prisons without walls."[15] And of course, any resistance is met with police aggression.

A key moment in the film occurs when John Nada, a homeless drifter, notices something strange about people hanging about a church near the homeless settlement where he lives. Nada decides to investigate. Entering the church, he sees graffiti on a door: *They live, We sleep.* Nada overhears two men, obviously resisters, talking about "robbing banks" and "manufacturing Hoffman lenses until we're blue in the face." Moments later, one of the resisters catches Nada fumbling in the church and tells him "it's the revolution." When Nada nervously backs off, the resister assures him, "You'll be back."[16]

Rummaging through a box, Nada discovers a handful of cheap-looking sunglasses, referred to earlier as Hoffman lenses. Grabbing a pair and exiting the church, he starts walking down a busy urban street.

Sliding the sunglasses on his face, Nada is shocked to see a society bombarded and controlled on every side by subliminal messages beamed at them from every direction. Billboards are transformed into authoritative messages: a bikini-clad woman in one ad is replaced with the words "MARRY AND REPRODUCE." Magazine racks scream "CONSUME" and "OBEY." A wad of dollar bills in a vendor's hand proclaims, "THIS IS YOUR GOD."[17] What's even more disturbing than the hidden messages, however, are the ghoulish-looking creatures—the elite—who appear human until viewed through the lens of truth.

This is the subtle message of *They Live*, an apt analogy of our own distorted vision of life in the American police state. These things are in plain sight, but from the time we are born until the time we die, we are indoctrinated into believing that those who rule us do it for our good. The

They Live serves as an apt analogy of our own distorted
vision of life in the American police state.

truth, far different, is that those who rule us don't really see us as human
beings with dignity and worth. They see us as if "we're livestock."[18]

It's only once Nada's eyes have been opened that he is able to see
the truth: "Maybe they've always been with us," he says. "Maybe they
love it—seeing us hate each other, watching us kill each other, feeding
on our own cold f**in' hearts."[19] Nada, disillusioned and fed up with the
lies and distortions, is finally ready to fight back. "I got news for them.
Gonna be hell to pay. Cause I ain't daddy's little boy no more."[20]

What about you?

The Warning Signs

The warning signs have been cautioning us for decades. Oblivious to
what lies ahead, most have ignored the obvious. We've been manipulated
into believing that if we continue to consume, obey, and have faith, things

will work out. But that's never been true of emerging regimes. And by the time we feel the hammer coming down upon us, it will be too late. As Rod Serling warned:

> All the Dachaus must remain standing. The Dachaus, the Belsens, the Buchenwalds, the Auschwitzes—all of them. They must remain standing because they are a monument to a moment in time when some men decided to turn the earth into a graveyard, into it they shoveled all of their reason, their logic, their knowledge, but worst of all their conscience. And the moment we forget this, the moment we cease to be haunted by its remembrance, then we become the gravediggers.[21]

The message: stay alert. Take the warning signs seriously. And take action because the paths to destruction are well disguised by those in control. This is the lesson of history.

The Baths

The signs at the entrances merely said "BATHS." They were not sinister looking places at all, especially with the well-kept lawns and flower borders.

The music was sweet and light—even beautiful. One survivor recalled that an orchestra of "young and pretty girls all dressed in white blouses and navy-blue skirts" played the music.

The place? The gas chambers at the Nazi concentration camp at Auschwitz. William Shirer in *The Rise and Fall of the Third Reich* describes what happened to the unsuspecting inmates who thought they were simply being taken to the baths for delousing (which was customary at all concentration camps). Accompanied by music, "the men, women and children were led into the 'bath houses,' where they were told to undress preparatory to taking a 'shower.'"[22]

> Sometimes they were given towels. Once they were inside the "shower-room"—and perhaps this was the first moment that they may have suspected something was amiss, for as many as two thousand of them were packed into the chamber like sardines, making it difficult to take a bath—the massive door was slid shut, locked and hermetically sealed. Up above where the

Jewish women and children who have been selected for death, walk in a line towards the gas chambers. (Photography: United States Holocaust Memorial Museum, courtesy of Yad Vashem)

well-groomed lawn and flower beds almost concealed the mushroom-shaped lids of vents that ran up from the hall of death, orderlies stood ready to drop into them the amethyst-blue crystals of hydrogen cyanide. . . .

Surviving prisoners watching from blocks nearby remembered how for a time the signal for the orderlies to pour the crystals down the vents was given by a Sergeant Moll. *"Na, gib ihnen schon zu fressen"* ("Alright, give 'em something to chew on"), he would laugh and the crystals would be poured through the openings, which were then sealed.

Through heavy-glass portholes the executioners could watch what happened. The naked prisoners below would be looking up at the showers from which no water spouted or perhaps at the floor wondering why there were no drains. It took some moments for the gas to have much effect. But soon the inmates became aware that it was issuing from the perforations in the vents. It was then that they usually panicked, crowding away from the pipes and finally stampeding toward the huge metal door where . . . "they piled up in one blue clammy blood-spattered pyramid, clawing and mauling each other even in death."[23]

Freedom Is a Choice

Often I have been asked: how could the German people not have seen the signs of the coming tyranny? What were they thinking? The same could well be said of the American people today.

Having allowed the government to expand and exceed our reach, we find ourselves on the losing end of a tug-of-war over control of our country and our lives. And for as long as we let them, government officials will continue to trample on our rights, always justifying their actions as being for the good of the people.

Yet the government can only go as far as "we the people" allow. Therein lies the problem. We have suspended our moral consciences in favor of the police state. As war correspondent Chris Hedges rightly told me years ago, "Not having to make moral choice frees you from a

A view of one of the concentration camp compounds for women inmates, April 1945

great deal of anxiety. It frees you from responsibility. And it assures that you will always be wrapped in the embrace of the powerful as long as, of course, you will do or dance to the tune the powers play . . . when you do what is right, you often have to understand that you are not going to be lauded and praised for it. Making a moral decision always entails risks, certainly to one's career and to one's standing in the community."24

The choice before us is clear, and it *is* a moral choice. It is the choice between tyranny and freedom, dictatorship and autonomy, peaceful slavery and dangerous freedom, and manufactured pipedreams of what America used to be versus the gritty reality of what she is today.

Most of all, perhaps, the choice before us is that of being a child or a parent, of obeying blindly, never questioning, and marching in lockstep with the police state or growing up, challenging injustice, standing up to tyranny, and owning up to our responsibilities as citizens, no matter how painful, risky, or uncomfortable.

The path to the baths, so to speak, is being constructed.

The question: Are you headed down the path? Will you resist?

The future is up to you.

Acknowledgments

Staying on the front lines of freedom is not an easy task. I certainly couldn't do it by myself. Indeed, many have helped me along the way. Without them, my work and my writings would not be as effective. To these, I owe a deep debt of gratitude.

First and foremost, I wish to thank my wife, Nisha, for her support, research, writing, editing, and ideas. Without Nisha, this book would not have been possible.

Christopher Combs' inventive cover art and illustrations definitely help in driving my points home.

Michael Khavari and John Frahm provided valuable research that is sprinkled throughout this book. I also appreciate the help provided by Peggy Kelly and Sam Carrigan with proofreading early drafts of the manuscript. Also Nancy Sugihara's editorial assistance was greatly appreciated.

I am particularly grateful to Tom and Judy Neuberger and Mike and Patrice Masters for their friendship and support through the years.

Finally, thank you to all those who risk criticism, ridicule, and even jail time in standing up for the principles of freedom.

Notes

Opening

1   John Rodden, ed., *Understanding Animal Farm* (Greenwood Publishing Group, 1999), p. 164.

2   Neil Postman, *Amusing Ourselves to Death: Public Discourse in the Age of Show Business* (Penguin, 2006), p. 156.

Part I: A Declaration of War

1   George Orwell, *1984* (Plume, 1983), p. 234.

2   Paul Craig Roberts, "The Empire Turns Its Guns on the Citizenry," Anti-War.com (Jan. 24, 2007), http://antiwar.com/roberts/?articleid=10382.

3   John Jessup, "'Overcriminalization' Making Us a Nation of Felons?" *CBN News* (July 89, 2012), http://www.cbn.com/cbnnews/us/2012/March/Overcriminalization-Making-Us-a-Nation-of-Felons/.

4   L. Gordon Crovitz, "You Commit Three Felonies a Day," *Wall Street Journal* (Sept. 27, 2009), http://online.wsj.com/news/articles/SB10001424052748704471504574438900830760842.

5   Gary Fields and John R. Emshwiller, "Many Failed Efforts to Count Nation's Federal Criminal Laws," *Wall Street Journal*, (July 23, 2011), http://online.wsj.com/news/articles/SB10001424052702304319804576389601079728920.

6   Richard A. Oppel Jr., "Steady Decline in Major Crime Baffles Experts," *The New York Times* (May 23, 2011), http://www.nytimes.com/2011/05/24/us/24crime.html?_r=0.

7   "Rough Justice in America," *The Economist* (July 22, 2010), http://www.economist.com/node/16636027.

8   Sasha Abramsky, "America's Shameful Poverty Stats," *The Nation* (Sept. 18, 2013), http://www.thenation.com/article/176242/americas-shameful-poverty-stats#.

9   "Childhood Hunger in America," No Kid Hungry, http://www.nokidhungry.org/pdfs/Facts-Childhood-Hunger-in-America-2013-grid.pdf.

10   "Veterans Stats, on Veterans Day," *The New York Times* (Nov. 11, 2013), http://takingnote.blogs.nytimes.com/2013/11/11/veterans-stats-on-veterans-day/?_php=true&_type=blogs&_r=0.

11   Malia Zimmerman, "Obama trips to Hawaii, Africa reportedly cost taxpayers nearly $16 million," *FOX News* (March 27, 2014), http://www.foxnews.com/politics/2014/03/27/obama-trips-to-hawaii-africa-reportedly-cost-taxpayers-nearly-16-million/.

12   Tom Coburn, *Wastebook 2013*, p. 54, http://www.coburn.senate.gov/public/index.cfm?a=Files.Serve&File_id=d204730e-4a24-4711-b1db-99bb6c29d4b6.

13   Tom Coburn, *Wastebook 2013*, p. 91, http://www.coburn.senate.gov/public/index.cfm?a=Files.Serve&File_id=d204730e-4a24-4711-b1db-99bb6c29d4b6.

CHAPTER 1

1   *As quoted in* Bertram Gross, *Friendly Fascism: The New Face of Power in America* (South End Press, 1986), p. 331.

2   "Former CIA director: In order to spy on domestic dissidents, just call them Terrorists," *PrivacySOS*, (January 31, 2014), http://privacysos.org/node/1318.

3   "Former CIA director: In order to spy on domestic dissidents, just call them Terrorists," *PrivacySOS*, (January 31, 2014), http://privacysos.org/node/1318.

4   Michael Snyder, "72 Types Of Americans That Are Considered "Potential Terrorists" In Official Government Documents," *Investment Watch*, (August 26, 2013), http://investmentwatchblog.com/72-types-of-americans-that-are-considered-potential-terrorists-in-official-government-documents/.

5   Jesse Hathaway, "Ohio National Guard Training Envisions Right-Wing Terrorism," *MediaTrackers*, (February 10, 2014), http://mediatrackers.org/ohio/2014/02/10/ohio-national-guard-training-envisions-right-wing-terrorism.

6   As quoted in Dahr Jamail, "Art Is a Necessary Element of Every Revolution," *Truthout* (July 30, 2014), http://www.truth-out.org/news/item/25209-erin-currier-art-is-a-necessary-element-of-every-revolution.

7   Sam Sloan, "Sci-Fi Writer's Success At Predicting the Future," *Slice of SciFi* (May 9, 2014), http://www.sliceofscifi.com/2014/05/09/sci-fi-writers-success-at-predicting-the-future/.

8   Sam Sloan, "Sci-Fi Writer's Success At Predicting the Future," *Slice of SciFi* (May 9, 2014), http://www.sliceofscifi.com/2014/05/09/sci-fi-writers-success-at-predicting-the-future/.

9   Sam Sloan, "Sci-Fi Writer's Success At Predicting the Future," *Slice of SciFi* (May 9, 2014), http://www.sliceofscifi.com/2014/05/09/sci-fi-writers-success-at-predicting-the-future/.

10 John Schwartz, "Novelists Predict Future With Eerie Accuracy," *The New York Times* (Sept. 3, 2011), http://www.nytimes.com/2011/09/04/sunday-review/novelists-predict-future-with-eerie-accuracy.html.

CHAPTER 2

1   Marc Scott Zicree, *The Twilight Zone Companion* (Bantam Books, 1982), p. 207.

2   Thom Patterson, "One JFK conspiracy theory that could be true," *CNN* (Nov. 18, 2013), http://www.cnn.com/2013/11/16/us/jfk-assassination-conspiracy-theories-debunked/.

3   Carl Gibson, "How the Government Killed Martin Luther King, Jr.," *Reader Supported News* (April 3, 2013), http://readersupportednews.org/opinion2/275-42/16784-how-the-government-killed-martin-luther-king-jr.

4   Tom Risen, "John Lennon: Rebel Beatle," *US News & World Report* (Jan. 22, 2014), http://www.usnews.com/news/special-reports/articles/2014/01/22/john-lennon-rebel-beatle.

5   Eric Posner, "Let's Make a Deal With Snowden," *Slate* (Jan. 27, 2014), http://www.slate.com/articles/news_and_politics/view_from_chicago/2014/01/making_a_deal_with_edward_snowden_the_grudging_case_for_a_plea_bargain.html.

6   Anthony M. Townsend, "Your city is spying on you: From iPhones to cameras, you are being watched right now," *Salon*, (October 13, 2013), http://www.salon.com/2013/10/13/your_city_is_spying_on_you_from_iphones_to_cameras_you_are_being_watched_right_now/.

CHAPTER 3

1   Henry Giroux, "Totalitarian Paranoia in the Post-Orwellian Surveillance State," *Truthout*, (February 10, 2014), http://truth-out.org/opinion/item/21656-totalitarian-paranoia-in-the-post-orwellian-surveillance-state.

2   Dannika Lewis, "Wisconsin natives in the midst of Boston's manhunt," WISC TV (April 19, 2013), http://www.channel3000.com/news/Wisconsin-natives-in-the-midst-of-Boston-s-manhunt/-/1648/19826118/-/kvgwot/-/index.html.

3   Matthew DeLuca, "Boston transit shut down, nearly 1 million sheltering in place amid terror hunt," *NBC News* (April 19, 2013), http://usnews.nbcnews.com/_news/2013/04/19/17822687-boston-transit-shut-down-nearly-1-million-sheltering-in-place-amid-terror-hunt?lite.

4   Helen Pow, "Incredible 'thermal imaging' technology that helped police helicopters detect HEAT of wounded suspect as he cowered in boat," *Daily Mail* (April 20, 2013), http://www.dailymail.co.uk/news/article-2312134/Boston-bombings-Incredible-thermal-imaging-technology-helped-police-helicopters-detect-HEAT-wounded-suspect-cowered-boat.html#ixzz2R7iNwXhe.

5   Dannika Lewis, "Wisconsin natives in the midst of Boston's manhunt," WISC TV (April 19, 2013), http://www.channel3000.com/news/Wisconsin-natives-in-the-midst-of-Boston-s-manhunt/-/1648/19826118/-/kvgwot/-/index.html.

6   Pete Williams, Richard Esposito, Michael Isikoff and Tracy Connor, "Boston Marathon Suspect Is Captured Alive: Police," *NBC News* (April 20, 2013), http://www.cnbc.com/id/100655686.

7   Justin Peters, "These Are the People Whose Houses Are Being Searched in Watertown," *Slate* (April 19, 2013), http://www.slate.com/blogs/crime/2013/04/19/watertown_manhunt_these_are_the_people_whose_houses_are_being_searched.html.

8   As quoted in David Welch and Jo Fox, ed., *Justifying War: Propaganda, Politics and the Modern Age* (Palgrave Macmillan, 2012), p. 378.

9   Andrew O'Hehir, "How Boston exposes America's dark post-9/11 bargain," *Salon* (April 20, 2013), http://www.salon.com/2013/04/20/how_boston_exposes_americas_dark_post_911_bargain/.

10 Will Bunch, "There's a police coup going on right now in Ferguson, Mo.," *Philadelphia Daily News* (Aug. 13, 2014), http://www.philly.com/philly/blogs/attytood/Theres-a-police-coup-right-now-n-Ferguson-Mo-.html#AgjyvLaJjMCGqMm2.99.

11 Justin Peters, "These Are the People Whose Houses Are Being Searched in Watertown," *Slate* (April 19, 2013), http://www.slate.com/blogs/crime/2013/04/19/watertown_manhunt_these_are_the_people_whose_houses_are_being_searched.html.

12 Will Bunch, "There's a police coup going on right now in Ferguson, Mo.," *Philadelphia Daily News* (Aug. 13, 2014), http://www.philly.com/philly/blogs/attytood/Theres-a-police-coup-right-now-n-Ferguson-Mo-.html#AgjyvLaJjMCGqMm2.99.

13 Will Bunch, "There's a police coup going on right now in Ferguson, Mo.," *Philadelphia Daily News* (Aug. 13, 2014), http://www.philly.com/philly/blogs/attytood/Theres-a-police-coup-right-now-n-Ferguson-Mo-.html#AgjyvLaJjMCGqMm2.99.

CHAPTER 4

1   "21 Best Tom Clancy Quotes," *Daily Beast* (Oct. 2, 2013), http://www.thedailybeast.com/articles/2013/10/02/21-best-tom-clancy-quotes.html.

2   Larry O'Dell, "Brandon J. Raub, Former Marine, Detained After Anti-Government Facebook Postings," *Associated Press* (Aug. 21, 2012), http://www.huffingtonpost.com/2012/08/21/brandon-j-raub-marine-detained_n_1817484.html.

3   Norman Solomon and Marcy Wheeler, "The Government War Against Reporter James Risen," *The Nation* (Oct. 8, 2014), http://www.thenation.com/article/181919/government-war-against-reporter-james-risen#.

4   Brent Kendall, "U.S. on Supreme Court Protest Restrictions: Sidewalk is Wide Enough," *Wall Street Journal* (Sept. 23, 2014), http://blogs.wsj.com/washwire/2014/09/23/u-s-on-supreme-court-protest-restrictions-sidewalk-is-wide-enough/.

5   Michael W. Hoskins, "Justices clarify police resistance ruling," *The Indiana Lawyer* (Sept. 28, 2011), http://www.theindianalawyer.com/supreme-court-upholds-barnes-ruling/PARAMS/article/27202.

6   Peter Jamison, "Internal review: Tampa SWAT team acted properly in fatal pot raid," *Tampa Bay Times* (Aug. 15, 2014), http://www.tampabay.com/news/publicsafety/internal-review-finds-tampa-swat-team-acted-properly-in-fatal-raid/2193215.

7   Radley Balko, "Scenes from a militarized America: Iowa family 'terrorized,'" *The Washington Post* (Feb. 4, 2014), http://www.washingtonpost.com/news/opinions/wp/2014/02/04/scenes-from-a-militarized-america-iowa-family-terrorized/.

8   Eric Tucker, "Focus on NSA Surveillance Limits Turns to Courts," *Associated Press* (Oct. 28, 2014), http://abcnews.go.com/Politics/wireStory/focus-nsa-surveillance-limits-turns-courts-26501570.

9   Natasha Lennard, "Obama signs NDAA 2014, indefinite detention remains," *Salon* (Dec. 27, 2013), http://www.salon.com/2013/12/27/obama_signs_ndaa_2014_indefinite_detention_remains/.

10   Spencer Ackerman, "US cited controversial law in decision to kill American citizen by drone," *The Guardian* (June 23, 2014), http://www.theguardian.com/world/2014/jun/23/us-justification-drone-killing-american-citizen-awlaki.

11   Jen Kalaidis, "Bring Back Social Studies," *The Atlantic* (Sept. 23, 2013), http://www.theatlantic.com/education/archive/2013/09/bring-back-social-studies/279891/.

12   *Trop v. Dulles* (1958) 356 U.S. 86, http://www.law.cornell.edu/supremecourt/text/356/86.

13   "Death Penalty Trial Flaws," *CBS News* (Feb. 11, 2002), http://www.cbsnews.com/news/death-penalty-trial-flaws/.

CHAPTER 5

1   Bill Moyers, *The Secret Government: The Constitution in Crisis* (1987), http://www.informationclearinghouse.info/article17720.htm.

2   Jacques Ellul, *The Political Illusion* (Vintage Books, 1972), p. 6.

3   Marcus K. Garner and Ben Gray, "Police: DeKalb officer shot teen skipping school," *Atlanta Journal Constitution* (Sept. 4, 2013), http://www.ajc.com/news/news/crime-law/police-dekalb-officer-shot-teen-skipping-school/nZmr6/.

4   Hojun Choi, "DOJ denies City of Austin request to review police policies following unarmed shooting," *The Horn* (Sept. 6, 2013), http://www.readthehorn.com/news/83051/doj_denies_city_of_austin_request_to_review_police_policies_following_unarmed_shooting.

5   "Police: Seattle officer accidentally shot unarmed woman," *KOMO News* (Sept. 5, 2013), http://www.komonews.com/news/local/Police-Seattle-officer-accidentally-shot-unarmed-woman-222608561.html.

6   Daniel Bergner, "Is Stop-and-Frisk Worth It?" *The Atlantic* (April 2014), http://www.theatlantic.com/features/archive/2014/03/is-stop-and-frisk-worth-it/358644/.

7   Andy Greenberg, "Full-Body Scan Technology Deployed In Street-Roving Vans," *Forbes* (Aug. 24, 2010), http://www.forbes.com/sites/andygreenberg/2010/08/24/full-body-scan-technology-deployed-in-street-roving-vans/.

8   Allison Klein and Josh White, "License plate readers: A useful tool for police comes with privacy concerns," *The Washington Post* (Nov. 19, 2011), http://www.washingtonpost.com/local/license-plate-readers-a-useful-tool-for-police-comes-with-privacy-concerns/2011/11/18/gIQAuEApcN_story.html.

9   Andrew Becker and G. W. Schulz, "Local Cops Ready for War With Homeland Security-Funded Military Weapons," *The Daily Beast*, (December 21, 2011), http://www.thedailybeast.com/articles/2011/12/20/local-cops-ready-for-war-with-homeland-security-funded-military-weapons.html.

10   Aviva Shen, "Why Taxpayers Will Get Stuck With The Bill For The Ferguson Lawsuit," *ThinkProgress* (Aug. 31, 2014), http://thinkprogress.org/justice/2014/08/31/3477604/ferguson-lawsuit-expensive-police-misconduct/.

11   Sabrina Siddiqui, "Obama Pledges Gun Control 'With Or Without Congress' In 2014 State of the Union Address," *Huffington Post* (Jan. 28, 2014), http://www.huffingtonpost.com/2014/01/28/obama-gun-control-state-of-the-union_n_4684426.html.

12   "Citing 2nd & 4th Amendments, Rutherford Institute Asks Texas Appeals Court to Ensure that Lawful Gun Ownership Is Not a Trigger for 'No-Knock' Police Raids," The Rutherford Institute (June 18, 2013), https://www.rutherford.org/publications_resources/on_the_front_lines/citing_2nd_4th_amendments_rutherford_institute_asks_texas_appeals_court_to.

13   Tom Jackson, "Gun Owner Unarmed, Unwelcome in Maryland," *Tampa Tribune* (Jan. 21, 2014), http://tbo.com/list/columns-tjackson/jackson-gun-owner-unarmed-unwelcome-in-maryland-20140112/.

14   John W. Whitehead, "Do Parents' Rights End at the Schoolhouse Gate?" The Rutherford Institute (May 9, 2011), https://www.rutherford.org/publications_resources/john_whiteheads_commentary/do_parents_rights_end_at_the_schoolhouse_gate/.

15 Scott Gordon, "North Texas Drivers Stopped at Roadblock Asked for Saliva, Blood," *NBC News*, (November 20, 2013), http://www.nbcdfw.com/news/local/North-Texas-Drivers-Stopped-at-Roadblock-Asked-for-Saliva-Blood-232438621.html.

16 Mike Sacks, "Supreme Court OKs Strip Searches Without Suspicion For New Jail Inmates," *The Huffington Post*, (April 2, 2012), http://www.huffingtonpost.com/2012/04/02/supreme-court-strip-search-jail-inmates-anthony-kennedy_n_1369532.html.

17 Leslie Salzillo, "2 More Women Internally Probed On Public Road By Texas Troopers," *Alternet*, (August 5, 2013), http://www.alternet.org/2-more-women-internally-probed-public-road-texas-troopers-video.

18 Steven Nelson, "New Mexico Man Given Forced Colonoscopy by Cops Wins $1.6 Million Settlement," *US News*, (January 14, 2014), http://www.usnews.com/news/articles/2014/01/14/new-mexico-man-given-forced-colonoscopy-by-cops-wins-16-million-settlement.

CHAPTER 6

1 Bertram Gross, *Friendly Fascism: The New Face of Power in America*, (South End Press, 1980), p. 3.

2 Llewellyn Rockwell, Jr., *Against The State: An Anarcho-Capitalist Manifesto*, (lewrockwell.com) 2014, p. 178.

3 Zachary Davies Boren, *The US Is An Oligarchy, Study Concludes*, "http://www.telegraph.co.uk" (April 16, 2014).

4 Zachary Davies Boren, *The US Is An Oligarchy, Study Concludes*, "http://www.telegraph.co.uk" (April 16, 2014).

5 Dwight D. Eisenhower, "Farewell Address," Eisenhower Presidential Library, Museum and Boyhood Home (Jan. 17, 1961), http://www.eisenhower.archives.gov/research/online_documents/farewell_address/1961_01_17_Press_Release.pdf.

6 John W. Whitehead, *The Change Manifesto: Join the Block by Block Movement to Remake America* (Source Books, 2008), p. 19.

7 Howard J. Wiarda, *Corporatism and Comparative Politics: The Other Great Ism* (M.E. Sharpe, 1996), p. 42.

8 Jonathan Lethem, *They Live* (Soft Skull Press, 2010), p. 125.

9 Bertram Gross, *Friendly Fascism: The New Face of Power in America*, (South End Press, 1980), p. 6.

10 Marc Scott Zicree, *The Twilight Zone Companion* (Bantam Books, 1982), p. 208.

CHAPTER 7

1 George Orwell, *1984* (Plume, 1983), p. 239.

2 *As quoted in* Bertram Gross, *Friendly Fascism: The New Face of Power in America* (Black Rose Books, 1990), p. 294.

3 Jeffrey Tucker, "Fascism is Real and Alive," *Beautiful Anarchy* (Aug. 31, 2008), http://tucker.liberty.me/2014/08/31/fascism-is-real-and-alive/.

4 Jeffrey Tucker, "Fascism is Real and Alive," *Beautiful Anarchy* (Aug. 31, 2008), http://tucker.liberty.me/2014/08/31/fascism-is-real-and-alive/.

5 Jeffrey Tucker, "Fascism is Real and Alive," *Beautiful Anarchy* (Aug. 31, 2008), http://tucker.liberty.me/2014/08/31/fascism-is-real-and-alive/.

6 John W. Whitehead, *"Faith and Democracy: The Role of Religion in a Police State,"* Liberty, (May/June, 2014).

7 Jeffrey Tucker, "Fascism is Real and Alive," *Beautiful Anarchy* (Aug. 31, 2008), http://tucker.liberty.me/2014/08/31/fascism-is-real-and-alive/.

8 Bertram Gross, *Friendly Fascism: The New Face of Power in America* (South End Press, 1980), p. 14.

9 Robert Gellately, *Backing Hitler: Consent and Coercion in Nazi Germany* (Oxford University Press, 2001), p. 6.

10 Robert Gellately, *Backing Hitler: Consent and Coercion in Nazi Germany* (Oxford University Press, 2001), p. 15.

11 Robert Gellately, *Backing Hitler: Consent and Coercion in Nazi Germany* (Oxford University Press, 2001), p. 3.

12 Robert Gellately, *Backing Hitler: Consent and Coercion in Nazi Germany* (Oxford University Press, 2001), p. 46.

13 Eric Lichtblau, "In Cold War, U.S. Spy Agencies Used 1,000 Nazis," *The New York Times* (Oct. 26, 2014), http://www.nytimes.com/2014/10/27/us/in-cold-war-us-spy-agencies-used-1000-nazis.html.

14 Bertram Gross, *Friendly Fascism: The New Face of Power in America* (South End Press, 1980), p. 14.

15 John W. Whitehead, *The Change Manifesto: Join the Block by Block Movement to Remake America* (Source Books, 2008), p. 259.

16 Jeffrey Tucker, "Fascism is Real and Alive," *Beautiful Anarchy* (Aug. 31, 2008), http://tucker.liberty.me/2014/08/31/fascism-is-real-and-alive/.

17 Jeffrey Tucker, "Fascism is Real and Alive," *Beautiful Anarchy* (Aug. 31, 2008), http://tucker.liberty.me/2014/08/31/fascism-is-real-and-alive/.

18 James Silver, *The Startling Accuracy of Referring to Politicians as Psychopaths*, http://www.theatlantic.com/health/archive/2012/07.

19 James Silver, *The Startling Accuracy of Referring to Politicians as Psychopaths*, http://www.theatlantic.com/health/archive/2012/07.

20 James G. Long, "The Road to Pathocracy," *The American Thinker* (Aug. 2, 2014), http://www.americanthinker.com/2014/08/the_road_to_pathocracy.html.

21 James G. Long, "The Road to Pathocracy," *The American Thinker* (Aug. 2, 2014), http://www.americanthinker.com/2014/08/the_road_to_pathocracy.html.

22 James Q. Wilson, "Hard Times, Fewer Crimes," *Wall Street Journal* (May 28, 2011), http://online.wsj.com/news/articles/SB10001424052702304066504576345553135009870.

23 "Fear Makes People Stupid" Zero Hedge (June 21, 2011), http://www.zerohedge.com/article/fear-terror-makes-people-stupid.

24 Ronald Bailey, "Fear Itself," *Reason* (April 12, 2011), http://reason.com/archives/2011/04/12/fear-itself.

25 George Orwell, *1984*, (Plume, 1983), p. 255.

26 George Orwell, *1984*, (Plume, 1983), p. 255.

27 George Orwell, *1984*, (Plume, 1983), p. 255.

28 George Orwell, *1984*, (Plume, 1983), p. 256.

29 George Orwell, *1984*, (Plume, 1983), p. 255.

30 George Orwell, *1984*, (Plume, 1983), p. 284.

Part II: The War on the American People

1 "Rough justice in America," *The Economist* (July 22, 2010), http://www.economist.com/node/16636027.

2 Radley Balko, "Illinois Traffic Stop Of Star Trek Fans Raises Concerns About Drug Searches, Police Dogs, Bad Cops," *The Huffington Post*, (March 31, 2012), http://www.huffingtonpost.com/2012/03/31/drug-search-trekies-stopped-searched-illinois_n_1364087.html.

3 Kevin Johnson, "Who's watching the kids when parents get arrested?" *USA Today* (July 31, 2014), http://www.usatoday.com/story/news/nation/2014/07/31/children-left-behind-parents-arrested/13333909/.

4 "Post-Sandy Hook, US school surveillance market rockets," *TechEye*, (July 18, 2013), http://news.techeye.net/security/post-sandy-hook-us-school-surveillance-market-rockets.

5 Bob Egelko, "City jail's blanket strip searches illegal," *San Francisco Chronicle*, (October 1, 2005), http://www.newdorf.com/articles/SF_County_Jail_strip-search_policy_overturned.pdf.

6 "Cost of National Security," *National Priorities Project*, http://nationalpriorities.org/cost-of/.

7 "Cost of National Security," *National Priorities Project*, http://nationalpriorities.org/cost-of/.

8 "Cost of National Security," *National Priorities Project*, http://nationalpriorities.org/cost-of/.

9 "Cost of National Security," *National Priorities Project*, http://nationalpriorities.org/cost-of/.

CHAPTER 8

1 "Martin Niemöller: 'First They Came for the Socialists...,'" United States Holocaust Memorial Museum, http://www.ushmm.org/wlc/en/article.php?ModuleId=10007392.

2 Joe Wolverton II, "Secret Military Training Blurs Lines Between Police and Soldiers," *The New American*, (January 24, 2014), http://www.thenewamerican.com/usnews/constitution/item/17474-secret-military-training-blurs-line-between-police-and-soldiers.

3 "TSA conducts operation at West Palm Beach Tri-Rail station," *WPTV*, (April 21, 2011), http://www.wptv.com/news/region-c-palm-beach-county/west-palm-beach/tsa-conducts-operation-at-west-palm-beach-tri-rail-station.

4 Carol Christian, "U.S. Army's special forces set to train in Galveston," *Houston Chronicle*, (January 30, 2013), http://www.chron.com/news/houston-texas/houston/article/U-S-Army-s-special-forces-set-to-train-in-4235761.php.

5 Department of Education, "Remington Shotguns, Solicitation Number: EDOOIG-10-000004" *FedBizOpps.gov* (March 11, 2010), https://www.fbo.gov/index?s=opportunity&mode=form&id=cb68cf9f3fa2fe18a83d1c3dee0039b2.

6 Department of the Treasury, "Acquiring Shotguns, Solicitation Number: TIRWR-10-Q-00023," *FedBizOpps.gov* (Feb. 3, 2010), https://www.fbo.gov/index?s=opportunity&mode=form&id=8d3b076bd4de14bbda5aba699e80621d&tab=core&_cview=1&cck=1&au=&.

7 Social Security Administration, "Request for Quote for Ammunition, Solicitation Number: SSA-RFQ-12-1851," *FedBizOpps.gov* (Aug. 7, 2012), https://www.fbo.gov/index?s=opportunity&mode=form&id=6c39a2a9f00a10187a1432388a3301e5&tab=core&_cview=0&fb_source=message.

8 Larry O'Dell, "Brandon J. Raub, Former Marine, Detained After Anti-Government Facebook Postings," *Huffington Post*, (August 20, 2012), http://www.huffingtonpost.com/2012/08/21/brandon-j-raub-marine-detained_n_1817484.html.

9 "The C.I.A. and the N.Y.P.D." *The New York Times*, (July 5, 2013), http://www.nytimes.com/2013/07/06/opinion/the-cia-and-the-nypd.html?_r=0.

10 April M. Short, "6 shocking revelations about how private prisons make money," *Salon*, (September 23, 2013), http://www.salon.com/2013/09/23/6_shocking_revelations_about_how_private_prisons_make_money_partner/.

11 Timothy Stenovec, "Michael Salman, Phoenix Pastor, Jailed For Holding Church Services Without Proper Permits," *Huffington Post*, (July 16, 2012), http://www.huffingtonpost.com/2012/07/16/michael-salman-phoenix-pastor-jailed-bible-study-video_n_1677943.html.

12 Larry McShane, "California farmer arrested for selling raw goat milk at illegal farm," *NY Daily News*, (August 4, 2011), http://www.nydailynews.com/news/national/california-farmer-arrested-selling-raw-goat-milk-illegal-farm-article-1.944257.

13 Chris Hedges, "A Victory for All of Us," *Truthdig*, (May 18, 2012), http://www.truthdig.com/report/item/a_victory_for_all_of_us_20120518.

14 Ilya Somin, "Justice Scalia on *Kelo* and *Korematsu*," *The Washington Post* (Feb. 8, 2014), http://www.washingtonpost.com/news/volokh-conspiracy/wp/2014/02/08/justice-scalia-on-kelo-and-korematsu/.

15 Peter Dale Scott, *The Road to 9/11: Wealth, Empire, and the Future of America* (University of California Press, 2007), p. 183, https://encrypted.google.com/books?id=eeYiVXWBGHIC&pg=PA183#v=onepage&q&f=false.

16 "Former CIA director: In order to spy on domestic dissidents, just call them Terrorists," *PrivacySOS*, (January 31, 2014), http://privacysos.org/node/1318.

17 "Former CIA director: In order to spy on domestic dissidents, just call them Terrorists," *PrivacySOS*, (January 31, 2014), http://privacysos.org/node/1318.

18 "Former CIA director: In order to spy on domestic dissidents, just call them Terrorists," *PrivacySOS*, (January 31, 2014), http://privacysos.org/node/1318.

19 Michael Snyder, "72 Types Of Americans That Are Considered "Potential Terrorists" In Official Government Documents," *Investment Watch*, (August 26, 2013), http://investmentwatchblog.com/72-types-of-americans-that-are-considered-potential-terrorists-in-official-government-documents/.

20 Rachel L. Swarns, "Halliburton Subsidiary Gets Contract to Add Temporary Immigration Detention Centers," *The New York Times*, (February 4, 2006), http://www.nytimes.com/2006/02/04/national/04halliburton.html.

21 Tim Shorrock, "Exposing Bush's historic abuse of power," *Salon*, (July 23, 2008), http://www.salon.com/2008/07/23/new_churchcomm/.

22 Tim Shorrock, "Exposing Bush's historic abuse of power," *Salon*, (July 23, 2008), http://www.salon.com/2008/07/23/new_churchcomm/.

23 "DHS Report Warns Of Right Wing Extremists," *CBS News* (April 14, 2009), http://www.cbsnews.com/8301-503544_162-4944701-503544.html.

24 U.S. Department of Homeland Security, "Leftwing Extremists Likely to Increase Use of Cyber Attacks over the Coming Decade," (January 26, 2009), https://www.fas.org/irp/eprint/leftwing.pdf.

25 Cam Simpson and Gary Fields, "Veterans a Focus of FBI Extremist Probe," *Wall Street Journal* (April 17, 2009), http://online.wsj.com/article/SB123992665198727459.html.

26 Richard L. Rubenstein, *The Cunning of History: The Holocaust and the American Future* (Harper Perennial, 1975), pp. 15-16.

27 Leo Stein, "NIEMOELLER Speaks!" *The National Jewish Monthly* (May 1941), pp. 284-5, 301-2, http://www.history.ucsb.edu/faculty/marcuse/projects/niem/njm415/NatJewMonthly415.htm.

CHAPTER 9

1 James Madison, "The Particular Structure of the New Government and the Distribution of Power Among Its Different Parts, *The Federalist No. 47* (Jan. 30, 1788), http://www.constitution.org/fed/federa47.htm.

2 Mark Guarino, "FBI reports a drop in crime in 2013: why the rate continues to fall," *CS Monitor* (Feb. 19, 2014), http://www.csmonitor.com/USA/Justice/2014/0219/FBI-reports-a-drop-in-crime-in-2013-why-the-rate-continues-to-fall.

3 Radley Balko, "Scenes from a militarized America: Iowa family 'terrorized'," *The Washington Post* (Feb. 4, 2014), http://www.washingtonpost.com/news/opinions/wp/2014/02/04/scenes-from-a-militarized-america-iowa-family-terrorized/.

4 Charlene Sakoda, "'Pure evil': City caps sewer of woman fighting to live 'off the grid'," *Yahoo News* (Feb. 25, 2014), http://news.yahoo.com/blogs/oddnews/%E2%80%98pure-evil%E2%80%99--city-caps-sewer-of-woman-fighting-to-live-%E2%80%98off-the-grid%E2%80%99-234050584.html.

5 "Elderly Woman To Remain Jailed For Feeding Birds," *My FOX Philly* (March 6, 2014), http://www.myfoxphilly.com/story/24907680/elderly-woman-to-remain-jailed-for-feeding-birds#ixzz2vVhLUwZs.

6 William Patrick, "Florida city uproots couple's 17-year-old garden, over new ordinance," *FOX News* (Nov. 19, 2013), http://www.foxnews.com/politics/2013/11/19/florida-city-uproots-couples-17-year-old-garden-over-new-ordinance/.

7 Kendra Alleyne, "Oregon Man Sentenced to 30 Days in Jail -- for Collecting Rainwater on His Property," *CNS News* (July 26, 2012), http://www.cnsnews.com/news/article/oregon-man-sentenced-30-days-jail-collecting-rainwater-his-property.

8 Christine Mai-Duc, "Man who watched police shoot his dog sues city of Hawthorne," *Los Angeles Times* (Feb. 14, 2014), http://www.latimes.com/local/lanow/la-me-ln-hawthorne-dog-shooting-lawsuit-20140214,0,3484941.story#ixzz2vWUyG8NJ.

9   "Female US cop caught on tape giving two women body cavity search during routine traffic stop...and 'using the SAME gloves on both'" *Daily Mail* (Dec. 18, 2012), http://www.dailymail.co.uk/news/article-2250218/Angel-Ashley-Dobbs-suing-Texas-troopers-shocking-BODY-CAVITY-search-caught-tape.html#ixzz2HxDDYDoh.

10 Natasha Lennard, "U.S. requests more and more Google user data," *Salon,* (January 23, 2013), http://www.salon.com/2013/01/23/us_requests_more_and_more_google_user_data/.

11 Matt Sledge and Ryan J. Reilly, "NDAA Signed Into Law By Obama Despite Guantanamo Veto Threat, Indefinite Detention Provisions," *The Huffington Post,* (January 3, 2013), http://www.huffingtonpost.com/2013/01/03/ndaa-obama-indefinite-detention_n_2402601.html.

12 Matt Taibbi, "Secrets and Lies of the Bailout," *Rolling Stone,* (January 4, 2013), http://www.rollingstone.com/politics/news/secret-and-lies-of-the-bailout-20130104#ixzz2HIrDzuGl.

13 Bill Mears, "High court rules strip search reasonable after traffic stop," CNN (April 2, 2012), http://www.cnn.com/2012/04/02/justice/scotus-strip-search-ruling/index.html.

14 Warren Richey, "Was Taser use on pregnant woman excessive force? Supreme Court declines case." *Christian Science Monitor* (May 29, 2012), http://www.csmonitor.com/USA/Justice/2012/0529/Was-Taser-use-on-pregnant-woman-excessive-force-Supreme-Court-declines-case.

15 "Pepper-spraying campus police won't face charges," *Yahoo! News,* (September 20, 2012), http://news.yahoo.com/pepper-spraying-campus-police-wont-face-charges-032232434.html.

16 Matt Taibbi, "Outrageous HSBC Settlement Proves the Drug War is a Joke," *Rolling Stone,* (December 13, 2013), http://www.rollingstone.com/politics/blogs/taibblog/outrageous-hsbc-settlement-proves-the-drug-war-is-a-joke-20121213.

17 Radley Balko, "And now: The criminalization of parenthood," *The Washington Post* (July 14, 2014), http://www.washingtonpost.com/news/the-watch/wp/2014/07/14/and-now-the-criminalization-of-parenthood/.

18 John Jessup, "'Overcriminalization' Making Us a Nation of Felons?" *CBN News* (July 9, 2012), http://www.cbn.com/cbnnews/us/2012/March/Overcriminalization-Making-Us-a-Nation-of-Felons/.

19 L. Gordon Crovitz, "You Commit Three Felonies a Day," *Wall Street Journal* (Sept. 27, 2009), http://online.wsj.com/news/articles/SB10001424052748704471504574438900830760842.

20 "Rough justice in America," *The Economist* (July 22, 2010), http://www.economist.com/node/16636027.

21 "Crime and punishment in America," *The Economist* (July 22, 2010), http://www.economist.com/node/16640389.

22 Gary Fields and John R. Emshwiller, "As Criminal Laws Proliferate, More Are Ensnared," *Wall Street Journal* (July 23, 2011), http://online.wsj.com/articles/SB10001424052748703749504576172714184601654.

23 Charlene Sakoda, "'Pure evil': City caps sewer of woman fighting to live 'off the grid'," *Yahoo News* (Feb. 25, 2014), http://news.yahoo.com/blogs/oddnews/%E2%80%98pure-evil%E2%80%99--city-caps-sewer-of-woman-fighting-to-live-%E2%80%98off-the-grid%E2%80%99-234050584.html.

24 "Elderly Woman To Remain Jailed For Feeding Birds," *My FOX Philly* (March 6, 2014), http://www.myfoxphilly.com/story/24907680/elderly-woman-to-remain-jailed-for-feeding-birds#ixzz2vVhLUwZs.

25 "Traffic-stop recording led to woman's wrongful arrest, suit claims," *RT* (Feb. 22, 2014), http://rt.com/usa/traffic-stop-recording-wrongful-arrest-183/.

26 Lisa Suhay, "Nicole Gainey arrested for letting son play in park alone: Overreaction or law?" *Christian Science Monitor* (July 30, 2014), http://www.csmonitor.com/The-Culture/Family/Modern-Parenthood/2014/0730/Nicole-Gainey-arrested-for-letting-son-play-in-park-alone-Overreaction-or-law.

27 "Rutherford Institute Defends Florida Mom Arrested, Handcuffed, Searched & Jailed for Allowing Her 7-Year-Old Son to Visit Playground Alone," The Rutherford Institute (July 30, 2014), https://www.rutherford.org/publications_resources/on_the_front_lines/rutherford_institute_defends_florida_mom_arrested_handcuffed_searched_jaile.

28 John Marzulli, Laura Dimon, Ginger Adams Otis, "Naked Brooklyn woman dragged from apartment, left topless in hallway for minutes by NYPD officers who say she beat 12-year-old daughter," NY Daily News (Aug. 1, 2014), http://www.nydailynews.com/new-york/brooklyn/nypd-officers-drag-naked-brooklyn-woman-apartment-video-article-1.1889292#ixzz39GJD54uj.

29 John Marzulli, Laura Dimon, Ginger Adams Otis, "Naked Brooklyn woman dragged from apartment, left topless in hallway for minutes by NYPD officers who say she beat 12-year-old daughter," NY Daily News (Aug. 1, 2014), http://www.nydailynews.com/new-york/brooklyn/nypd-officers-drag-naked-brooklyn-woman-apartment-video-article-1.1889292#ixzz39GJD54uj.

30 Trevor Burrus, "How Destroying Fish Is Not Like Destroying Financial Records," Cato at Liberty (July 10, 2014), http://www.cato.org/blog/how-destroying-fish-not-destroying-financial-records.

31 Jessica Grose, "Parents Are Now Getting Arrested for Letting Their Kids Go to the Park Alone," Slate (July 15, 2014), http://www.slate.com/blogs/xx_factor/2014/07/15/debra_harrell_arrested_for_letting_her_9_year_old_daughter_go_to_the_park.html.

32 Christopher Brito, "Mom arrested after 7-year-old boy left alone at Lego Store," PIX11 (Aug. 6, 2014), http://pix11.com/2014/08/06/long-island-woman-arrested-after-leaving-her-child-at-lego-store/.

33 Mark O'Mara, "Does leaving kids alone make parents 'criminals'?" CNN (July 31, 2014), http://www.cnn.com/2014/07/31/opinion/omara-parents-children-unattended/.

34 Brandon Todd, "Mom arrested for letting kids play outside," My FOX DFW (Sept. 20, 2012), http://www.myfoxdfw.com/story/19600642/mom-arrested-for-letting-kids-play-outside.

35 C.S. Lewis, God in the Dock (1948), http://online.wsj.com/news/articles/SB10001424052702304527504579170134126854254.

36 Richard A. Oppel Jr., "Steady Decline in Major Crime Baffles Experts," The New York Times (May 23, 2011), http://www.nytimes.com/2011/05/24/us/24crime.html?_r=0.

37 "Rough justice in America," The Economist (July 22, 2010), http://www.economist.com/node/16636027.

38 Melissa Hipolit, "Former police officer exposes Chesterfield's ticket quota goals," WTVR (July 14, 2014), http://wtvr.com/2014/07/14/chesterfield-quota-investigation/.

39 Kevin Johnson, "Private purchasing of prisons locks in occupancy rates," USA Today (March 8, 2012), http://www.usatoday.com/news/nation/story/2012-03-01/buying-prisons-require-high-occupancy/53402894/1.

40 Joe Weisenthal, "This Investor Presentation For A Private Prison Is One Of The Creepiest Presentations We've Ever Seen," Business Insider (March 12, 2012), http://www.businessinsider.com/the-private-prison-business-2012-3#-4.

41 Kevin Johnson, "Private purchasing of prisons locks in occupancy rates," USA Today (March 8, 2012), http://www.usatoday.com/news/nation/story/2012-03-01/buying-prisons-require-high-occupancy/53402894/1.

42 Adam Liptak, "U.S. prison population dwarfs that of other nations," The New York Times (April 23, 2008), http://www.nytimes.com/2008/04/23/world/americas/23iht-23prison.12253738.html?pagewanted=all.

43 Sadhbh Walshe, "How US prison labour pads corporate profits at taxpayers' expense," The Guardian, (July 6, 2012), http://www.theguardian.com/commentisfree/2012/jul/06/prison-labor-pads-corporate-profits-taxpayers-expense.

44 Simon McCormack, "Prison Labor Booms As Unemployment Remains High; Companies Reap Benefits," *The Huffington Post*, (December 10, 2012), http://www.huffingtonpost.com/2012/12/10/prison-labor_n_2272036.html.

45 Caroline Winter, "What Do Prisoners Make for Victoria's Secret?" *Mother Jones*, (July 2008), http://www.motherjones.com/politics/2008/07/what-do-prisoners-make-victorias-secret.

46 Wendy McElroy, "Cage Complex," *The Freeman*, (January 21, 2014), http://www.fee.org/the_freeman/detail/cage-complex#ixzz2rWSrOAwg.

47 John Nichols, "ALEC Exposed," *The Nation* (Aug. 1-8, 2011), http://www.thenation.com/article/161978/alec-exposed.

48 Gracy Olmstead, "Parenting in an Age of Bad Samaritans," *The American Conservative* (July 17, 2014), http://www.theamericanconservative.com/parenting-in-an-age-of-bad-samaritans/.

49 William Styron, Introduction to *The Cunning of History: The Holocaust and the American Future*, by Richard L. Rubenstein (New York: Harper Perennial, 1987), xi.

50 Viktor Frankl, *Man's Search for Meaning* (Beacon Press, 2006), p. 7.

CHAPTER 10

1 Adam Summers, "Master of Your Domain: The Impact of the Kelo Decision," *Reason*, (June 26, 2006), http://reason.org/news/show/122529.html.

2 Steve Horrell, "Man may lose $22,870 to law enforcement after recent stop," *The Edwardsville Intelligencer*, (November 1, 2010), http://www.theintelligencer.com/local_news/article_c27b45aa-3395-5064-8542-2d4c4d66bc3d.html.

3 Lindsay Abrams, "Couple who had been growing their own food for 17 years forced to stop because it isn't "aesthetic,"" *Salon*, (November 20, 2013), http://www.salon.com/2013/11/20/couple_that_had_been_growing_their_own_food_for_17_years_forced_to_stop_because_it_isnt_aesthetic/.

4 Suzanne Goldenberg and Ed Pilkington, "ALEC calls for penalties on 'freerider' homeowners in assault on clean energy," *The Guardian*, (December 4, 2013), http://www.theguardian.com/world/2013/dec/04/alec-freerider-homeowners-assault-clean-energy.

5 Mikael Thalen, "City Takes Veteran To Trial For Raising Backyard Chickens," *StoryLeak* (Dec. 4, 2013), http://www.storyleak.com/city-takes-veteran-trial-owning-chickens/#ixzz2mcusqyv7.

6 Andy Fox, "Boys punished for airsoft guns in yard," *WAVY*, (September 24, 2013), http://www.wavy.com/news/local/va-beach/has-zero-tolerance-gone-too-far.

7 Radley Balko, "Family Of Jose Guerena, Former Marine Killed By SWAT Team, To Receive $3.4 Million," *Huffington Post*, (September 26, 2013), http://www.huffingtonpost.com/2013/09/26/jose-guerena_n_3988658.html.

8 "FBI targets wrong apartment in Fitchburg raid," *WHDH*, (January 31, 2012), http://www1.whdh.com/news/articles/local/north/12006574418493/fbi-targets-wrong-apartment-in-fitchburg-raid/.

9 Aaron C. Davis, "Police Raid Berwyn Heights Mayor's Home, Kill His 2 Dogs," *The Washington Post*, (July 31, 2008), http://articles.washingtonpost.com/2008-07-31/news/36921174_1_police-dog-trinity-tomsic-mayor-cheye-calvo.

10 Scott Gordon, "North Texas Drivers Stopped at Roadblock Asked for Saliva, Blood," *NBC News*, (November 20, 2013), http://www.nbcdfw.com/news/local/North-Texas-Drivers-Stopped-at-Roadblock-Asked-for-Saliva-Blood-232438621.html.

11 Mike Sacks, "Supreme Court OKs Strip Searches Without Suspicion For New Jail Inmates," *The Huffington Post*, (April 2, 2012), http://www.huffingtonpost.com/2012/04/02/supreme-court-strip-search-jail-inmates-anthony-kennedy_n_1369532.html.

12 Leslie Salzillo, "2 More Women Internally Probed On Public Road By Texas Troopers," *Alternet*, (August 5, 2013), http://www.alternet.org/2-more-women-internally-probed-public-road-texas-troopers-video.

13   "Massachusetts Body of Liberties," http://www.mass.gov/anf/research-and-tech/legal-and-legislative-resources/body-of-liberties.html.

14   Nick Gillespie, "One DC Traffic Camera Generates $12 Million in Revenue!" *Reason* (October 25, 2012), http://reason.com/blog/2012/10/25/one-dc-traffic-camera-generates-12-milli.

15   Radley Balko, "Illinois Traffic Stop Of Star Trek Fans Raises Concerns About Drug Searches, Police Dogs, Bad Cops," *The Huffington Post*, (March 31, 2012), http://www.huffingtonpost.com/2012/03/31/drug-search-trekies-stopped-searched-illinois_n_1364087.html.

16   Radley Balko, "Illinois Traffic Stop Of Star Trek Fans Raises Concerns About Drug Searches, Police Dogs, Bad Cops," *The Huffington Post*, (March 31, 2012), http://www.huffingtonpost.com/2012/03/31/drug-search-trekies-stopped-searched-illinois_n_1364087.html.

17   Stephen J. Dunn, "Nothing Civil About Asset Forfeiture," *Forbes*, (February 18, 2013), http://www.forbes.com/sites/stephendunn/2013/02/18/asset-forfeiture-is-anything-but-civil/.

18   Dave Smith, "Bill Would Extend Forfeiture Actions to Petty Misdemeanors," *Big Island Now*, (February 15, 2013), http://bigislandnow.com/2013/02/15/bill-would-extend-forfeiture-actions-to-petty-misdemeanors/.

19   Radley Balko, "Tennessee Asset Forfeiture Bill Seeks To Abolish Abusive Police Practice," *Huffington Post* (March 22, 2013), http://www.huffingtonpost.com/2013/03/22/tennessee-asset-forfeiture_n_2933246.html.

20   J. Reynolds Hutchins, "Albemarle monitoring bribery probe of red-light camera vendor," *Daily Progress*, (May 17, 2013), http://www.dailyprogress.com/news/local/albemarle-monitoring-bribery-probe-of-red-light-camera-vendor/article_0d65cdb4-bf58-11e2-a71a-001a4bcf6878.html.

21   J. Reynolds Hutchins, "Albemarle monitoring bribery probe of red-light camera vendor," *Daily Progress*, (May 17, 2013), http://www.dailyprogress.com/news/local/albemarle-monitoring-bribery-probe-of-red-light-camera-vendor/article_0d65cdb4-bf58-11e2-a71a-001a4bcf6878.html.

22   Noah Pransky, "Florida quietly shortened yellow light standards & lengths, resulting in more red light camera tickets for you," *NBC 10*, (May 19, 2013), http://www.wtsp.com/news/local/story.aspx?storyid=316418.

23   Justin Peters, "Did Florida Shorten Its Yellow Lights to Rake in Traffic Camera Revenue?" *Slate*, (May 21, 2013), http://www.slate.com/blogs/crime/2013/05/21/traffic_cameras_did_florida_shorten_its_yellow_lights_to_rake_in_traffic.html.

24   Annette Fuentes, "The Truancy Trap," *The Atlantic*, (September 5, 2012), http://www.theatlantic.com/national/archive/2012/09/the-truancy-trap/261937/.

25   Barbara Ehrenreich, "Is It Now a Crime to Be Poor?" *The New York Times*, (August 8, 2009), http://www.nytimes.com/2009/08/09/opinion/09ehrenreich.html?pagewanted=all&_r=0.

26   Alexia Campbell, "New court could mean jail for parents of truant kids," *Sun Sentinel* (Dec. 11, 2011), http://articles.sun-sentinel.com/2011-12-11/news/fl-palm-truancy-court-20111209_1_truancy-court-absences-parents-of-truant-kids.

CHAPTER 11

1   Herman Schwartz, "How the Supreme Court Came to Embrace Strip Searches for Trivial Offenses," *The Nation* (Aug. 16, 2012), http://www.thenation.com/article/169419/how-supreme-court-came-embrace-strip-searches-trivial-offenses#.

2   *Florence v. Burlington*, http://www.scotusblog.com/case-files/cases/florence-v-board-of-chosen-freeholders-of-the-county-of-burlington/.

3   *Florence v. Burlington*, http://www.supremecourt.gov/opinions/11pdf/10-945.pdf.

4   "Searches of Arrested Persons," http://www.aele.org/search1.html#What%20are%20some%20examples%20of%20strip%20searches%20that%20the.

5   Chris Sweeney, "Cops Strip Search Mom, "Forcibly" Pull Tampon Out of Her for Maybe Rolling Through Stop Sign," *Broward Palm Beach NewTimes* (Aug. 9, 2012), http://blogs.browardpalmbeach.com/pulp/2012/08/cops_strip_search_mom_pull_tam.php.

6   *Cox v. Sampson County School Board*, No. 7:12-CV-00344-FL (E.D.N.C. 2012).

7   "Ga. Tech Fan Claims Strip Search Over Sandwich," WSBTV (Aug. 2, 2011), http://www.wsbtv.com/news/news/ga-tech-fan-claims-strip-search-over-sandwich/nDKwF/.

8   Brendan J. Lyons and Alysia Santo, "Stripped of dignity?" *Times Union* (Dec. 10, 2012), http://www.timesunion.com/local/article/Stripped-of-dignity-4102501.php.

9   Pam Zekman, "Parents Of Teen Strip-Searched At School Sue Assistant Principal, Police," CBS Chicago, (December 5, 2012), http://chicago.cbslocal.com/2012/12/05/parents-of-teen-strip-searched-at-school-sue-assistant-principal-police/.

10 Gina Barton and John Diedrich, "4 Milwaukee police officers charged in strip-search case," *Milwaukee-Wisconsin Journal Sentinel* (Oct. 9, 2012), http://www.jsonline.com/news/crime/criminal-charges-against-police-in-strip-search-case-expected-today-gf5cb94-173312411.html.

11 Henry K. Lee, "Strip searches cost Oakland $4.6 million," *SF Gate* (Nov. 15, 2012), http://www.sfgate.com/crime/article/Strip-searches-cost-Oakland-4-6-million-4035103.php.

12 "Female US cop caught on tape giving two women body cavity search during routine traffic stop ... and 'using the SAME gloves on both'" *Daily Mail* (Dec. 18, 2012), http://www.dailymail.co.uk/news/article-2250218/Angel-Ashley-Dobbs-suing-Texas-troopers-shocking-BODY-CAVITY-search-caught-tape.html#ixzz2HxDDYDoh.

13 Kevin Krause, "Texas trooper being sued in Irving body cavity search case has been suspended," *The Dallas Morning News*, (December 19, 2012), http://crimeblog.dallasnews.com/2012/12/irving-women-sue-state-troopers-in-federal-court-alleging-roadside-body-cavity-searches.html/.

CHAPTER 12

1   "Foucauldian Discourse on Punishment," *UKEssays*, http://www.ukessays.com/essays/philosophy/foucauldian-discourse-on-punishment.php.

2   Niall McLaren, "Dumbing Down America: The Decline of Education in the US as Seen From Down Under," *Truthout* (November 22, 2013), http://www.truth-out.org/opinion/item/20043-dumbing-down-america-the-decline-of-education-in-the-us-as-seen-from-down-under.

3   Stacy Teicher Khadaroo, "Atlanta school shooting raises doubts about metal detectors," *The Christian Science Monitor*, (February 1, 2013), http://www.csmonitor.com/USA/Education/2013/0201/Atlanta-school-shooting-raises-doubts-about-metal-detectors.

4   Emma Brown, "Fairfax board authorizes high school surveillance cameras," *The Washington Post*, (December 16, 2011), http://www.washingtonpost.com/local/education/fairfax-board-authorizes-high-school-surveillance-cameras/2011/12/15/gIQAmb6HxO_story.html.

5   "Police Dogs Roam N.J. High School In Search Of Illegal Drugs," *New York CBS*, (December 22, 2013), http://newyork.cbslocal.com/2013/12/11/drug-sniffing-dogs-roam-n-j-high-school-in-search-of-illegal-drugs/.

6   Editorial Board, "Torturing Children at School," *The New York Times* (April 11, 2014), http://www.nytimes.com/2014/04/12/opinion/torturing-children-at-school.html.

7   Patrik Jonsson, "Ohio boy suspended for pointing finger like a gun. 'Zero tolerance' run amok?" *Christian Science Monitor*, (March 4, 2014), http://www.csmonitor.com/USA/Education/2014/0304/Ohio-boy-suspended-for-pointing-finger-like-a-gun.-Zero-tolerance-run-amok.

8   Stephanie Chen, "Girl's arrest for doodling raises concerns about zero tolerance," *CNN*, (February 18, 2010), http://www.cnn.com/2010/CRIME/02/18/new.york.doodle.arrest/.

9   Mykal Washington, "Zero Tolerance: A Student's Perspective," *ACLU-PA*, (February 19, 2014), http://blog.aclupa.org/2014/02/19/zero-tolerance-a-students-perspective/.

10   Aaron Cantu, "The latest dangerous education "reform": Tracking students' data," *Salon*, (January 30, 2014), http://www.salon.com/2014/01/30/new_idea_from_the_surveillance_state_collect_students_data_partner/.

11   Erik Eckholm, "With Police in Schools, More Children in Court," *The New York Times* (April 12, 2013), http://www.nytimes.com/2013/04/12/education/with-police-in-schools-more-children-in-court.html.

12   Erik Eckholm, "With Police in Schools, More Children in Court," *The New York Times* (April 12, 2013), http://www.nytimes.com/2013/04/12/education/with-police-in-schools-more-children-in-court.html.

13   Martin Hart-Landsberg, "Security Guards Now Outnumber High School Teachers," *The Society Pages* (March 24, 2014), http://thesocietypages.org/socimages/2014/03/24/security-guards-now-outnumber-high-school-teachers/.

14   Erik Eckholm, "With Police in Schools, More Children in Court," *The New York Times* (April 12, 2013), http://www.nytimes.com/2013/04/12/education/with-police-in-schools-more-children-in-court.html.

15   Editorial Board, "Torturing Children at School," *The New York Times* (April 11, 2014), http://www.nytimes.com/2014/04/12/opinion/torturing-children-at-school.html.

16   Niall McLaren, "Dumbing Down America: The Decline of Education in the US as Seen From Down Under," *Truthout* (November 22, 2013), http://www.truth-out.org/opinion/item/20043-dumbing-down-america-the-decline-of-education-in-the-us-as-seen-from-down-under.

17   Robert Higgs, "Supreme Court rules firing justified for teacher accused of advancing religion in classroom," *Cleveland Plain Dealer* (Nov. 19, 2013), http://www.cleveland.com/open/index.ssf/2013/11/supreme_court_rules_firing_jus.html.

18   Roy A. Barnes, "Public Schools' Politically Correct Assault on Childhood Innocence is Outrageous," *Yahoo! News* (Dec. 5, 2011), http://news.yahoo.com/public-schools-politically-correct-assault-childhood-innocence-outrageous-183100753.html.

19   Michael Martinez, "California school district hires firm to monitor students' social media," *CNN* (Sept. 18, 2013), http://www.cnn.com/2013/09/14/us/california-schools-monitor-social-media/.

20   Jennifer Steinhauer, "Scouts Train to Fight Terrorists, and More," *The New York Times* (May 13, 2009), http://www.nytimes.com/2009/05/14/us/14explorers.html?_r=0.

21   Jennifer Steinhauer, "Scouts Train to Fight Terrorists, and More," *The New York Times* (May 13, 2009), http://www.nytimes.com/2009/05/14/us/14explorers.html?_r=0.

22   Hamza Shaban, "Playing War: How the Military Uses Video Games," *The Atlantic* (Oct. 10, 2013), http://www.theatlantic.com/technology/archive/2013/10/playing-war-how-the-military-uses-video-games/280486/.

23   Nick Turse, "Torturing Iron Man," *Southern Cross Review* (2008), http://southerncrossreview.org/60/ironman.htm.

24   Associated Press, "US school districts given free machine guns and grenade launchers," *The Guardian* (Sept. 18, 2014), http://www.theguardian.com/world/2014/sep/18/us-school-districts-given-free-machine-guns-and-grenade-launchers.

25   Associated Press, "US school districts given free machine guns and grenade launchers," *The Guardian* (Sept. 18, 2014), http://www.theguardian.com/world/2014/sep/18/us-school-districts-given-free-machine-guns-and-grenade-launchers.

26   Emily Bloomenthal, "Inadequate Discipline: Challenging Zero Tolerance Policies As Violating State Constitution Education Clauses," 35 N.Y.U. Rev. L. & Soc. Change 303, 311-12 (2011).

27   "Rutherford Institute Defends 10-Year-Old Suspended for Shooting Imaginary Arrow, Threatened with Expulsion Under Weapons Policy," The Rutherford Institute (Dec. 4, 2013), https://www.rutherford.org/publications_resources/on_the_front_lines/rutherford_institute_defends_10_year_old_suspended_for_shooting_imaginary_a.

28 Steven K. Paulson, "6-year-old Colorado boy suspended for kissing a girl," *KBOI*, (December 10, 2013), http://www.kboi2.com/news/national/6-year-old-boy-suspended-for-kissing-a-girl-235230651.html.

29 Kevin Koeninger, "Arrested & Beaten for Dozing in Class," *Courthouse News Service*, (May 7, 2013), http://www.courthousenews.com/2013/05/07/57383.htm.

30 "NC high school students charged in water balloon prank, parents outraged," *WBTW*, (May 17, 2013), http://www.wbtw.com/story/22286425/nc-high-school-students-charged-in-water-balloon-prank-near-graduation.

31 *As quoted in* Malcolm Gladwell, "The Crooked Ladder," *The New Yorker* (Aug. 11, 2014), http://www.newyorker.com/magazine/2014/08/11/crooked-ladder.

32 United States Holocaust Memorial Museum. "Indoctrinating Youth." Holocaust Encyclopedia. http://www.ushmm.org/wlc/en/article.php?ModuleId=10007820. Accessed on April 28, 2014.

33 United States Holocaust Memorial Museum. "Indoctrinating Youth." Holocaust Encyclopedia. http://www.ushmm.org/wlc/en/article.php?ModuleId=10007820. Accessed on April 28, 2014.

34 United States Holocaust Memorial Museum. "Indoctrinating Youth." Holocaust Encyclopedia. http://www.ushmm.org/wlc/en/article.php?ModuleId=10007820. Accessed on April 28, 2014.

35 United States Holocaust Memorial Museum. "Indoctrinating Youth." Holocaust Encyclopedia. http://www.ushmm.org/wlc/en/article.php?ModuleId=10007820. Accessed on April 28, 2014.

36 *The Trial of German Major War Criminals: Proceedings of the International Military Tribunal Sitting at Nuremberg, Germany* (International Military Tribunal, 1946), p. 120.

CHAPTER 13

1 Robert Gellately, *Backing Hitler: Consent and Coercion in Nazi Germany* (Oxford University Press, May 16, 2002).

2 Robert Gellately, *Backing Hitler: Consent and Coercion in Nazi Germany* (Oxford University Press, May 16, 2002).

3 Mike Riggs, "Ten Years of 'If You See Something, Say Something," *Reason* (March 19, 2012), http://reason.com/blog/2012/03/19/ten-years-of-if-you-see-something-say-so.

4 Rachel Green, "See Something, Say Something campaign to be launched on campus," *Daily Iowan* (Aug. 29, 2014), http://www.dailyiowan.com/2014/08/29/Metro/38760.html.

5 Anna Stolzenburg, "Bills introduce gameday 'See Something Say Something' app," *Buffalo Bills* (Sept. 9, 2014), http://www.buffalobills.com/news/article-1/Bills-introduce-gameday-See-Something-Say-Something-app/3f79d7b7-fd26-4815-b46b-af6d57ee48ff.

6 Catherine Foti, "If You See Something, Say Something, But Maybe Only to the SEC," *Forbes* (June 18, 2014), http://www.forbes.com/sites/insider/2014/06/18/if-you-see-something-say-something-but-maybe-only-to-the-sec/.

7 "Community Policing Defined," US Dept. of Justice (accessed 9/22/14), http://www.cops.usdoj.gov/Publications/e030917193-CP-Defined.pdf.

8 "Use of Force," *US Department of Justice* (accessed 9/16/14), http://www.cops.usdoj.gov/default.asp?Item=1374.

9 Ron Barnett and Paul Alongi, "Critics knock no-knock police raids," *USA Today* (Feb. 13, 2011), http://usatoday30.usatoday.com/news/nation/2011-02-14-noknock14_ST_N.htm.

10 Jenna Ross, "Atwater police chief's killing of pet chicken stirs outrage," *Star Tribune* (9/2/14), http://www.startribune.com/local/273684271.html.

11 Jenna Ross, "Atwater police chief's killing of pet chicken stirs outrage," *Star Tribune* (9/2/14), http://www.startribune.com/local/273684271.html.

12 Katherine Paterson, "First, Families," *The New York Times* (Feb. 11, 1996), http://www.nytimes.com/books/97/04/13/bsp/19162.html.

13 "Community Policing Defined," US Dept. of Justice (accessed 9/22/14), http://www.cops. usdoj.gov/Publications/e030917193-CP-Defined.pdf.

14 Robert Gellately, *Backing Hitler: Consent and Coercion in Nazi Germany* (Oxford University Press, 2001), p. 188.

CHAPTER 14

1 Adam Liptak, "A Liberal Case for Gun Rights Sways Judiciary," *The New York Times*, (May 6, 2007), http://www.nytimes.com/2007/05/06/us/06firearms.html?pagewanted=all&_ r=0.

2 George Orwell, Ian Angus, Sheila Davison, *The Complete Works of George Orwell: A Patriot After All, 1940-1941* (Secker & Warburg, 1998), p. 365.

3 Thomas Jefferson, "Thomas Jefferson, Resolutions Relative to the Alien and Sedition Acts," http://press-pubs.uchicago.edu/founders/documents/v1ch8s41.html.

4 Tom Jackson, "Gun owner unarmed, unwelcome in Maryland," *The Tampa Tribune*, (January 12, 2014), http://tbo.com/list/columns-tjackson/jackson-gun-owner-unarmed-unwelcome-in-maryland-20140112/.

5 Wynton Hall, "Washington State Bill to Search Gun Owner Homes First Introduced in 2005,) *Breitbart* (Feb. 19, 2013), http://www.breitbart.com/Big-Government/2013/02/19/ Washington-State-Bill-To-Search-Gun-Owner-Homes-Introduced-Since-2005.

6 Jonathan Turley, "ACLU Files On Behalf Of Gun Owner Abusively Arrested By Philadelphia Police," *Jonathan Turley* (Feb. 17, 2012), http://jonathanturley.org/2012/02/17/aclu-files-on-behalf-of-gun-owner-abusively-arrested-by-philadelphia-police/.

7 David Sherfinski, "NRA: Federal surveillance policies could lead to gun registry," *Washington Times* (March 16, 2014), http://www.washingtontimes.com/news/2014/ mar/16/nra-federal-surveillance-policies-could-undermine-/.

8 Claire Healey, "NEW SMARTPHONE APP INVADES GUN OWNERS' PRIVACY," *American Spectator* (July 11, 2013), http://spectator.org/blog/54297/new-smartphone-app-invades-gun-owners-privacy.

9 "U.S. Supreme Court Rejects Appeal in Second Amendment Case, Refuses to Prohibit Police from Using Lawful Gun Ownership as a Trigger for 'No-Knock' Police Raids," The Rutherford Institute (March 12, 2014), https://www.rutherford.org/ publications_resources/on_the_front_lines/us_supreme_court_rejects_appeal_in_second_ amendment_case.

10 "U.S. Supreme Court Rejects Appeal in Second Amendment Case, Refuses to Prohibit Police from Using Lawful Gun Ownership as a Trigger for 'No-Knock' Police Raids," The Rutherford Institute (March 12, 2014), https://www.rutherford.org/ publications_resources/on_the_front_lines/us_supreme_court_rejects_appeal_in_second_ amendment_case.

11 Tom Jackson, "Gun owner unarmed, unwelcome in Maryland," *The Tampa Tribune*, (January 12, 2014), http://tbo.com/list/columns-tjackson/jackson-gun-owner-unarmed-unwelcome-in-maryland-20140112/.

12 Jonathan Turley, "ACLU Files On Behalf Of Gun Owner Abusively Arrested By Philadelphia Police," *Jonathan Turley* (Feb. 17, 2012), http://jonathanturley.org/2012/ 02/17/aclu-files-on-behalf-of-gun-owner-abusively-arrested-by-philadelphia-police/.

13 Wynton Hall, "Washington State Bill to Search Gun Owner Homes First Introduced in 2005,) *Breitbart* (Feb. 19, 2013), http://www.breitbart.com/Big-Government/ 2013/02/19/Washington-State-Bill-To-Search-Gun-Owner-Homes-Introduced-Since-2005.

14 Associated Press, "Connecticut Gun Control Law Upheld By Federal Judge," *Huffington Post* (Jan. 30, 2014), http://www.huffingtonpost.com/2014/01/30/connecticut-gun-control-_n_4698342.html.

15 Matt Friedman, "Lower capacity for gun magazines approved by NJ Assembly panel," *NJ Star Ledger* (March 13, 2014), http://www.nj.com/politics/index.ssf/2014/03/assembly_ committee_approves_lower_limit_for_gun_magazines.html.

16 Michael E. Hammond, "Should you lose your gun rights if you visit a shrink?" *The Washington Times*, (January 7, 2014), http://www.washingtontimes.com/news/2014/jan/7/hammond-see-a-shrink-lose-your-weapon/.

17 Michael E. Hammond, "Should you lose your gun rights if you visit a shrink?" *The Washington Times*, (January 7, 2014), http://www.washingtontimes.com/news/2014/jan/7/hammond-see-a-shrink-lose-your-weapon/.

18 William Orville Douglas, *The Court Years, 1939-1975: The Autobiography of William O. Douglas* (Vintage Books, 1981), p. 8.

19 "Sandy Hook shooting: What happened?" *CNN* (December 2012), http://www.cnn.com/interactive/2012/12/us/sandy-hook-timeline/.

20 Rong-Gong Lin II, "Gunman kills 12 at 'Dark Knight Rises' screening in Colorado," *LA Times* (July 20, 2012), http://articles.latimes.com/2012/jul/20/nation/la-na-nn-dark-knight-shooting-20120720.

21 Joseph Straw In Washington, Rocco Parascandola, Bev Ford, Chelsia Rose Marcius and Larry Mcshane, "Bombs at Boston Marathon were made from pressure cookers and ball bearings," *NY Daily News* (April 16, 2013), http://www.nydailynews.com/news/national/apartment-searched-connection-boston-marathon-bombing-article-1.1317904#ixzz2wErdJ6tB.

22 Julie Makinen, "China knife attack leaves 28 dead, scores injured at train station," *Los Angeles Times*, (March 1, 2014), http://www.latimes.com/world/asia/la-fg-china-knife-attack-20140302,0,7598776.story.

23 Awr Hawkins, "Study: Concealed Carry Saves Lives, Assault Weapon Ban Ineffective," *Breitbart* (Jan. 4, 2014), http://www.breitbart.com/Big-Government/2014/01/03/Study-Concealed-Carry-Saves-Lives-Assault-Weapons-Ban-Had-Little-to-No-Effect.

24 Kevin Carson, "Some Observations on the Gun Control Debate," *Counter Punch*, (December 17, 2012), http://www.counterpunch.org/2012/12/17/some-observations-on-the-gun-control-debate/.

25 *Essays on Liberty, Volume XII* (Foundation for Economic Education, 1965), p. 372.

26 Norman Cameron and R.H. Stevens, *Hitler's Table Talk 1941–1944: His Private Conversations*, (2000), p. 425, https://www.archive.org/stream/HitlersTableTalk#page/n1/mode/2up.

27 Robert Gellately, *Backing Hitler*, Oxford University Press, 2001, p. 307.

28 Robert Gellately, *Backing Hitler*, Oxford University Press, 2001, p. 127.

CHAPTER 15

1 Rod Serling, "The Monsters Are Due on Maple Street," *Twilight Zone* (March 4, 1960).

2 David Grant, "Its approval rating at new low, Congress plows ahead on immigration, taxes," *Christian Science Monitor*, (June 14, 2013), http://www.csmonitor.com/USA/Politics/2013/0614/Its-approval-rating-at-new-low-Congress-plows-ahead-on-immigration-taxes.

3 Jo Becker and Scott Shane, "Secret 'Kill List' Proves a Test of Obama's Principles and Will," *The New York Times*, (May 29, 2012), http://www.nytimes.com/2012/05/29/world/obamas-leadership-in-war-on-al-qaeda.html?pagewanted=all&_r=0.

4 Charlie Savage and Peter Baker, "Obama, in a Shift, to Limit Targets of Drone Strikes," *The New York Times*, (May 22, 2013), http://www.nytimes.com/2013/05/23/us/us-acknowledges-killing-4-americans-in-drone-strikes.html?pagewanted=all.

5 Scott Wilson, "Obama move to arm Syrian rebels comes as Assad gains upper hand," *The Washington Post*, (June 14, 2013), http://articles.washingtonpost.com/2013-06-14/politics/39970680_1_assad-syrian-rebels-bashar.

6 http://www.scotusblog.com/case-files/cases/maryland-v-king/.

7 Brandon L. Garrett, "You Don't Have the Right to Remain Silent," *Slate*, (June 19, 2013), http://www.slate.com/articles/news_and_politics/jurisprudence/2013/06/salinas_v_texas_right_to_remain_silent_supreme_court_right_to_remain_silent.html.

8 Bernie Sanders, "The American People Have Spoken: No More War Abroad, More Jobs at Home," *Huffington Post* (Sept. 12, 2013), http://www.huffingtonpost.com/rep-bernie-sanders/the-american-people-have_b_3916584.html.

9 "Iraq war 10th anniversary: A dark mark for news media," *Los Angeles Times*, (March 19, 2013), http://latimesblogs.latimes.com/lanow/2013/03/iraq-war-anniversary-a-dark-mark-for-the-news-media.html.

10 Carl Bernstein, "The CIA and the Media," *Carl Bernstein* (Accessed on October 29, 2014), http://www.carlbernstein.com/magazine_cia_and_media.php.

11 Carl Bernstein, "The CIA and the Media," *Carl Bernstein* (Accessed on October 29, 2014), http://www.carlbernstein.com/magazine_cia_and_media.php.

12 Hannah Arendt, *Responsibility and Judgment* (Knopf Doubleday Publishing Group, 2009), p. 111.

13 Mike Patton, "The Growth Of Government: 1980 To 2012," *Forbes* (Jan. 24, 2013), http://www.forbes.com/sites/mikepatton/2013/01/24/the-growth-of-the-federal-government-1980-to-2012/.

14 Julie Hanus, "Overcoming Fear Culture and Fear Itself," *Utne* (Jan.-Feb. 2009), https://www.utne.com/politics/overcoming-american-fear-culture-on-eve-of-new-presidency.aspx.

15 David Freeman, "Are Politicians Psychopaths?" *Huffington Post* (Aug. 27, 2012), http://www.huffingtonpost.com/david-freeman/are-politicians-psychopaths_b_1818648.html.

16 James Silver, "The Startling Accuracy of Referring to Politicians as 'Psychopaths,'" *The Atlantic* (July 31, 2012), http://www.theatlantic.com/health/archive/2012/07/the-startling-accuracy-of-referring-to-politicians-as-psychopaths/260517/#.

17 James G. Long, "The Road to Pathocracy," *American Thinker* (Aug. 2, 2014), http://www.americanthinker.com/2014/08/the_road_to_pathocracy.html.

18 Anthony Ramirez, "Outcry Over Use of Hitler Quote in Yearbook," *The New York Times* (June 18, 1999), http://www.nytimes.com/1999/06/18/nyregion/outcry-over-use-of-hitler-quote-in-yearbook.html.

Part III: The American Police State

1 C.S. Lewis, *Five Best Books in One Volume* (Canon Press, 1969), p. 6.

2 Hunter S. Thompson, *Kingdom of Fear: Loathsome Secrets of a Star-Crossed Child in the Final Days of the American Century* (Simon and Schuster, 2011), p. 107.

3 Sam Wood, "Ex-Philly police captain protests in Ferguson, blasts American policing," *Philly.com* (Nov. 26, 2014), http://www.philly.com/philly/news/Ex-Philly_police_captain_blasts_American_policing.html.

4 "Epidemic of Killer Cops: No Justice, No Peace!" *Media Roots*, (October 24, 2013), http://www.mediaroots.org/epidemic-of-killer-cops-no-justice-no-peace/.

5 "Fear of Terror Makes People Stupid," *Washington's Blog*, (June 21, 2011), http://www.washingtonsblog.com/2011/06/fear-of-terror-makes-people-stupid.html.

6 Michael Meurer, "Cantaloupe vs. al-Qaeda: What's More Dangerous?" *Truthout*, (September 15, 2013), http://truth-out.org/opinion/item/18715-cantaloupe-vs-al-qaeda.

7 Bill Gertz, "Inside the Ring: Memo outlines Obama's plan to use the military against citizens," *Washington Times* (May 28, 2014), http://www.washingtontimes.com/news/2014/may/28/inside-the-ring-directive-outlines-obamas-policy-t/?page=all#pagebreak.

8 Radley Balko, "How did America's police become a military force on the streets?" *ABA Journal*, (July 1, 2013), http://www.abajournal.com/magazine/article/how_did_americas_police_become_a_military_force_on_the_streets.

9 Danielle Kurtzleben, "Let Them Eat Cake: Members of Congress 14 Times More Wealthy Than Average American," *U.S. News* (Jan. 9, 2014), http://www.usnews.com/news/blogs/data-mine/2014/01/09/let-them-eat-cake-members-of-congress-14-times-more-wealthy-than-average-american.

10 Martin Gilens and Benjamin I. Page, "Testing Theories of American Politics: Elites, Interest Groups, and Average Citizens," *Princeton*, (April 9, 2014), https://www. princeton.edu/~mgilens/Gilens%20homepage%20materials/Gilens%20and%20 Page/Gilens%20and%20Page%202014-Testing%20Theories%203-7-14.pdf.

11 Joanna C. Schwartz, "Police Indemnification," *New York University Law, Volume 89:885* (June 2014), file:///Users/nishawhitehead/Desktop/SSRN-id2297534.pdf.

CHAPTER 16

1 Glenn Harlan Reynolds, "SWAT Overkill: The Danger of a Paramilitary Police Force," *Popular Mechanics* (Aug. 14, 2014), http://www.popularmechanics.com/technology/ military/paramilitary-police-force-ferguson?click=main_sr.

2 Patrick Henningsen, "Kafka's Amerika: A Society At War With Itself," *21st Century Wire* (April 9, 2014), http://21stcenturywire.com/2014/04/09/kafkas-amerika-a-society-at-war-with-itself/.

3 Ron Barnett and Paul Alongi, "Critics knock no-knock police raids," *USA Today* (Feb. 13, 2011), http://usatoday30.usatoday.com/news/nation/2011-02-14-noknock14_ST_N.htm.

4 Elina Shatkin, "Cops Raid Rawesome Foods; Owner James Stewart Arrested," *LA Weekly* (Aug. 3, 2011), http://www.laweekly.com/squidink/2011/08/03/cops-raid-rawesome-foods-owner-james-stewart-arrested.

5 Elizabeth Flock, "Occupy Wall Street protesters beaten, maced by police," *The Washington Post* (Oct. 6, 2011)< http://www.washingtonpost.com/blogs/worldviews/post/occupy-wall-street-protesters-get-beaten-maced-by-police-videos/2011/10/06/gIQAVdA3PL_blog.html.

6 Steve Almasy, "Newtown shooter's guns: What we know," *CNN* (Dec. 19, 2012), http://www.cnn.com/2012/12/18/us/connecticut-lanza-guns/index.html.

7 Christopher Ingraham, "The Pentagon gave nearly half a billion dollars of military gear to local law enforcement last year," *The Washington Post* (Aug. 14, 2014), http://www.washingtonpost.com/blogs/wonkblog/wp/2014/08/14/the-pentagon-gave-nearly-half-a-billion-dollars-of-military-gear-to-local-law-enforcement-last-year/.

8 Arezou Rezvani, Jessica Pupovac, David Eads and Tyler Fisher, "MRAPs And Bayonets: What We Know About The Pentagon's 1033 Program," *NPR* (Sept. 2, 2014), http://www.npr. org/2014/09/02/342494225/mraps-and-bayonets-what-we-know-about-the-pentagons-1033-program.

9 Michael Kunzelman, "Little restraint in military giveaways," *AP*, (July 31, 2013), http:// news.yahoo.com/ap-impact-little-restraint-military-giveaways-174255839.html.

10 Taylor Wofford, "How America's Police Became an Army: The 1033 Program," *Newsweek* (Aug. 13, 2014), http://www.newsweek.com/how-americas-police-became-army-1033-program-264537.

11 Michael Kunzelman, "Little restraint in military giveaways," *AP*, (July 31, 2013), http:// news.yahoo.com/ap-impact-little-restraint-military-giveaways-174255839.html.

12 Radley Balko, "How did America's police become a military force on the streets?" *ABA Journal*, (July 1, 2013), http://www.abajournal.com/magazine/article/how_did_ americas_police_become_a_military_force_on_the_streets.

13 Radley Balko, "How did America's police become a military force on the streets?" *ABA Journal*, (July 1, 2013), http://www.abajournal.com/magazine/article/how_did_ americas_police_become_a_military_force_on_the_streets.

14 "Practice Relating to Rule 77. Expanding Bullets," International Committee of the Red Cross (Accessed on October 14, 2014), https://www.icrc.org/customary-ihl/eng/docs/ v2_rul_rule77.

15 Eloise Lee and Robert Johnson, "The Department Of Homeland Security Is Buying 450 Million New Bullets," *Business Insider*, (March 28, 2012), http://www.businessinsider. com/us-immigration-agents-are-loading-up-on-as-many-as-450-million-new-rounds-of-ammo-2012-3.

16   Paul Joseph Watson, "DHS To Purchase Another 750 Million Rounds Of Ammo," *Prison Planet*, (August 13, 2012), http://www.prisonplanet.com/dhs-to-purchase-another-750-million-rounds-of-ammo.html.

17   "Request for Quote for Ammunition," *Federal Business Opportunities*, https://www.fbo.gov/index?s=opportunity&mode=form&id=6c39a2a9f00a10187a1432388a3301e5&tab=core&_cview=0&fb_source=message.

18   Paul Joseph Watson, "Social Security Administration To Purchase 174 Thousand Rounds Of Hollow Point Bullets," *Infowars*, (August 15, 2012), http://www.infowars.com/social-security-administration-to-purchase-174-thousand-rounds-of-hollow-point-bullets/.

19   Leonard Williams Levy, *Origins of the Bill of Rights* (Yale University Press, 2001), p. 158.

20   James Otis, *Against Writs of Assistance* (February 24, 1761), http://www.constitution.org/bor/otis_against_writs.htm.

21   "I call it the law of the instrument, and it may be formulated as follows: Give a small boy a hammer, and he will find that everything he encounters needs pounding."—Abraham Kaplan, *The Conduct of Inquiry: Methodology for Behavioral Science* (1964).

22   Speech by James Madison, *Constitutional Convention* (June 29, 1787).

CHAPTER 17

1   Kristian Williams, *Our Enemies in Blue* (South End Press, 2007), p. 9.

2   Woody Guthrie, "Vigilante Man," Woody Guthrie Publications, Inc. (1960), http://woodyguthrie.org/Lyrics/Vigilante_Man.htm.

3   Jim Harper, "You're Eight Times More Likely to be Killed by a Police Officer than a Terrorist," CATO Institute (Aug. 10, 2012), http://www.cato.org/blog/youre-eight-times-more-likely-be-killed-police-officer-terrorist.

4   Ted Conover, "A Snitch's Dilemma," *The New York Times*, (June 29, 2012), http://www.nytimes.com/2012/07/01/magazine/alex-white-professional-snitch.html?_r=4&ref=magazine&pagewanted=all&.

5   Christina Pascucci, "Widow to Sue Over Fatal Shooting of Husband, 80, by Sheriff's Deputies," *KTLA*, (October 2013), http://ktla.com/2013/10/10/widow-to-sue-over-fatal-shooting-of-husband-80-by-sheriffs-deputies/.

6   Jason Howerton, "Police Fatally Shoot Grandfather, 72, While Searching the Wrong Home for Burglar, Blame 'Poor Lighting,'" *The Blaze*, (July 27, 2013), http://www.theblaze.com/stories/2013/07/27/police-shoot-dead-grandfather-72-while-searching-the-wrong-home-for-burglar-blame-poor-lighting/#.

7   Ron Barnett and Paul Alongi, "Critics knock no-knock police raids," *USA Today* (Feb. 13, 2011), http://usatoday30.usatoday.com/news/nation/2011-02-14-noknock14_ST_N.htm.

8   Tom Lyons, "Police raid felt like home invasion," *The Herald-Tribune*, (July 18, 2013), http://www.heraldtribune.com/article/20130718/COLUMNIST/130719612?p=1&tc=pg.

9   Tom Lyons, "Police raid felt like home invasion," *The Herald-Tribune*, (July 18, 2013), http://www.heraldtribune.com/article/20130718/COLUMNIST/130719612?p=1&tc=pg.

10   Tom Lyons, "Police raid felt like home invasion," *The Herald-Tribune*, (July 18, 2013), http://www.heraldtribune.com/article/20130718/COLUMNIST/130719612?p=1&tc=pg.

11   Shawn Gude, "The Bad Kind of Unionism," *Jacobin*, https://www.jacobinmag.com/2014/01/the-bad-kind-of-unionism/.

12   Lucy Steigerwald, "What Happens to Cops Who Arrest Other Cops?" *VICE*, (February 18, 2014), http://www.vice.com/read/what-happens-to-cops-who-arrest-other-cops.

13   David Packman, "The Problem with Prosecuting Police in Washington State," *CATO Institute* (Feb. 27, 2011), http://www.policemisconduct.net/the-problem-with-prosecuting-police-in-washington-state/.

14   Erwin Chemerinsky, "How the Supreme Court Protects Bad Cops," *The New York Times* (Aug. 26, 2014), http://www.nytimes.com/2014/08/27/opinion/how-the-supreme-court-protects-bad-cops.html?_r=0.

15 Daniel Politi, "Police Shoot Bystanders in New York, Kill Unarmed Man in North Carolina," *Slate* (Sept. 15, 2013), http://www.slate.com/blogs/the_slatest/2013/09/15/police_shoot_bystanders_in_new_york_kill_unarmed_man_in_north_carolina.html.

CHAPTER 18

1 *As quoted in* Malcolm Gladwell, "The Crooked Ladder," *The New Yorker* (Aug. 11, 2014), http://www.newyorker.com/magazine/2014/08/11/crooked-ladder.

2 "Texas Gunowner Appeals No-Knock Raid On His Home," *The Rutherford Institute* (June 24, 2013), https://www.rutherford.org/publications_resources/tri_in_the_news/texas_gunowner_appeals_no_knock_raid_on_his_home.

3 Kevin Drum, "South Carolina Cop Unloads on Unarmed Driver Reaching for His License," *Mother Jones* (Sept. 25, 2014), http://www.motherjones.com/kevin-drum/2014/09/south-carolina-cop-unloads-unarmed-driver-reaching-his-license.

4 Rachel Dissell, "Cleveland police chase and shooting portrayed as chaotic scene by Ohio Attorney General Mike DeWine (video)," *Plain Dealer* (Feb. 5, 2013), http://www.cleveland.com/metro/index.ssf/2013/02/cleveland_police_chase_and_shooting_scene.html.

5 "Police officers admit shooting dead father who was holding a GARDEN HOSE nozzle after mistaking it for a gun," *Daily Mail* (Dec. 14, 2010), http://www.dailymail.co.uk/news/article-1338571/Douglas-Zerby-shot-dead-police-holding-GARDEN-HOSE-nozzle-gun-chief-admits.html#ixzz2YO9Fbgvq.

6 "Forced to fire?" KTLA, http://www.youtube.com/watch?v=Ow8bJ14VEvY#at=94.

7 "Police officers admit shooting dead father who was holding a GARDEN HOSE nozzle after mistaking it for a gun," *Daily Mail* (Dec. 14, 2010), http://www.dailymail.co.uk/news/article-1338571/Douglas-Zerby-shot-dead-police-holding-GARDEN-HOSE-nozzle-gun-chief-admits.html#ixzz2YO9Fbgvq.

8 "Calif. boy with pellet gun shot 7 times by deputy, autopsy finds," *FOX News*, (October 25, 2013), http://www.foxnews.com/us/2013/10/25/13-year-old-with-pellet-gun-shot-7-times-by-sheriff-deputy-autopsy-finds/.

9 "Calif. boy with pellet gun shot 7 times by deputy, autopsy finds," *FOX News*, (October 25, 2013), http://www.foxnews.com/us/2013/10/25/13-year-old-with-pellet-gun-shot-7-times-by-sheriff-deputy-autopsy-finds/.

10 William Norman Grigg, "A 'Fearful' Police Mindset Leads to a Dead Child," Lew Rockwell (Oct. 24, 2013), http://www.lewrockwell.com/lrc-blog/a-fearful-police-mindset-leads-to-a-dead-child/.

11 Lawrence Downes, "The Mayor, the Cops and the Chorus of Outrage," *The New York Times* (Aug. 17, 2014), http://www.nytimes.com/2014/08/18/opinion/the-mayor-the-police-and-eric-garner.html?_r=0.

12 Ryan Devereaux, "Eyewitness: Police Shot Kimani Gray While The 16-Year-Old Was On The Ground," *Village Voice* (March 18, 2013), http://blogs.villagevoice.com/runninscared/2013/03/kimani_gray_4.php.

13 Scott Kaufman, "NYC cops arrest human rights lawyer waiting outside restaurant while her kids used restroom," *Raw Story* (Sept. 4, 2014), http://www.rawstory.com/rs/2014/09/04/nyc-cops-arrest-human-rights-lawyer-waiting-outside-restaurant-while-her-kids-used-restroom/?onswipe_redirect=no&oswrr=1.

14 "Muslim lawyer sues NYPD after arrest for 'blocking the sidewalk' during pro-Palestinian rally," *RT* (Sept. 6, 2014), http://rt.com/usa/185596-lawyer-sues-nypd-muslim/.

15 Carlos Miller, "Oregon Man Arrested for Recording Militarized Police Raid in Neighborhood," *Photography Is Not a Crime* (Sept. 8, 2014), http://photographyisnotacrime.com/2014/09/08/oregon-man-arrested-recording-militarized-police-raid-neighborhood/.

16   Jason Howerton, "Man Was Recording 'Militarized' SWAT Raid When Things Took a Sudden Turn: 'At First I Was Scared to Post This Video…'" *The Blaze* (Sept. 8, 2014), http://www.theblaze.com/stories/2014/09/08/man-was-recording-militarized-swat-raid-when-things-took-a-sudden-turn-at-first-i-was-scared-to-post-this-video/.

17   Lawrence Downes, "The Mayor, the Cops and the Chorus of Outrage," *The New York Times* (Aug. 17, 2014), http://www.nytimes.com/2014/08/18/opinion/the-mayor-the-police-and-eric-garner.html?_r=0.

18   Yoav Goen and Amber Jamieson, "De Blasio Tells NYers: 'Don't resist arrest,'" *NY Post* (Aug. 13, 2014), http://nypost.com/2014/08/13/de-blasio-tells-new-yorkers-dont-resist-arrest/.

19   Philip Messing, Kirstan Conley and Daniel Prendergast, "Only a fraction of 'arrest resisters' are prosecuted," *NY Post* (Aug. 15, 2014), http://nypost.com/2014/08/15/too-few-resisting-arrest-suspects-are-prosecuted-nypd-official/.

20   Tiffany Madison, "The case of Brandon Raub: Can government detain you over Facebook?" *The Washington Times* (Aug. 22, 2012), http://communities.washingtontimes.com/neighborhood/citizen-warrior/2012/aug/22/can-government-detain-you-over-facebook-posts/#ixzz3GcQRwjVm.

21   Aaron Feis, "Bratton: Criminal suspects should not resist arrest," *NY Post* (Aug. 12, 2014), http://nypost.com/2014/08/12/bratton-criminal-suspects-should-not-resist-arrest/.

22   "Teen Says Police Overreacted To Incident," CBS Miami (May 28, 2013), http://miami.cbslocal.com/2013/05/28/teen-says-police-overreacted-to-incident/.

23   "Teen Says Police Overreacted To Incident," CBS Miami (May 28, 2013), http://miami.cbslocal.com/2013/05/28/teen-says-police-overreacted-to-incident/.

24   Titania Kumeh, "When Police Shoot And Kill Unarmed Men," *Mother Jones* (July 14, 2010), http://www.motherjones.com/mojo/2010/07/when-police-shoot-unarmed-man-oscar-grant-verdict-Mehserle.

25   "Fatal occupational injuries," *Bureau of Labor Statistics*, (2012), http://www.bls.gov/iif/oshwc/cfoi/cfoi_rates_2012hb.pdf.

26   "Epidemic of Killer Cops: No Justice, No Peace!" *Media Roots*, (October 24, 2013), http://www.mediaroots.org/epidemic-of-killer-cops-no-justice-no-peace/.

27   Kristian Williams, *Our Enemies in Blue* (South End Press, 2007), p. 19.

28   Katie Rucke, "Trained To Kill: The Policing Tactics The Public Isn't Supposed To Know About," *MintPress News* (June 2, 2014), http://www.mintpressnews.com/trained-to-kill-the-policing-tactics-the-public-isnt-supposed-to-know-about/191639/.

29   Katie Rucke, "Trained To Kill: The Policing Tactics The Public Isn't Supposed To Know About," *MintPress News* (June 2, 2014), http://www.mintpressnews.com/trained-to-kill-the-policing-tactics-the-public-isnt-supposed-to-know-about/191639/.

30   Katie Rucke, "Trained To Kill: The Policing Tactics The Public Isn't Supposed To Know About," *MintPress News* (June 2, 2014), http://www.mintpressnews.com/trained-to-kill-the-policing-tactics-the-public-isnt-supposed-to-know-about/191639/.

31   Katie Rucke, "Trained To Kill: The Policing Tactics The Public Isn't Supposed To Know About," *MintPress News* (June 2, 2014), http://www.mintpressnews.com/trained-to-kill-the-policing-tactics-the-public-isnt-supposed-to-know-about/191639/.

32   Jaclyn Belczyk, "Supreme Court rules for police in fatal car chase," *Jurist* (May 27, 2014), http://jurist.org/paperchase/2014/05/supreme-court-rules-for-police-in-fatal-car-chase.php.

CHAPTER 19

1   William Norman Grigg, "'We Have Been a Paramilitary Organization': How the Police Talk When They Think We're Not Listening," *Lew Rockwell.com* (Sept. 22, 2014), https://www.lewrockwell.com/2014/09/william-norman-grigg/chilling-lingo-of-cops/.

2   J.D. Tuccille, "All Police Shootings of Dogs Have Been Justified, Says Houston Police Department," *Reason* (May 17, 2013), http://reason.com/blog/2013/05/17/all-police-shootings-of-dogs-have-been-j.

3   "Family pet shot in the head by plainclothes cops searching at wrong address," *Police State USA* (Aug. 6, 2014), http://www.policestateusa.com/2014/justice-for-lady-erie-county-ny/#prettyPhoto.

4   "Toddler critically burned during SWAT raid," *WSB-TV*, (May 30, 2014), http://www.wsbtv.com/news/news/local/toddler-critically-burned-during-swat-raid/nf9SJ/?GxbuEu.

5   "Times Square shooting: NYPD officers shoot two innocent bystanders near Times Square," *CBS News* (Sept. 15, 2013), http://www.cbsnews.com/8301-201_162-57602998/times-square-shooting-nypd-officers-shoot-two-innocent-bystanders-near-times-square/.

6   "Homeland Security agents use 1,000 more bullets each than Army soldiers," *RT*, (April 26, 2013), http://rt.com/usa/army-million-rounds-dhs-472/.

7   Sadhbh Walshe, "How US prison labour pads corporate profits at taxpayers' expense," *The Guardian*, (July 6, 2012), http://www.theguardian.com/commentisfree/2012/jul/06/prison-labor-pads-corporate-profits-taxpayers-expense/.

8   Kristian Williams, *Our Enemies in Blue* (South End Press, 2007), p. 20.

9   Mike Riggs, "St. Paul Cops Shoot Dog in Wrong-Door Raid, Force Handcuffed Kids to Sit Near the Corpse," *Reason* (Aug. 10, 2012), http://reason.com/blog/2012/08/10/st-paul-cops-shoot-dog-in-wrong-door-rai.

10   Virginia Hennessey, "Monterey County agrees to pay $2.6 million in 'flash-bang' death of Greenfield man," *Monterey Herald* (Aug. 19, 2013), http://www.montereyherald.com/crime_courts/ci_23897554/monterey-county-agrees-pay-2-6-million-flash.

11   Virginia Hennessey, "Monterey County agrees to pay $2.6 million in 'flash-bang' death of Greenfield man," *Monterey Herald* (Aug. 19, 2013), http://www.montereyherald.com/crime_courts/ci_23897554/monterey-county-agrees-pay-2-6-million-flash.

12   "Cops or soldiers?" *The Economist*, (March 22, 2014), http://www.economist.com/news/united-states/21599349-americas-police-have-become-too-militarised-cops-or-soldiers?src=prb%2Fcopsorsoldiers.

13   "SWAT locks down California school for 4 hours during class-by-class weapons search," *Police State USA* (June 2, 2014), http://www.policestateusa.com/2014/dana-point-high-school-swat-lockdown/.

14   Kevin Mathews, "5 Unnecessary SWAT Team Raids Gone Terribly Wrong," *Care2* (Dec. 13, 2013), http://www.care2.com/causes/5-unnecessary-swat-team-raids-gone-terribly-wrong.html#ixzz33Q3eMvaK.

15   Kevin Johnson, "Police get help with vets who are ticking bombs," *USA Today* (Jan. 26, 2012), http://usatoday30.usatoday.com/news/washington/story/2012-01-24/police-training-combative-veterans/52794974/1.

16   Marcella Lee and Richard Allyn, "Gunman killed in standoff identified as Vietnam veteran," CBS 8 (Feb. 26, 2014), http://www.cbs8.com/story/24830627/gunman-making-threats-downtown.

17   Shern-Min Chow, "Soldier speaks out about 'target practice' that triggered SWAT scene," KHOU Houston (Feb. 19, 2014), http://www.khou.com/news/local/Man-accused-of-being-active-shooter-in--246189281.html.

18   Kevin Mathews, "5 Unnecessary SWAT Team Raids Gone Terribly Wrong," *Care2* (Dec. 13, 2013), http://www.care2.com/causes/5-unnecessary-swat-team-raids-gone-terribly-wrong.html#ixzz33Q3eMvaK.

19   "Cops or soldiers?" *The Economist*, (March 22, 2014), http://www.economist.com/news/united-states/21599349-americas-police-have-become-too-militarised-cops-or-soldiers?src=prb%2Fcopsorsoldiers.

20   Kevin Mathews, "5 Unnecessary SWAT Team Raids Gone Terribly Wrong," *Care2* (Dec. 13, 2013), http://www.care2.com/causes/5-unnecessary-swat-team-raids-gone-terribly-wrong.html#ixzz33Q3eMvaK.

21 Radley Balko, "How did America's police become a military force on the streets?" *ABA Journal*, (July 1, 2013), http://www.abajournal.com/magazine/article/how_did_ americas_police_become_a_military_force_on_the_streets.

22 Ron Barnett and Paul Alongi, "Critics knock no-knock police raids," *USA Today* (Feb. 13, 2011), http://usatoday30.usatoday.com/news/nation/2011-02-14-noknock14_ST_N. htm.

23 Radley Balko, "How did America's police become a military force on the streets?" *ABA Journal*, (July 1, 2013), http://www.abajournal.com/magazine/article/how_did_ americas_police_become_a_military_force_on_the_streets.

24 Colleen Henry, "Armed agents raid animal shelter for baby deer," *WISN*, (August 1, 2013), http://www.wisn.com/armed-agents-raid-animal-shelter-for-baby-deer/- /9374034/21272108/-/98e07f/-/index.html.

25 Colleen Henry, "Armed agents raid animal shelter for baby deer," *WISN*, (August 1, 2013), http://www.wisn.com/armed-agents-raid-animal-shelter-for-baby-deer/- /9374034/21272108/-/98e07f/-/index.html.

26 Michael Kunzelman, "Little restraint in military giveaways," *AP*, (July 31, 2013), http:// news.yahoo.com/ap-impact-little-restraint-military-giveaways-174255839.html.

27 Radley Balko, "How did America's police become a military force on the streets?" *ABA Journal*, (July 1, 2013), http://www.abajournal.com/magazine/article/how_did_ americas_police_become_a_military_force_on_the_streets.

28 Radley Balko, "How did America's police become a military force on the streets?" *ABA Journal*, (July 1, 2013), http://www.abajournal.com/magazine/article/how_did_ americas_police_become_a_military_force_on_the_streets.

29 "Anthony Mitchell Lawsuit: Cops Violated Third Amendment, Occupied Home, Complaint States," *The Huffington Post*, (July 7, 2013), http://www.huffingtonpost. com/2013/07/07/anthony-mitchell-lawsuit-third-amendment-_n_3557431.html.

30 Radley Balko, "How did America's police become a military force on the streets?" *ABA Journal*, (July 1, 2013), http://www.abajournal.com/magazine/article/how_did_ americas_police_become_a_military_force_on_the_streets.

31 Radley Balko, "How did America's police become a military force on the streets?" *ABA Journal*, (July 1, 2013), http://www.abajournal.com/magazine/article/how_did_ americas_police_become_a_military_force_on_the_streets.

CHAPTER 20

1 Andrew Becker and G. W. Schulz, "Local Cops Ready for War With Homeland Security-Funded Military Weapons," *The Daily Beast*, (December 21, 2011), http://www. thedailybeast.com/articles/2011/12/20/local-cops-ready-for-war-with-homeland-security-funded-military-weapons.html.

2 Terry Frieden, "U.S. violent crime down for fifth straight year," *CNN*, (October 29, 2012), http://www.cnn.com/2012/10/29/justice/us-violent-crime.

3 James Rainey and Joel Rubin, "LAPD's 'magic number' of 10,000 officers losing some luster," *The Los Angeles Times*, (April 28, 2013), http://www.latimes.com/news/local/ la-me-lapd-10k-20130429,0,7160383.story?track=lat-email-topofthetimes.

4 "Bloomberg: 'I have my own army,'" *RT*, (November 30, 2011), http://rt.com/usa/bloomberg-nypd-army-york-599/.

5 James Rainey and Joel Rubin, "LAPD's 'magic number' of 10,000 officers losing some luster," *The Los Angeles Times*, (April 28, 2013), http://www.latimes.com/news/local/ la-me-lapd-10k-20130429,0,7160383.story?track=lat-email-topofthetimes.

6 Whet Moser, "City Size and Police Presence," *Chicago Mag* (Aug. 30, 2012), http://www. chicagomag.com/Chicago-Magazine/The-312/August-2012/City-Size-and-Police-Presence/.

7 Whet Moser, "City Size and Police Presence," *Chicago Mag* (Aug. 30, 2012), http://www. chicagomag.com/Chicago-Magazine/The-312/August-2012/City-Size-and-Police-Presence/.

8 James Rainey and Joel Rubin, "LAPD's 'magic number' of 10,000 officers losing some luster," *The Los Angeles Times*, (April 28, 2013), http://www.latimes.com/news/local/la-me-lapd-10k-20130429,0,7160383.story?track=lat-email-topofthetimes.

9 James Rainey and Joel Rubin, "LAPD's 'magic number' of 10,000 officers losing some luster," *The Los Angeles Times*, (April 28, 2013), http://www.latimes.com/news/local/la-me-lapd-10k-20130429,0,7160383.story?track=lat-email-topofthetimes.

10 "Reality TV's Top Cop Shows," *MSN Entertainment*, http://tv.msn.com/reality-tv-cop-shows/photo-gallery/feature/.

11 Andrew Becker and G. W. Schulz, "Local Cops Ready for War With Homeland Security-Funded Military Weapons," *The Daily Beast*, (December 21, 2011), http://www.thedailybeast.com/articles/2011/12/20/local-cops-ready-for-war-with-homeland-security-funded-military-weapons.html.

12 Michael Kunzelman, "Military Surplus Diverted to Political Departments with Little Oversight," *Huffington Post*, (July 31, 2013), http://www.huffingtonpost.com/2013/07/31/military-surplus-police_n_3684683.html.

13 Andrew Becker and G. W. Schulz, "Local Cops Ready for War With Homeland Security-Funded Military Weapons," *The Daily Beast*, (December 21, 2011), http://www.thedailybeast.com/articles/2011/12/20/local-cops-ready-for-war-with-homeland-security-funded-military-weapons.html.

14 Andrew Becker and G. W. Schulz, "Local Cops Ready for War With Homeland Security-Funded Military Weapons," *The Daily Beast*, (December 21, 2011), http://www.thedailybeast.com/articles/2011/12/20/local-cops-ready-for-war-with-homeland-security-funded-military-weapons.html.

15 Michael Shank and Elizabeth Beavers, "America's police are looking more and more like the military," *The Guardian*, (October 7, 2013), http://www.theguardian.com/commentisfree/2013/oct/07/militarization-local-police-america.

16 Michael Shank and Elizabeth Beavers, "The militarization of U.S. police forces," *Reuters*, (October 22, 2013), http://blogs.reuters.com/great-debate/2013/10/22/the-militarization-of-u-s-police-forces/.

17 Justin L. Mack, "West Lafayette police acquire military vehicle," *jconline.com*, (October 31, 2013), http://www.jconline.com/article/20131031/NEWS/310310038/Purdue-tank-police-riot?nclick_check=1.

18 Eric Owens, "The cops at Ohio State have an armored fighting vehicle now," *The Daily Caller*, (September 17, 2013), http://dailycaller.com/2013/09/17/the-cops-at-ohio-state-have-an-armored-fighting-vehicle-now/.

19 Benjamin Preston, "Police Are Getting the Military's Leftover Armored Trucks," *The New York Times*, (October 11, 2013), http://wheels.blogs.nytimes.com/2013/10/11/police-are-getting-the-militarys-leftover-armored-trucks/?_r=0.

20 Michael Shank and Elizabeth Beavers, "America's police are looking more and more like the military," *The Guardian*, (October 7, 2013), http://www.theguardian.com/commentisfree/2013/oct/07/militarization-local-police-america.

21 Michael Shank and Elizabeth Beavers, "The militarization of U.S. police forces," *Reuters*, (October 22, 2013), http://blogs.reuters.com/great-debate/2013/10/22/the-militarization-of-u-s-police-forces/.

22 Scott Kaufman, "Seattle police department has network that can track all Wi-Fi enabled devices," *Raw Story*, (November 10, 2013), http://www.rawstory.com/rs/2013/11/10/seattle-police-department-has-network-that-can-track-all-wi-fi-enabled-devices/.

23 "Police deactivating controversial WiFi network in Seattle," *KOMO News*, (November 13, 2013), http://www.komonews.com/news/local/Police-deactivating-controversial-WiFi-network-in-Seattle-231692161.html.

24 Andrew Becker and G. W. Schulz, "Local Cops Ready for War With Homeland Security-Funded Military Weapons," *The Daily Beast*, (December 21, 2011), http://www.thedailybeast.com/articles/2011/12/20/local-cops-ready-for-war-with-homeland-security-funded-military-weapons.html.

25 Jodie Gummow, "The Shocking Tales of 11 of the Most Over the Top US Police Paramilitary Raids and the Innocent People They Victimized," *Alternet*, (August 20, 2013), http://www.alternet.org/civil-liberties/shocking-tales-11-most-over-top-us-police-paramilitary-raids-and-innocent-people?paging=off&current_page=1#bookmark.

CHAPTER 21

1 *Terry v. Ohio*, 1967, http://www.law.cornell.edu/supremecourt/text/392/1.

2 Anthony M. Townsend, "Your city is spying on you: From iPhones to cameras, you are being watched right now," *Salon*, (October 13, 2013), http://www.salon.com/2013/10/13/your_city_is_spying_on_you_from_iphones_to_cameras_you_are_being_watched_right_now/.

3 Robert Faturechi and Matt Stevens, "Police seeking Dorner opened fire in a second case of mistaken identity," *Los Angeles Times* (Feb. 9, 2013), http://articles.latimes.com/2013/feb/09/local/la-me-torrance-shooting-20130210.

4 http://www.scotusblog.com/case-files/cases/plumhoff-v-rickard/.

5 http://www.scotusblog.com/case-files/cases/navarette-v-california/.

6 Nat Hentoff, "Suddenly More Americanized Supreme Court Has Long Way Ahead to Do More," Cato Institute (July 2, 2014), http://www.cato.org/publications/commentary/suddenly-more-americanized-supreme-court-has-long-way-ahead-do-more.

7 http://www.scotusblog.com/case-files/cases/wood-v-moss/.

8 Richard F. Albert, "The Supreme Court's Decision In Salinas v. Texas: Implications For White Collar Investigations," Forbes (June 19, 2013), http://www.forbes.com/sites/insider/2013/06/19/the-supreme-courts-decision-in-salinas-v-texas-implications-for-white-collar-investigations/.

9 http://www.scotusblog.com/case-files/cases/florida-v-harris/.

10 Alexandra Horowitz, "What the Dog Knows," *New Yorker* (Feb. 23, 2013), http://www.newyorker.com/online/blogs/newsdesk/2013/02/what-the-dog-knows.html.

11 Barry Friedman, "The Supreme Court Fails the Fourth Amendment Test," *Slate* (June 5, 2013), http://www.slate.com/articles/news_and_politics/jurisprudence/2013/06/dna_collection_in_maryland_v_king_the_supreme_court_fails_on_the_fourth.html.

12 Robert Barnes, "Supreme Court upholds key part of Arizona law for now, strikes down other provisions," *The Washington Post* (June 25, 2012), http://www.washingtonpost.com/politics/supreme-court-rules-on-arizona-immigration-law/2012/06/25/gJQA0Nrm1V_story.html.

13 http://www.scotusblog.com/case-files/cases/florence-v-board-of-chosen-freeholders-of-the-county-of-burlington/.

14 "Supreme Court Decision: Reichle v. Howards," *The New York Times* (June 5, 2012), http://www.nytimes.com/interactive/2012/06/05/us/05scotus-document.html?ref=us.

15 Andy Kroll, "The Supreme Court Just Gutted Another Campaign Finance Law. Here's What Happened." *Mother Jones* (April 2, 2014), http://www.motherjones.com/politics/2014/03/supreme-court-mccutcheon-citizens-united.

16 Adam Liptak, "Search Allowed if Police Hear Evidence Being Destroyed," *The New York Times* (May 16, 2011), http://www.nytimes.com/2011/05/17/us/17scotus.html?_r=0.

17 http://www.scotusblog.com/case-files/cases/alford-v-greene/.

18 Charles Lane, "Refusing to Give Name a Crime," *The Washington Post* (June 22, 2004), http://www.washingtonpost.com/wp-dyn/articles/A57604-2004Jun21.html.

19 Katie Rucke, "Does The 4th Amendment Apply To Gun Owners?" *MintPress News* (March 17, 2014), http://www.mintpressnews.com/does-the-4th-amendment-apply-to-gun-owners/186627/.

20 Lawrence Hurley, "Supreme Court rejects hearing on military detention case," *Reuters* (April 28, 2014), http://www.reuters.com/article/2014/04/28/us-usa-court-security-idUSBREA3R0YH20140428.

21 "Supreme Court Won't Hear Central High Drug Search Case," *Ozarks First* (Oct. 9, 2013), http://www.ozarksfirst.com/story/supreme-court-wont-hear-central-high-drug-search-case/d/story/aYOdeKEJDEyD5kQdn6hxig.

22   *Brooks v. City of Seattle,* http://cdn.ca9.uscourts.gov/datastore/opinions/2010/03/26/08-35526.pdf.

23   Robert Gellately, *Backing Hitler: Consent and Coercion in Nazi Germany* (Oxford University Press, 2001), p. 49.

CHAPTER 22

1   James Madison, *Journal of the Federal Convention* (The Lawbook Exchange, 2008), p. 265.

2   Michael Coleman, "MISSION CREEP: NM footprint grows: 'We've up-armored,'" *Albuquerque Journal,* (April 28, 2014), http://www.abqjournal.com/390807/news/nm-footprint-grows-weve-uparmored.html.

3   Michael Coleman, "MISSION CREEP: Homeland Security a 'runaway train,'" *Albuquerque Journal,* (April 27, 2014), http://www.abqjournal.com/390438/news/homeland-security-a-runaway-train.html.

4   Michael Coleman, "MISSION CREEP: Homeland Security a 'runaway train,'" *Albuquerque Journal,* (April 27, 2014), http://www.abqjournal.com/390438/news/homeland-security-a-runaway-train.html.

5   Michael Coleman, "MISSION CREEP: Homeland Security a 'runaway train,'" *Albuquerque Journal,* (April 27, 2014), http://www.abqjournal.com/390438/news/homeland-security-a-runaway-train.html.

6   Jennifer Levitz, "Towns Say 'No Tanks' to Militarized Police," *Wall Street Journal* (Feb. 7, 2014), http://online.wsj.com/news/articles/SB10001424052702304450904579366963588434656.

7   Andrew Becker and G.W. Schulz, "Local Cops Ready for War With Homeland Security-Funded Military Weapons," *Daily Beast* (Dec. 21, 2011), http://www.thedailybeast.com/articles/2011/12/20/local-cops-ready-for-war-with-homeland-security-funded-military-weapons.html.

8   Ralph Benko, "1.6 Billion Rounds Of Ammo For Homeland Security? It's Time For A National Conversation," *Forbes* (March 11, 2013), http://www.forbes.com/sites/ralphbenko/2013/03/11/1-6-billion-rounds-of-ammo-for-homeland-security-its-time-for-a-national-conversation/.

9   Maria Cramer, "Police response training planned, but bombs hit first," *Boston Globe* (June 8, 2013), http://www.bostonglobe.com/metro/2013/06/07/before-police-could-plan-for-terrorist-attack-real-thing-happened/ufxjb9OORXyzVZNPFyGkiI/story.html.

10   Bruce Finley, "Terror watch uses local eyes," *Denver Post* (June 29, 2008), http://www.denverpost.com/news/ci_9725077.

11   "Letter to Rep. Bennie G. Thompson and Peter T. King," Privacy Coalition (Oct. 23, 2009), http://privacycoalition.org/DHS_CPO_Priv_Coal_Letter.pdf.

12   Susan Stellin, "Security Check Now Starts Long Before You Fly," *The New York Times,* (October 21, 2013), http://www.nytimes.com/2013/10/22/business/security-check-now-starts-long-before-you-fly.html.

13   Susan Stellin, "Security Check Now Starts Long Before You Fly," *The New York Times,* (October 21, 2013), http://www.nytimes.com/2013/10/22/business/security-check-now-starts-long-before-you-fly.html.

14   Charlie Savage, "US doles out millions for street cameras," *Boston Globe* (Aug. 12, 2007), http://www.boston.com/news/nation/washington/articles/2007/08/12/us_doles_out_millions_for_street_cameras/?page=full.

15   Darwin Bond-Graham and Ali Winston, "Forget the NSA, the LAPD Spies on Millions of Innocent Folks," *LA Weekly* (Feb. 27, 2014), http://www.laweekly.com/2014-02-27/news/forget-the-nsa-la-cops-spy-on-millions-of-innocent-folks/.

16   C.J. Ciaramella, "DHS Building National License Plate Reader Database," *Free Beacon* (Feb. 17, 2014), http://freebeacon.com/issues/dhs-building-national-license-plate-reader-database/.

17   Tim Cushing, "The DHS May Have (Publicly) Dumped Its License Plate Database Plans But It Still Has Access To Millions Of Records," *Techdirt* (March 18, 2014), https://www.techdirt.com/articles/20140312/12072426552/dhs-may-have-publicly-dumped-its-license-plate-database-plans-it-still-has-access-to-millions-records.shtml.

18   Ken Broder, "Local Cops Throughout the State Use Anti-Terrorism Stingrays to Track Cellphone Users," *AllGov* (June 13, 2014), http://www.allgov.com/usa/ca/news/top-stories/local-cops-throughout-the-state-use-anti-terrorism-stingrays-to-track-cellphone-users-140613?news=853393.

19   Ken Broder, "Local Cops Throughout the State Use Anti-Terrorism Stingrays to Track Cellphone Users," *AllGov* (June 13, 2014), http://www.allgov.com/usa/ca/news/top-stories/local-cops-throughout-the-state-use-anti-terrorism-stingrays-to-track-cellphone-users-140613?news=853393.

20   Michael Coleman, "MISSION CREEP: NM footprint grows: 'We've up-armored,'" *Albuquerque Journal*, (April 28, 2014), http://www.abqjournal.com/390807/news/nm-footprint-grows-weve-uparmored.html.

21   Michael Coleman, "MISSION CREEP: NM footprint grows: 'We've up-armored,'" *Albuquerque Journal*, (April 28, 2014), http://www.abqjournal.com/390807/news/nm-footprint-grows-weve-uparmored.html.

22   Michael Coleman, "MISSION CREEP: NM footprint grows: 'We've up-armored,'" *Albuquerque Journal*, (April 28, 2014), http://www.abqjournal.com/390807/news/nm-footprint-grows-weve-uparmored.html.

23   Robert Beckhusen, "5 Homeland Security 'Bots Coming to Spy on You (If They Aren't Already)," *Wired* (Feb. 8, 2013), http://www.wired.com/2013/02/dhs-drones/?pid=1804&viewall=true.

24   Trevor Timm, "Homeland Security Wants to More Than Double Its Predator Drone Fleet Inside the US, Despite Safety and Privacy Concerns," *Electronic Frontier Foundation* (Nov. 20, 2012), https://www.eff.org/deeplinks/2012/11/homeland-security-wants-more-double-its-predator-drone-fleet-inside-us-despite.

25   Trevor Timm, "Homeland Security Wants to More Than Double Its Predator Drone Fleet Inside the US, Despite Safety and Privacy Concerns," *Electronic Frontier Foundation* (Nov. 20, 2012), https://www.eff.org/deeplinks/2012/11/homeland-security-wants-more-double-its-predator-drone-fleet-inside-us-despite.

26   Andrea Stone, "Drone Program Aims To 'Accelerate' Use Of Unmanned Aircraft By Police," *Huffington Post* (May 22, 2012), http://www.huffingtonpost.com/2012/05/22/drones-dhs-program-unmanned-aircraft-police_n_1537074.html.

27   Rachel L. Swarns, "Halliburton Subsidiary Gets Contract to Add Temporary Immigration Detention Centers," *The New York Times* (Feb. 4, 2006), http://www.nytimes.com/2006/02/04/national/04halliburton.html?_r=3&.

28   Rachel L. Swarns, "Halliburton Subsidiary Gets Contract to Add Temporary Immigration Detention Centers," *The New York Times* (Feb. 4, 2006), http://www.nytimes.com/2006/02/04/national/04halliburton.html?_r=3&.

29   O. Ricardo Pimentel, "Beware, that 'border' is actually 100 miles deep," *San Antonio Express-News* (Aug. 1, 2014), http://www.mysanantonio.com/opinion/opinion_columnists/o_ricardo_pimentel/article/Beware-that-border-is-actually-100-miles-deep-5660862.php.

30   "Constitution 'exemption' zone spans 100 miles inland of US border– judge," *RT*, (December 31, 2013), http://rt.com/usa/court-upholds-laptop-border-searches-041/.

31   Ron Nixon, "T.S.A. Expands Duties Beyond Airport Security," *The New York Times* (Aug. 5, 2013), http://www.nytimes.com/2013/08/06/us/tsa-expands-duties-beyond-airport-security.html?pagewanted=all&_r=0.

32   Millard K. Ives, "Training exercise startles locals," *Daily Commercial* (Jan. 4, 2012), http://assets.mediaspanonline.com/prod/7511966/01-04-2012_A-01.pdf.

33 Radley Balko, "DHS: A wasteful, growing, fear-mongering beast," *The Washington Post* (May 7, 2014), http://www.washingtonpost.com/news/the-watch/wp/2014/05/07/dhs-a-wasteful-growing-fear-mongering-beast/.

34 Charles Kenny, "The Case for Abolishing the DHS," *Business Week* (July 15, 2013), http://www.businessweek.com/articles/2013-07-15/the-case-for-abolishing-the-dhs.

35 Joe O'Sullivan, "State gets millions in homeland security grants, but where does it go?" *Rapid City Journal* (June 8, 2014), http://rapidcityjournal.com/news/local/state-gets-millions-in-homeland-security-grants-but-where-does/article_1be9acf1-b8e6-5bdb-a01d-5d2e4e2362ca.html.

CHAPTER 23

1 McLean Gordon, "You're as Evil as Your Social Network—What the Prison Experiment Got Wrong," *Motherboard* (Dec. 11, 2012), http://motherboard.vice.com/blog/you-are-as-evil-as-your-social-network-alexander-haslam-on-what-the-prison-experiment-got-wrong.

2 McLean Gordon, "You're as Evil as Your Social Network—What the Prison Experiment Got Wrong," *Motherboard* (Dec. 11, 2012), http://motherboard.vice.com/blog/you-are-as-evil-as-your-social-network-alexander-haslam-on-what-the-prison-experiment-got-wrong.

3 Fred Kaplan, "The Woman Who Saw Banality in Evil," *The New York Times* (May 24, 2013), http://www.nytimes.com/2013/05/26/movies/hannah-arendt-directed-by-margarethe-von-trotta.html?pagewanted=all.

4 McLean Gordon, "You're as Evil as Your Social Network—What the Prison Experiment Got Wrong," *Motherboard* (Dec. 11, 2012), http://motherboard.vice.com/blog/you-are-as-evil-as-your-social-network-alexander-haslam-on-what-the-prison-experiment-got-wrong.

5 Stanley Milgram, "Behavioral Study of Obedience," *Journal of Abnormal and Social Psychology 67*, no. 4 (1963): 371-8, http://psycnet.apa.org/journals/abn/67/4/371.pdf.

6 A confederate is a person who is hired by the experimenter to play a subject. In reality, confederates are actors who are aware of the purpose of the experiment. In Milgram the confederates pretended to receive painful shocks, but in reality, no shocks were administered.

7 Jerry Burger, "Replicating Milgram: Would people still obey today?," *American Psychologist* 64, no. 1 (2009): 1-11, accessed June 20, 2012, http://psycnet.apa.org/journals/amp/64/1/1.

8 Philip Zimbardo, "Stanford Prison Experiment: A Simulation Study of the Psychology of Imprisonment," (1971), www.prisonexp.org.

9 Norm Stamper, "Occupy the Police," *Nation 293*, no. 22, (2011): 6-8, http://web.ebscohost.com/ehost/pdfviewer/pdfviewer?sid=9ccce215-f1d0-4873-9c52-57192c54859c%40sessionmgr114&vid=4&hid=126.

10 Eungkyoon Lee, "Socio-Political Contexts, Identity Formation and Regulatory Compliance," *Administration and Society 40*, no. 7, (2008): 741-769, http://aas.sagepub.com/content/40/7/741.full.pdf+html.

11 McLean Gordon, "You're as Evil as Your Social Network—What the Prison Experiment Got Wrong," *Motherboard* (Dec. 11, 2012), http://motherboard.vice.com/blog/you-are-as-evil-as-your-social-network-alexander-haslam-on-what-the-prison-experiment-got-wrong.

12 McLean Gordon, "You're as Evil as Your Social Network—What the Prison Experiment Got Wrong," *Motherboard* (Dec. 11, 2012), http://motherboard.vice.com/blog/you-are-as-evil-as-your-social-network-alexander-haslam-on-what-the-prison-experiment-got-wrong.

13 McLean Gordon, "You're as Evil as Your Social Network—What the Prison Experiment Got Wrong," *Motherboard* (Dec. 11, 2012), http://motherboard.vice.com/blog/you-are-as-evil-as-your-social-network-alexander-haslam-on-what-the-prison-experiment-got-wrong.

14   McLean Gordon, "You're as Evil as Your Social Network—What the Prison Experiment Got Wrong," *Motherboard* (Dec. 11, 2012), http://motherboard.vice.com/blog/you-are-as-evil-as-your-social-network-alexander-haslam-on-what-the-prison-experiment-got-wrong.

15   Bonnie Kristian, "Seven Reasons Police Brutality Is Systemic, Not Anecdotal," *The American Conservative* (July 2, 2014), http://www.theamericanconservative.com/seven-reasons-police-brutality-is-systematic-not-anecdotal/.

16   Charles Davis, "Is Obedience the Only Way to Avoid Police Brutality?" *Vice* (Sept. 15, 2014), http://www.vice.com/read/is-obedience-the-only-way-to-avoid-police-brutality-915.

17   Charles Davis, "Is Obedience the Only Way to Avoid Police Brutality?" *Vice* (Sept. 15, 2014), http://www.vice.com/read/is-obedience-the-only-way-to-avoid-police-brutality-915.

18   Bernie Suarez, "Are Police One of the Mental Casualties of the New World Order?" *Truth and Art TV* (April 27, 2014), http://truthandarttv.com/read_91098.

19   Bernie Suarez, "Are Police One of the Mental Casualties of the New World Order?" *Truth and Art TV* (April 27, 2014), http://truthandarttv.com/read_91098.

20   Bonnie Kristian, "Seven Reasons Police Brutality Is Systemic, Not Anecdotal," *The American Conservative* (July 2, 2014), http://www.theamericanconservative.com/seven-reasons-police-brutality-is-systematic-not-anecdotal/.

21   Bonnie Kristian, "Seven Reasons Police Brutality Is Systemic, Not Anecdotal," *The American Conservative* (July 2, 2014), http://www.theamericanconservative.com/seven-reasons-police-brutality-is-systematic-not-anecdotal/.

22   Conor Friedersdorf, "Police Have a Much Bigger Domestic-Abuse Problem Than the NFL Does," *The Atlantic* (Sept. 19, 2014), http://www.theatlantic.com/national/archive/2014/09/police-officers-who-hit-their-wives-or-girlfriends/380329/.

23   *As quoted in* Lindsay Krishna Coleman, "The Whore with the Vampire Heart," *Undead in the West: Vampires, Zombies, Mummies, and Ghosts on the Cinematic Frontier* (Scarecrow Press, 2012), p. 40.

Part IV: The American Surveillance State

1   Pratap Chatterjee, "The Data Hackers," *Truthdig*, (October 11, 2013), http://www.truthdig.com/report/page2/the_data_hackers_20131011.

2   *Osborn v. United States*, 385 U.S. 323, 343 (1966) (dissenting).

3   Kristin Tate, "Latest Assault on Privacy: Grocery Store Shelves That Watch You," *Ben Swann*, (October 2013), http://benswann.com/latest-assault-on-privacy-grocery-store-shelves-that-watch-you/.

4   Jennifer Lynch, "FBI to have 52 million photos in its NGI face recognition database by next year," *ArsTechnica*, (April 14, 2014), http://arstechnica.com/tech-policy/2014/04/fbi-to-have-52-million-photos-in-its-ngi-face-recognition-database-by-next-year/.

5   Jennifer Lynch, "FBI to have 52 million photos in its NGI face recognition database by next year," *ArsTechnica*, (April 14, 2014), http://arstechnica.com/tech-policy/2014/04/fbi-to-have-52-million-photos-in-its-ngi-face-recognition-database-by-next-year/.

6   Sarah Kellogg, "Drones: Coming to the Skies Near You," *DC Bar Journal*, (August 2013), http://www.dcbar.org/for_lawyers/resources/publications/washington_lawyer/august_2013/drones.cfm.

7   Sarah Kellogg, "Drones: Coming to the Skies Near You," *DC Bar Journal*, (August 2013), http://www.dcbar.org/for_lawyers/resources/publications/washington_lawyer/august_2013/drones.cfm.

8   Bruno Waterfield and Matthew Day, "EU has secret plan for police to 'remote stop' cars," *The Telegraph*, (January 29, 2014), http://www.telegraph.co.uk/news/worldnews/europe/eu/10605328/EU-has-secret-plan-for-police-to-remote-stop-cars.html.

9 John Danaher, "Is Modern Technology Creating a Borg-like Society?" Institute for Ethics & Emerging Technologies (June 9, 2014), http://ieet.org/index.php/IEET/more/danaher20140609.

CHAPTER 24

1 Michael Walsh, "Canada Gains A Noted Science Fiction Writer," *Vancouver Provence*, (February 21, 1972), http://www.philipkdickfans.com/resources/articles/canada-gains-a-noted-science-fiction-writer/.

2 N. Gangulee, ed., *The Mind and Face of Nazi Germany* (London: John Murray, 1942), p. 26.

3 Julia Angwin and Jennifer Valentino-Devries, "New Tracking Frontier: Your License Plates," *Wall Street Journal*, (October 13, 2012), http://online.wsj.com/article/SB1000087 2396390443995604578004723603576296.html.

4 James Risen and Charlie Savage, "N.S.A. Director Lobbies House on Eve of Critical Vote," *The New York Times*, (July 23, 2013), http://www.nytimes.com/2013/07/24/us/politics/nsa-director-lobbies-house-on-eve-of-critical-vote.html?_r=0.

5 Jose Pagliery, "How the NSA can 'turn on' your phone remotely," *CNN* (June 6, 2014), http://money.cnn.com/2014/06/06/technology/security/nsa-turn-on-phone/.

6 Pratap Chatterjee, "The Data Hackers," *Truthdig*, (October 11, 2013), http://www.truthdig.com/report/page2/the_data_hackers_20131011.

7 Dustin Slaughter, "The Murky Legality of Philadelphia Police Department's License Plate Reader Program," *The Public Record* (May 28, 2014), http://pubrecord.org/nation/11262/murky-legality-philadelphia-police/.f

8 "You Are Being Tracked: How License Plate Readers Are Being Used to Record Americans' Movements," *ACLU*, (July 2013), http://www.aclu.org/technology-and-liberty/you-are-being-tracked-how-license-plate-readers-are-being-used-record.

9 "You Are Being Tracked: How License Plate Readers Are Being Used to Record Americans' Movements," *ACLU*, (July 2013), http://www.aclu.org/technology-and-liberty/you-are-being-tracked-how-license-plate-readers-are-being-used-record.

10 "You Are Being Tracked: How License Plate Readers Are Being Used to Record Americans' Movements," *ACLU*, (July 2013), http://www.aclu.org/technology-and-liberty/you-are-being-tracked-how-license-plate-readers-are-being-used-record.

11 Julia Angwin and Jennifer Valentino-Devries, "New Tracking Frontier: Your License Plates," *Wall Street Journal*, (October 13, 2012), http://online.wsj.com/article/SB100008 7239639044399560457800472360576296.html.

12 "You Are Being Tracked: How License Plate Readers Are Being Used to Record Americans' Movements," *ACLU*, (July 2013), http://www.aclu.org/technology-and-liberty/you-are-being-tracked-how-license-plate-readers-are-being-used-record.

13 Neal Ungerleider, "Some Florida Police Are Using Data to Predict Crime," *Fast Company*, (October 24, 2013), http://www.fastcompany.com/3020608/fast-feed/some-florida-police-are-using-data-to-predict-crime?partner.

14 Somini Sengupta, "Privacy Fears Grow as Cities Increase Surveillance," *The New York Times*, (October 13, 2013), http://www.nytimes.com/2013/10/14/technology/privacy-fears-as-surveillance-grows-in-cities.html?partner=rss&emc=rss&_r=0.

15 Chrissie Thompson and Jessie Balmert, "Ohio database access rules loosest in U.S.," *Cincinnati.com*, (September 22, 2013), http://news.cincinnati.com/article/20130922/NEWS010801/309220022?nclick_check=1.

16 Charlie Savage, "Facial Scanning Is Making Gains in Surveillance," *The New York Times*, (August 21, 2013), http://www.nytimes.com/2013/08/21/us/facial-scanning-is-making-gains-in-surveillance.html?_r=0.

17 Megan Garber, "I Know What You Did Last Errand," *The Atlantic*, (July 15, 2013), http://www.theatlantic.com/technology/archive/2013/07/i-know-what-you-did-last-errand/277785/.

18 Bob Egelko, "FBI reports show widespread domestic surveillance," *SFGate*, (September 20, 2013), http://www.sfgate.com/nation/article/FBI-reports-show-widespread-domestic-surveillance-4828272.php.

19 Charles Duhigg, "How Companies Learn Your Secrets," *The New York Times*, (February 16, 2012), http://www.nytimes.com/2012/02/19/magazine/shopping-habits.html?pagewanted=all&_r=1&.

20 Kristin Tate, "Latest Assault on Privacy: Grocery Store Shelves That Watch You," *Ben Swann*, (October 2013), http://benswann.com/latest-assault-on-privacy-grocery-store-shelves-that-watch-you/.

21 John Knefel, "Meet the Private Companies Helping Cops Spy on Protesters," *Rolling Stone*, (October 24, 2013), http://www.rollingstone.com/politics/news/meet-the-private-companies-helping-cops-spy-on-protesters-20131024.

22 Pratap Chatterjee, "The Data Hackers," *Truthdig*, (October 11, 2013), http://www.truthdig.com/report/page2/the_data_hackers_20131011.

23 Jathan Sadowski, "In-Store Tracking Companies Try to Self-Regulate Privacy," *Slate*, (July 23, 2013), http://www.slate.com/blogs/future_tense/2013/07/23/privacy_self_regulation_and_consumer_tracking_euclid_and_the_future_of_privacy.html.

24 Helen A.S. Popkin, "Careful what you tweet: Police, schools tap social media to track behavior," *NBC News*, (October 6, 2013), http://www.nbcnews.com/technology/careful-what-you-tweet-police-schools-tap-social-media-track-4B11215908.

25 Jathan Sadowski, "Ron Wyden's Warning: America May Be on Track to Become Surveillance State," *Slate*, (July 23, 2013), http://www.slate.com/blogs/future_tense/2013/07/23/ron_wyden_dangers_of_nsa_surveillance_and_the_patriot_act.html.

26 George Orwell, *Animal Farm* and *1984* (Houghton Mifflin Harcourt, 2003), p. 91.

CHAPTER 25

1 Cindy Cohn and Trevor Timm, "In Response to the NSA, We Need A New Church Committee and We Need It Now," *EFF*, (June 7, 2013), https://www.eff.org/deeplinks/2013/06/response-nsa-we-need-new-church-commission-and-we-need-it-now.

2 Bill Moyers, *The Secret Government: The Constitution in Crisis* (1987), http://www.informationclearinghouse.info/article17720.htm.

3 "Sen. Frank Church Warns of How Easily Government Can Abuse Expanding Surveillance Capabilities," *Meet the Press* (Aug. 17, 1975), https://grabien.com/file.php?id=7701.

4 James Bamford, "Private Lives: The Agency That Could Be Big Brother," *The New York Times* (December 25, 2005), http://www.nytimes.com/2005/12/25weekinreview/25bamford.html?ex=1293166800&en=3d09922ebe6b2eac&ei=5090.

5 Todd Beamon, "Secret Court Renews NSA's Phone Records Collection," *Newsmax* (July 19, 2013), http://www.newsmax.com/Newsfront/surveillance-Verizon-cellphone-renewal/2013/07/19/id/516082/.

6 James Risen and Charlie Savage, "N.S.A. Director Lobbies House on Eve of Critical Vote," *The New York Times*, (July 23, 2013), http://www.nytimes.com/2013/07/24/us/politics/nsa-director-lobbies-house-on-eve-of-critical-vote.html?_r=0.

7 Bill Quigley, "13 Things the Government is Trying to Keep Secret From You," *CounterPunch* (Aug. 23-25, 2013), http://www.counterpunch.org/2013/08/23/13-things-the-government-is-trying-to-keep-secret-from-you/.

8 Bill Quigley, "13 Things the Government is Trying to Keep Secret From You," *CounterPunch* (Aug. 23-25, 2013), http://www.counterpunch.org/2013/08/23/13-things-the-government-is-trying-to-keep-secret-from-you/.

9 James Bamford, *Body of Secrets: Anatomy of the Ultra-Secret National Security Agency* (DoubleDay, 2001), p. 4.

10 "Frequently Asked Questions," *National Security Agency* (September 28, 2006), http://www.nsa.gov/careers/faqs_1.cfm#ahp_2.

11 "Frequently Asked Questions," *National Security Agency* (September 28, 2006), http://www.nsa.gov/about/about00018.cfm#7.

12 Barton Gellman and Ashkan Soltani, "NSA tracking cellphone locations worldwide, Snowden documents show," *The Washington Post*, (December 4, 2013), http://www.washingtonpost.com/world/national-security/nsa-tracking-cellphone-locations-worldwide-snowden-documents-show/2013/12/04/5492873a-5cf2-11e3-bc56-c6ca94801fac_story.html?wpisrc=al_national.

13 David E. Sanger and Thom Shanker, "N.S.A. Devises Radio Pathway Into Computers," *The New York Times*, (January 14, 2014), http://www.nytimes.com/2014/01/15/us/nsa-effort-pries-open-computers-not-connected-to-internet.html?smid=re-share&_r=0.

14 Bill Quigley, "13 Things the Government is Trying to Keep Secret From You," *CounterPunch* (Aug. 23-25, 2013), http://www.counterpunch.org/2013/08/23/13-things-the-government-is-trying-to-keep-secret-from-you/.

15 James Bamford, "The NSA Is Building the Country's Biggest Spy Center (Watch What You Say)," *Wired*, (March 15, 2012), http://www.wired.com/threatlevel/2012/03/ff_nsadatacenter/.

16 Justice Sharrock, "The NSA's Massive Data Center Is Coming Online Ahead Of Schedule — And It's More Powerful Than You Thought," *BuzzFeed*, (July 15, 2013), http://www.buzzfeed.com/justinesharrock/the-nsas-massive-data-center-is-coming-online-ahead-of-sched.

17 James Risen and Laura Poitras, "N.S.A. Gathers Data on Social Connections of U.S. Citizens," *The New York Times*, (September 28, 2013), http://www.nytimes.com/2013/09/29/us/nsa-examines-social-networks-of-us-citizens.html?partner=rss&emc=rss&src=igw&_r=1&.

18 James Risen and Laura Poitras, "N.S.A. Gathers Data on Social Connections of U.S. Citizens," *The New York Times*, (September 28, 2013), http://www.nytimes.com/2013/09/29/us/nsa-examines-social-networks-of-us-citizens.html?partner=rss&emc=rss&src=igw&_r=1&.

19 Sara M. Watson, "Data Doppelgängers and the Uncanny Valley of Personalization," *The Atlantic*, (June 16, 2014), http://www.theatlantic.com/technology/archive/2014/06/data-doppelgangers-and-the-uncanny-valley-of-personalization/372780/.

20 James Risen and Laura Poitras, "N.S.A. Gathers Data on Social Connections of U.S. Citizens," *The New York Times*, (September 28, 2013), http://www.nytimes.com/2013/09/29/us/nsa-examines-social-networks-of-us-citizens.html?partner=rss&emc=rss&src=igw&_r=1&.

21 James Risen and Laura Poitras, "N.S.A. Gathers Data on Social Connections of U.S. Citizens," *The New York Times*, (September 28, 2013), http://www.nytimes.com/2013/09/29/us/nsa-examines-social-networks-of-us-citizens.html?partner=rss&emc=rss&src=igw&_r=1&.

22 Ryan Gallagher and Glenn Greenwald, "How the NSA Plans to Infect 'Millions' of Computers with Malware," *The Intercept*, (March 12, 2014), https://firstlook.org/theintercept/article/2014/03/12/nsa-plans-infect-millions-computers-malware/.

23 Ryan Gallagher and Glenn Greenwald, "How the NSA Plans to Infect 'Millions' of Computers with Malware," *The Intercept*, (March 12, 2014), https://firstlook.org/theintercept/article/2014/03/12/nsa-plans-infect-millions-computers-malware/.

24 Barton Gellman and Ashkan Soltani, "NSA surveillance program reaches 'into the past' to retrieve, replay phone calls," *The Washington Post*, (March 18, 2014), http://www.washingtonpost.com/world/national-security/nsa-surveillance-program-reaches-into-the-past-to-retrieve-replay-phone-calls/2014/03/18/226d2646-ade9-11e3-a49e-76adc9210f19_story.html.

25 John Baker, "Revisiting the Explosive Growth of Federal Crimes," The Heritage Foundation (June 16, 2008), http://www.heritage.org/research/reports/2008/06/revisiting-the-explosive-growth-of-federal-crimes.

CHAPTER 26

1 Yasha Levine, "Google's for-profit surveillance problem," *Pandodaily*, (December 16, 2013), http://pando.com/2013/12/16/googles-for-profit-surveillance-problem/.

2 Yasha Levine, "Google's for-profit surveillance problem," *Pandodaily*, (December 16, 2013), http://pando.com/2013/12/16/googles-for-profit-surveillance-problem/.

3 Eric Sommer, "Google's Deep CIA Connections," *Pravda*, (January 14, 2010), http://english. pravda.ru/world/asia/14-01-2010/111657-google_china-0/.

4 Barton Gellman, Ashkan Soltani, and Andrea Peterson, "How we know the NSA had access to internal Google and Yahoo cloud data," *The Washington Post*, (November 4, 2013), http:// www.washingtonpost.com/blogs/the-switch/wp/2013/11/04/how-we-know-the-nsa-had-access-to-internal-google-and-yahoo-cloud-data/.

5 Yasha Levine, "Google's for-profit surveillance problem," *Pandodaily*, (December 16, 2013), http://pando.com/2013/12/16/googles-for-profit-surveillance-problem/.

6 Bruce Schneier, "Don't Listen to Google and Facebook: The Public-Private Surveillance Partnership Is Still Going Strong," *The Atlantic*, (March 25, 2013), http://www.theatlantic. com/technology/archive/2014/03/don-t-listen-to-google-and-facebook-the-public-private-surveillance-partnership-is-still-going-strong/284612/.

7 Carole Cadwalladr, "Are the robots about to rise? Google's new director of engineering thinks so..." *The Guardian*, (February 22, 2014), http://www.theguardian.com/technology/2014/ feb/22/robots-google-ray-kurzweil-terminator-singularity-artificial-intelligence.

8 Frank Konkel, "How the CIA Partnered With Amazon and Changed Intelligence," *Defense One*, (July 11, 2014), http://www.defenseone.com/technology/2014/07/how-cia-partnered-amazon-and-changed-intelligence/88555/.

9 Eric Sommer, "Google's Deep CIA Connections," *Pravda*, (January 14, 2010), http://english. pravda.ru/world/asia/14-01-2010/111657-google_china-0/.

10 Yasha Levine, "Google's for-profit surveillance problem," *Pandodaily*, (December 16, 2013), http://pando.com/2013/12/16/googles-for-profit-surveillance-problem/.

11 Yasha Levine, "Google's for-profit surveillance problem," *Pandodaily*, (December 16, 2013), http://pando.com/2013/12/16/googles-for-profit-surveillance-problem/.

12 Yasha Levine, "Google's for-profit surveillance problem," *Pandodaily*, (December 16, 2013), http://pando.com/2013/12/16/googles-for-profit-surveillance-problem/.

13 Yasha Levine, "Google's for-profit surveillance problem," *Pandodaily*, (December 16, 2013), http://pando.com/2013/12/16/googles-for-profit-surveillance-problem/.

14 Colin Koopman, "The Age of 'Infopolitics,'" *The New York Times*, (January 26, 2014), http://opinionator.blogs.nytimes.com/2014/01/26/the-age-of-infopolitics/.

15 Colin Koopman, "The Age of 'Infopolitics,'" *The New York Times*, (January 26, 2014), http://opinionator.blogs.nytimes.com/2014/01/26/the-age-of-infopolitics/.

16 "Google will 'know you better than your intimate partner,'" *RT*, (February 23, 2014), http://rt.com/news/google-kurzweil-robots-transhumanism-312/.

17 Carole Cadwalladr, "Are the robots about to rise? Google's new director of engineering thinks so..." *The Guardian*, (February 22, 2014), http://www.theguardian.com/ technology/2014/feb/22/robots-google-ray-kurzweil-terminator-singularity-artificial-intelligence.

18 Carole Cadwalladr, "Are the robots about to rise? Google's new director of engineering thinks so..." *The Guardian*, (February 22, 2014), http://www.theguardian.com/ technology/2014/feb/22/robots-google-ray-kurzweil-terminator-singularity-artificial-intelligence.

19 Carole Cadwalladr, "Are the robots about to rise? Google's new director of engineering thinks so..." *The Guardian*, (February 22, 2014), http://www.theguardian.com/ technology/2014/feb/22/robots-google-ray-kurzweil-terminator-singularity-artificial-intelligence.

20 Ron Amadeo, "Google to buy Nest for $3.2 billion," *ArsTechnica*, (January 13, 2014), http://arstechnica.com/gadgets/2014/01/google-to-buy-nest-for-3-2-billion/.

21 Samuel Gibbs, "What is Boston Dynamics and why does Google want robots?" *The Guardian*, (December 17, 2013), http://www.theguardian.com/technology/2013/dec/17/google-boston-dynamics-robots-atlas-bigdog-cheetah?CMP=fb_gu.

22 Carole Cadwalladr, "Are the robots about to rise? Google's new director of engineering thinks so" *The Guardian*, (February 22, 2014), http://www.theguardian.com/technology/2014/feb/22/robots-google-ray-kurzweil-terminator-singularity-artificial-intelligence.

23 Carole Cadwalladr, "Are the robots about to rise? Google's new director of engineering thinks so..." *The Guardian*, (February 22, 2014), http://www.theguardian.com/technology/2014/feb/22/robots-google-ray-kurzweil-terminator-singularity-artificial-intelligence.

24 William J. Broad, "Why They Called It the Manhattan Project," *The New York Times* (Oct. 30, 2007), http://www.nytimes.com/2007/10/30/science/30manh.html?pagewanted=all.

CHAPTER 27

1 Tom Simonite, "Google's Boss Envisions a Utopian Future," *Technology Review* (Sept. 28, 2010), http://www.technologyreview.com/view/420962/googles-boss-envisions-a-utopian-future/?p1=A1.

2 Jemima Kiss, "Worried about your privacy? Wait until the drones start stalking you," *The Guardian*, (February 8, 2014), http://www.theguardian.com/technology/2014/feb/09/privacy-concerns-google-streetview-facebook-drones.

3 Charlie Warzel, "Your Next Phone Will Be The Ultimate Surveillance Machine," *BuzzFeed*, (November 27, 2013), http://www.buzzfeed.com/charliewarzel/your-next-phone-will-be-the-ultimate-surveillance-machine.

4 Peter Bright, "Smart TVs, smart fridges, smart washing machines? Disaster waiting to happen," *ArsTechnica*, (January 9, 2014), http://arstechnica.com/gadgets/2014/01/smart-tvs-smart-fridges-smart-washing-machines-disaster-waiting-to-happen/.

5 Peter Bright, "Smart TVs, smart fridges, smart washing machines? Disaster waiting to happen," *ArsTechnica*, (January 9, 2014), http://arstechnica.com/gadgets/2014/01/smart-tvs-smart-fridges-smart-washing-machines-disaster-waiting-to-happen/.

6 Michelle Starr, "Facial recognition app matches strangers to online profiles," *Cnet*, (January 7, 2014), http://news.cnet.com/8301-17938_105-57616799-1/facial-recognition-app-matches-strangers-to-online-profiles/?part=propeller&subj=crave&tag=title.

7 "You Are Being Tracked: How License Plate Readers Are Being Used to Record Americans' Movements," *ACLU*, (July 2013), http://www.aclu.org/technology-and-liberty/you-are-being-tracked-how-license-plate-readers-are-being-used-record.

8 Paul A. Eisenstein, "Spying, glitches spark concern over driverless cars," *CNBC*, (February 8, 2014), http://www.cnbc.com/id/101386129.

9 Adam Snider, "DOT pushing connected cars — But privacy, tech concerns remain — Winter of discontented travelers — CSA program comes under fire," *Politico*, (February 4, 2014), http://www.politico.com/morningtransportation/0214/morningtransportation12904.html.

10 "U.S. Department of Transportation Announces Decision to Move Forward with Vehicle-to-Vehicle Communication Technology for Light Vehicles," *National Highway Traffic Safety Administration*, (February 3, 2014), http://www.nhtsa.gov/About+NHTSA/Press+Releases/2014/USDOT+to+Move+Forward+with+Vehicle-to-Vehicle+Communication+Technology+for+Light+Vehicles.

11 "U.S. Department of Transportation Announces Decision to Move Forward with Vehicle-to-Vehicle Communication Technology for Light Vehicles," *National Highway Traffic Safety Administration*, (February 3, 2014), http://www.nhtsa.gov/About+NHTSA/Press+Releases/2014/USDOT+to+Move+Forward+with+Vehicle-to-Vehicle+Communication+Technology+for+Light+Vehicles.

12 Jaclyn Trop, "The Next Data Privacy Battle May Be Waged Inside Your Car," *The New York Times*, (January 10, 2014), http://www.nytimes.com/2014/01/11/business/the-next-privacy-battle-may-be-waged-inside-your-car.html?_r=1.

13   Jaclyn Trop, "The Next Data Privacy Battle May Be Waged Inside Your Car," *The New York Times*, (January 10, 2014), http://www.nytimes.com/2014/01/11/business/the-next-privacy-battle-may-be-waged-inside-your-car.html?_r=1.

14   Jim Edwards, "Ford Exec: 'We Know Everyone Who Breaks The Law' Thanks To Our GPS In Your Car," *Business Insider*, (January 8, 2014), http://www.businessinsider.com/ford-exec-gps-2014-1#ixzz2puo4Oq5f.

15   Bruno Waterfield and Matthew Day, "EU has secret plan for police to 'remote stop' cars," *The Telegraph*, (January 29, 2014), http://www.telegraph.co.uk/news/worldnews/europe/eu/10605328/EU-has-secret-plan-for-police-to-remote-stop-cars.html.

16   Jaclyn Trop, "The Next Data Privacy Battle May Be Waged Inside Your Car," *The New York Times*, (January 10, 2014), http://www.nytimes.com/2014/01/11/business/the-next-privacy-battle-may-be-waged-inside-your-car.html?_r=1.

17   Patrick Lin, "What If Your Autonomous Car Keeps Routing You Past Krispy Kreme?" *Slate*, (January 22, 2014), http://www.theatlantic.com/technology/archive/2014/01/what-if-your-autonomous-car-keeps-routing-you-past-krispy-kreme/283221/.

18   "Obama Signs Bill Modernizing Aviation System," *Huffington Post* (Feb. 15, 2012), http://www.huffingtonpost.com/2012/02/15/obama-signs-bill-moderniz_0_n_1278594.html.

19   Shaun Waterman, "Drones over U.S. get OK by Congress," *The Washington Times* (Feb. 7, 2012), http://www.washingtontimes.com/news/2012/feb/7/coming-to-a-sky-near-you/.

20   Buck Sexton, "Aerial 'Shadowhawk' Police Drones Can Now Deploy Tasers & Tear Gas," *The Blaze* (March 12, 2012), http://www.theblaze.com/stories/want-to-see-the-aerial-drone-police-could-soon-deploy-in-your-town/.

21   Morley, Jefferson. "Drones for "urban warfare"." *Salon*, April 24, 2012. http://www.salon.com/2012/04/24/drones_for_urban_warfare/singleton/ (accessed April 26, 2012).

22   Sarah Kellogg, "Drones: Coming to the Skies Near You," *DC Bar Journal*, (August 2013), http://www.dcbar.org/for_lawyers/resources/publications/washington_lawyer/august_2013/drones.cfm.

23   Jennifer Lynch, "Are Drones Watching You?" Electronic Frontier Foundation (Jan. 10, 2012), https://www.eff.org/deeplinks/2012/01/drones-are-watching-you.

24   Jennifer Lynch, "Are Drones Watching You?" Electronic Frontier Foundation (Jan. 10, 2012), https://www.eff.org/deeplinks/2012/01/drones-are-watching-you.

25   Noah Shachtman, "Army Tracking Plan: Drones That Never Forget a Face," *Wired* (Sept. 29, 2011), http://www.wired.com/dangerroom/2011/09/drones-never-forget-a-face/.

26   Peter Finn, "A future for drones: automated killing," *The Washington Post* (Sept. 19, 2011), http://www.washingtonpost.com/national/national-security/a-future-for-drones-automated-killing/2011/09/15/gIQAVy9mgK_story.html.

27   Morley, Jefferson. "Drones for "urban warfare"." *Salon*, April 24, 2012. http://www.salon.com/2012/04/24/drones_for_urban_warfare/singleton/.

28   Morley, Jefferson. "The drones are coming — to America." *Salon*, April 10, 2012. http://www.salon.com/2012/04/10/the_drones_are_coming_to_america/singleton/.

29   Gregory Wallace, "Amazon says drone deliveries are the future," *CNN Money* (Dec. 2, 2013), http://money.cnn.com/2013/12/01/technology/amazon-drone-delivery/.

30   Julianne Pepitone, "Domino's tests drone pizza delivery," *CNN Money* (June 4, 2013), http://money.cnn.com/2013/06/04/technology/innovation/dominos-pizza-drone/index.html?iid=EL.

31   Julianne Pepitone, "Domino's tests drone pizza delivery," *CNN Money* (June 4, 2013), http://money.cnn.com/2013/06/04/technology/innovation/dominos-pizza-drone/index.html?iid=EL.

32   Market Research, "Robotics: Technologies and Global Markets." Last modified July 1, 2011. Accessed April 26, 2012. http://www.marketresearch.com/BCC-Research-v374/Robotics-Technologies-Global-6481848/.

33 Mitch Horowitz, "Why Rod Serling Still Matters," *Huffington Post*, (August 21, 2013), http://www.huffingtonpost.com/mitch-horowitz/why-rod-serling-still-mat_ b_3791602.html.

34 Anne Serling, *As I Knew Him: My Dad, Rod Serling* (Citadel, 2014), p. 212.

CHAPTER 28

1 George Orwell, *Nineteen Eighty-Four* (Knopf Doubleday, 2009), p. 21.

2 Jennifer Medina, "Warning: The Literary Canon Could Make Students Squirm," *The New York Times*, (May 17, 2014), http://www.nytimes.com/2014/05/18/us/warning-the-literary-canon-could-make-students-squirm.html.

3 Stacy St. Clair, "Police raid over tweets leads to lawsuit against Peoria mayor," *Chicago Tribune*, (June 13, 2014), http://www.chicagotribune.com/news/local/breaking/chi-peoria-mayor-twitter-20140612,0,5493686.story.

4 Shane Harris, "Meet the Spies Doing the NSA's Dirty Work," *Foreign Policy*, (November 21, 2013), http://www.foreignpolicy.com/articles/2013/11/21/the_obscure_fbi_team_that_does_the_nsa_dirty_work.

5 Cyrus Farivar, "New documents: NSA provided 2-3 daily "tips" to FBI for at least 3 years," *ArsTechnica*, (January 20, 2014), http://arstechnica.com/tech-policy/2014/01/new-documents-nsa-provided-2-3-daily-tips-to-fbi-for-at-least-3-years/.

6 Shane Harris, "Meet the Spies Doing the NSA's Dirty Work," *Foreign Policy*, (November 21, 2013), http://www.foreignpolicy.com/articles/2013/11/21/the_obscure_fbi_team_that_does_the_nsa_dirty_work.

7 Jennifer Lynch, "FBI to have 52 million photos in its NGI face recognition database by next year," *ArsTechnica*, (April 14, 2014), http://arstechnica.com/tech-policy/2014/04/fbi-to-have-52-million-photos-in-its-ngi-face-recognition-database-by-next-year/.

8 Jennifer Lynch, "FBI to have 52 million photos in its NGI face recognition database by next year," *ArsTechnica*, (April 14, 2014), http://arstechnica.com/tech-policy/2014/04/fbi-to-have-52-million-photos-in-its-ngi-face-recognition-database-by-next-year/.

9 Jennifer Lynch, "FBI to have 52 million photos in its NGI face recognition database by next year," *ArsTechnica*, (April 14, 2014), http://arstechnica.com/tech-policy/2014/04/fbi-to-have-52-million-photos-in-its-ngi-face-recognition-database-by-next-year/.

10 Jennifer Lynch, "FBI to have 52 million photos in its NGI face recognition database by next year," *ArsTechnica*, (April 14, 2014), http://arstechnica.com/tech-policy/2014/04/fbi-to-have-52-million-photos-in-its-ngi-face-recognition-database-by-next-year/.

11 Jessica Hughes, "FBI Facial Recognition System Gives Officers an Investigative Lead," *GovTech* (Oct. 20, 2014), http://www.govtech.com/public-safety/FBI-Facial-Recognition-System-Gives-Officers-an-Investigative-Lead.html.

12 Natasha Singer, "Never Forgetting a Face," *The New York Times* (May 17, 2014), http://www.nytimes.com/2014/05/18/technology/never-forgetting-a-face.html?_r=0.

13 Rawlson King, "FBI seeks to add Rapid DNA to biometric database," *Biometric Update* (Oct. 1, 2014), http://www.biometricupdate.com/201410/fbi-seeks-to-add-rapid-dna-to-biometric-database.

14 Valerie Ross, "Forget Fingerprints: Law Enforcement DNA Databases Poised To Expand," *NOVA Next PBS* (Jan. 2m 2014), http://www.pbs.org/wgbh/nova/next/body/dna-databases/.

15 Valerie Ross, "Forget Fingerprints: Law Enforcement DNA Databases Poised To Expand," *NOVA Next PBS* (Jan. 2m 2014), http://www.pbs.org/wgbh/nova/next/body/dna-databases/.

16 Kwame Opam, "Scientists can now create accurate mugshots using only DNA," *The Verge* (March 21, 2014), http://www.theverge.com/2014/3/21/5533976/scientists-can-now-create-accurate-mugshots-using-only-dna.

17 Valerie Ross, "Forget Fingerprints: Law Enforcement DNA Databases Poised To Expand," *NOVA Next PBS* (Jan. 2m 2014), http://www.pbs.org/wgbh/nova/next/body/dna-databases/.

18 Valerie Ross, "Forget Fingerprints: Law Enforcement DNA Databases Poised To Expand," *NOVA Next PBS* (Jan. 2m 2014), http://www.pbs.org/wgbh/nova/next/body/dna-databases/.

19 Kevin Gosztola, "'Inventing Terrorists' Study Offers Critical Examination of Government's Use of Preemptive Prosecutions," *The Dissenter*, (June 9, 2014), http://dissenter.firedoglake.com/2014/06/09/inventing-terrorists-study-offers-critical-examination-of-governments-use-of-preemptive-prosecutions/.

20 Project SALAM and National Coalition to Protect Civil Freedoms, "Inventing Terrorists: The Lawfare of Preemptive Prosecution," (May 2014), p. 1, http://www.projectsalam.org/Inventing-Terrorists-study.pdf.

21 Project SALAM and National Coalition to Protect Civil Freedoms, "Inventing Terrorists: The Lawfare of Preemptive Prosecution," (May 2014), p. 40, http://www.projectsalam.org/Inventing-Terrorists-study.pdf.

22 Project SALAM and National Coalition to Protect Civil Freedoms, "Inventing Terrorists: The Lawfare of Preemptive Prosecution," (May 2014), p. 3, http://www.projectsalam.org/Inventing-Terrorists-study.pdf.

23 Project SALAM and National Coalition to Protect Civil Freedoms, "Inventing Terrorists: The Lawfare of Preemptive Prosecution," (May 2014), p. 27, http://www.projectsalam.org/Inventing-Terrorists-study.pdf.

24 Project SALAM and National Coalition to Protect Civil Freedoms, "Inventing Terrorists: The Lawfare of Preemptive Prosecution," (May 2014), p. 40, http://www.projectsalam.org/Inventing-Terrorists-study.pdf.

25 Trevor Aaronson, "The Informants," *Mother Jones* (Sept./Oct. 2011), pp. 32 – 43, http://www.motherjones.com/politics/2011/08/fbi-terrorist-informants.

26 Project SALAM and National Coalition to Protect Civil Freedoms, "Inventing Terrorists: The Lawfare of Preemptive Prosecution," (May 2014), p. 4, http://www.projectsalam.org/Inventing-Terrorists-study.pdf.

27 Trevor Aaronson, "The Informants," *Mother Jones* (Sept./Oct. 2011), pp. 32 – 43, http://www.motherjones.com/politics/2011/08/fbi-terrorist-informants.

28 James Bovard, *Terrorism and Tyranny: Trampling Freedom, Justice, and Peace to Rid the World of Evil* (Palgrave Macmillan, 2004), p. 150.

29 Adam Fairclough, *Martin Luther King, Jr.* (University of Georgia Press, 1995), p. 96.

30 Allan M. Jallon, "A break-in to end all break-ins," *Los Angeles Times* (March 8, 2006), http://articles.latimes.com/2006/mar/08/opinion/oe-jalon8.

31 Matt Sledge, "Homeland Security Tracked Occupy Wall Street 'Peaceful Activist Demonstrations,'" *The Huffington Post*, (April 3, 2013), http://www.huffingtonpost.com/2013/04/02/homeland-security-occupy-wall-street_n_3002445.html.

CHAPTER 29

1 Bruce Levine, "How TV Zombifies and Pacifies Us and Subverts Democracy," (Oct. 30, 2012), http://brucelevine.net/how-tv-zombifies-and-pacifies-us-and-subverts-democracy/.

2 John Lennon, "Working Class Hero," *John Lennon / Plastic Ono Band* (Apple, 1970).

3 *As quoted in* Bertram Gross, *Friendly Fascism: The New Face of Power in America* (South End Press, 1980), p. 259.

4 Bo Moore, "Terry Gilliam on His Epic New Dystopian Film *The Zero Theorem*," *Wired* (Sept. 18, 2014), http://www.wired.com/2014/09/zero-theorem/.

5 Bertram Gross, "Friendly Fascism: The New Face of Power in America" (South End Press, 1980), p. 256.

6 Kadhim Shubber, "MRI Scan Reveal Effect of 'Mob Mentality' on the Brain," http://www.co.uk/news/archive/2014-06-12/mobmentality.

7 Kadhim Shubber, "MRI Scans Reveal Effect of 'Mob Mentality' on the Brain," *Wired* (June 12, 2014), http://www.wired.co.uk/news/archive/2014-06-12/mob-mentality.

8 Bruce Levine, "How TV Zombifies and Pacifies Us and Subverts Democracy," (Oct. 30, 2012), http://brucelevine.net/how-tv-zombifies-and-pacifies-us-and-subverts-democracy/.

9 Bruce Levine, "How TV Zombifies and Pacifies Us and Subverts Democracy," (Oct. 30, 2012), http://brucelevine.net/how-tv-zombifies-and-pacifies-us-and-subverts-democracy/.

10 Bruce Levine, "How TV Zombifies and Pacifies Us and Subverts Democracy," (Oct. 30, 2012), http://brucelevine.net/how-tv-zombifies-and-pacifies-us-and-subverts-democracy/.

11 Bruce Levine, "How TV Zombifies and Pacifies Us and Subverts Democracy," (Oct. 30, 2012), http://brucelevine.net/how-tv-zombifies-and-pacifies-us-and-subverts-democracy/.

12 Bertram Gross, *"Friendly Fascism: The New Face of Power in America"* (South End Press, 1980), p. 261.

13 Bruce Levine, "How TV Zombifies and Pacifies Us and Subverts Democracy," (Oct. 30, 2012), http://brucelevine.net/how-tv-zombifies-and-pacifies-us-and-subverts-democracy/.

14 Bruce Levine, "How TV Zombifies and Pacifies Us and Subverts Democracy," (Oct. 30, 2012), http://brucelevine.net/how-tv-zombifies-and-pacifies-us-and-subverts-democracy/.

15 Bruce Levine, "How TV Zombifies and Pacifies Us and Subverts Democracy," (Oct. 30, 2012), http://brucelevine.net/how-tv-zombifies-and-pacifies-us-and-subverts-democracy/.

16 Bruce Levine, "How TV Zombifies and Pacifies Us and Subverts Democracy," (Oct. 30, 2012), http://brucelevine.net/how-tv-zombifies-and-pacifies-us-and-subverts-democracy/.

17 Marshall McLuhan, *Understanding Media: The Extension of Man* (New American Library, 1964), p. 293.

18 Bruce Levine, "How TV Zombifies and Pacifies Us and Subverts Democracy," (Oct. 30, 2012), http://brucelevine.net/how-tv-zombifies-and-pacifies-us-and-subverts-democracy/.

19 Neil Postman *Amusing Ourselves to Death: Discourse in the Age of Show Business,* (Viking Books, 1985), p. 155, 156.

20 Edward R. Murrow, *Speech to the Radio and Television News Directors (RTNDA) in Chicago,* (Oct. 15, 1958).

21 Neil Postman, *Amusing Ourselves to Death: Public Discourse in the Age of Show Business* (Viking Press, 1980), p. 163.

CHAPTER 30

1 Andy Wachowski and Lana Wachowski, *The Matrix* (Warner Bros., 1999).

2 Aldous Huxley, *Brave New World Revisited* (RosettaBooks, 2010), p. 27 and Chapter 12.

3 Daniel Taylor, "The Scientific Dictator," *Dark Government* (June 13, 2014), http://www.darkgovernment.com/news/the-scientific-dictator/.

4 Stuart Clark, "Artificial intelligence could spell end of human race – Stephen Hawking," *The Guardian* (Dec. 2, 2014), http://www.theguardian.com/science/2014/dec/02/stephen-hawking-intel-communication-system-astrophysicist-software-predictive-text-type.

5 Charles Arthur, "Google+ isn't a social network; it's The Matrix," *The Guardian* (June 4, 2013), http://www.theguardian.com/technology/blog/2013/jun/04/google-plus-the-matrix.

6 John Danaher, "Is Modern Technology Creating a Borg-like Society?" Institute for Ethics & Emerging Technologies (June 9, 2014), http://ieet.org/index.php/IEET/more/danaher20140609.

7 Antony Loewenstein, "The Ultimate Goal of the NSA is Total Population Control," http://www.theguardian.com (July 11, 2014).

8 Carol Cadwalladr, "Are the robots about to rise? Google's new director of engineering thinks so...," *The Guardian* (Feb. 22, 2014), http://www.theguardian.com/technology/2014/feb/22/robots-google-ray-kurzweil-terminator-singularity-artificial-intelligence.

9 "Google will 'know you better than your intimate partner,'" *RT* (Feb. 24, 2014), http://rt.com/news/google-kurzweil-robots-transhumanism-312/.

10 David Auerbach, "The Most Terrifying Thought Experiment of All Time," *Slate* (July 17, 2014), http://www.slate.com/articles/technology/bitwise/2014/07/roko_s_basilisk_the_most_terrifying_thought_experiment_of_all_time.html.

11 Carol Cadwalladr, "Are the robots about to rise? Google's new director of engineering thinks so…," *The Guardian* (Feb. 22, 2014), http://www.theguardian.com/technology/2014/feb/22/robots-google-ray-kurzweil-terminator-singularity-artificial-intelligence.

12 Carol Cadwalladr, "Are the robots about to rise? Google's new director of engineering thinks so…," *The Guardian* (Feb. 22, 2014), http://www.theguardian.com/technology/2014/feb/22/robots-google-ray-kurzweil-terminator-singularity-artificial-intelligence.

13 Carol Cadwalladr, "Are the robots about to rise? Google's new director of engineering thinks so…," *The Guardian* (Feb. 22, 2014), http://www.theguardian.com/technology/2014/feb/22/robots-google-ray-kurzweil-terminator-singularity-artificial-intelligence.

14 Carol Cadwalladr, "Are the robots about to rise? Google's new director of engineering thinks so…," *The Guardian* (Feb. 22, 2014), http://www.theguardian.com/technology/2014/feb/22/robots-google-ray-kurzweil-terminator-singularity-artificial-intelligence.

15 "Meet ATLAS!" https://www.youtube.com/watch?v=zkBnFPBV3f0.

16 Carol Cadwalladr, "Are the robots about to rise? Google's new director of engineering thinks so…," *The Guardian* (Feb. 22, 2014), http://www.theguardian.com/technology/2014/feb/22/robots-google-ray-kurzweil-terminator-singularity-artificial-intelligence.

17 "Google will 'know you better than your intimate partner,'" *RT* (Feb. 24, 2014), http://rt.com/news/google-kurzweil-robots-transhumanism-312/.

18 Adam Rawnsley, "The Pentagon Basically Wants to Merge You With a Robot," *Daily Beast* (March 6, 2014), http://www.thedailybeast.com/articles/2014/03/06/the-pentagon-basically-wants-to-merge-you-with-a-robot.html.

19 Adam Rawnsley, "The Pentagon Basically Wants to Merge You With a Robot," *Daily Beast* (March 6, 2014), http://www.thedailybeast.com/articles/2014/03/06/the-pentagon-basically-wants-to-merge-you-with-a-robot.html.

20 Dan Lohrmann, "Robots are Coming: Even to the Cloud," *Government Technology* (August 31, 2014), http://www.govtech.com/blogs/lohrmann-on-cybersecurity/Robots-are-Coming-Even-to-the-Cloud-.html.

21 Kamil Muzyka, "The Internet of Things, The Industry and AI," *Institute for Ethics & Emerging Technologies* (June 2, 2014), http://ieet.org/index.php/IEET/more/muzyka20140601.

22 Michael Price, "I'm terrified of my new TV: Why I'm scared to turn this thing on — and you'd be, too," *Salon* (Oct. 30, 2014), http://www.salon.com/2014/10/30/im_terrified_of_my_new_tv_why_im_scared_to_turn_this_thing_on_and_youd_be_too/.

23 Kamil Muzyka, "The Internet of Things, The Industry and AI," *Institute for Ethics & Emerging Technologies* (June 2, 2014), http://ieet.org/index.php/IEET/more/muzyka20140601.

24 Kamil Muzyka, "The Internet of Things, The Industry and AI," *Institute for Ethics & Emerging Technologies* (June 2, 2014), http://ieet.org/index.php/IEET/more/muzyka20140601.

25 John Danaher, "Is Modern Technology Creating a Borg-like Society?" Institute for Ethics & Emerging Technologies (June 9, 2014), http://ieet.org/index.php/IEET/more/danaher20140609.

26 John Danaher, "Is Modern Technology Creating a Borg-like Society?" Institute for Ethics & Emerging Technologies (June 9, 2014), http://ieet.org/index.php/IEET/more/danaher20140609.

27 Michael Haederle, "Brain scans of inmates turn up possible link to risks of reoffending," *Los Angeles Times*, (July 15, 2013), http://www.latimes.com/news/nationworld/nation/la-na-prisoner-brains-20130715,0,5130358.story.

28 Elise Ackerman, "How Smart Dust Could Be Used To Monitor Human Thought," *Forbes*, (July 19, 2013), http://www.forbes.com/sites/eliseackerman/2013/07/19/how-smart-dust-could-be-used-to-monitor-human-thought/.

29 Elise Ackerman, "How Smart Dust Could Be Used To Monitor Human Thought," *Forbes*, (July 19, 2013), http://www.forbes.com/sites/eliseackerman/2013/07/19/how-smart-dust-could-be-used-to-monitor-human-thought/.

30 Sebastian Anthony, "Hackers backdoor the human brain, successfully extract sensitive data," *ExtremeTech*, (August 17, 2012), http://www.extremetech.com/extreme/134682-hackers-backdoor-the-human-brain-successfully-extract-sensitive-data.

31 Mo Costandi, "Brain-to-brain interface transmits information from one rat to another," *The Guardian*, (February 28, 2013), http://www.theguardian.com/science/neurophilosophy/2013/feb/28/brain-to-brain-interface.

CHAPTER 31

1 Lawrence Sutin, *Divine Invasions: A Life of Philip K. Dick* (Harmony Books, 1989), p. 244.

2 Jim Edwards, "Here's A Look At The Finger-Vein Scanner Barclays Is Going to Use On Its Customers," *Business Insider* (Sept. 5, 2014), http://www.businessinsider.com/barclays-finger-vein-scanner-2014-9.

3 Marcelo Gleiser, "The Transhuman Future: Be More Than You Can Be," *NPR* (June 11, 2014), http://www.npr.org/blogs/13.7/2014/06/11/320961912/the-transhuman-future-be-more-than-you-can-be.

4 "Google will 'know you better than your intimate partner,'" *RT* (Feb. 24, 2014), http://rt.com/news/google-kurzweil-robots-transhumanism-312/.

5 Robert Sorokanich, "Scientists Have Located the Brain's On/Off Switch for Consciousness," *Gizmodo* (July 6, 2014), http://gizmodo.com/scientists-find-the-brains-on-off-switch-that-controls-1600783245.

6 Iain Gillespie, "Human Microchipping: I've Got You Under My Skin," *Sydney Morning Herald* (April 17, 2014), http://www.smh.com.au/digital-life/digital-life-news/human-microchipping-ive-got-you-under-my-skin-20140416-zqvho.html.

7 "Facebook's Psychological Experiments Connected to Department of Defense Research on Civil Unrest," *SCG News* (July 1, 2014), http://scgnews.com/facebooks-psychological-experiments-connected-to-department-of-defense-research-on-civil-unrest.

8 Robinson Meyer, "Everything We Know About Facebook's Secret Mood Manipulation Experiment," *The Atlantic*, (June 28, 2014), http://www.theatlantic.com/technology/archive/2014/06/everything-we-know-about-facebooks-secret-mood-manipulation-experiment/373648/.

9 "Facebook's Psychological Experiments Connected to Department of Defense Research on Civil Unrest," *SCG News* (July 1, 2014), http://scgnews.com/facebooks-psychological-experiments-connected-to-department-of-defense-research-on-civil-unrest.

10 Nafeez Ahmed, "Pentagon preparing for mass civil breakdown," *The Guardian*, (June 12, 2014), http://www.theguardian.com/environment/earth-insight/2014/jun/12/pentagon-mass-civil-breakdown.

11 "Facebook's Psychological Experiments Connected to Department of Defense Research on Civil Unrest," *SCG News*, (July 1, 2014), http://scgnews.com/facebooks-psychological-experiments-connected-to-department-of-defense-research-on-civil-unrest.

12 Nafeez Ahmed, "Pentagon preparing for mass civil breakdown," *The Guardian*, (June 12, 2014), http://www.theguardian.com/environment/earth-insight/2014/jun/12/pentagon-mass-civil-breakdown.

13 Conor Friedersdorf, "The Latest Snowden Leak Is Devastating to NSA Defenders," *The Atlantic*, (July 7, 2014), http://www.theatlantic.com/politics/archive/2014/07/a-devastating-leak-for-edward-snowdens-critics/373991/.

14 "The Conspiracy Theory Is True: Agents Infiltrate Websites Intending To 'Manipulate, Deceive, And Destroy Reputations,'" *Zero Hedge*, (February 25, 2014), http://www.zerohedge.com/news/2014-02-24/conspiracy-theory-true-agents-infiltrate-websites-intending-manipulate-deceive-and-d.

15 Robert Lemos, "Surveillance, Commercialization Threaten Web Freedom, Pew Study Finds," *eWeek*, (July 5, 2014), http://www.eweek.com/security/surveillance-commercialization-threaten-web-freedom-pew-study-find.html.

16 Sherry Turkle, *The Second Self: Computers and the Human Spirit* (Simon and Schuster, 1984), p. 296.

17 John W. Whitehead, "Blade Runner: What It Means to Be Human in the Cybernetic State," *Huffington Post* (April 24, 2012), http://www.huffingtonpost.com/john-w-whitehead/blade-runner_b_1445387.html.

18 John W. Whitehead, "Blade Runner: What It Means to Be Human in the Cybernetic State," *Huffington Post* (April 24, 2012), http://www.huffingtonpost.com/john-w-whitehead/blade-runner_b_1445387.html.

19 Christopher Riche Evans, *The Micro Millennium* (Pocket Books, 1981), p. 281.

20 Jaron Lanier, "One Half a Manifesto," *Edge* (Nov. 10, 2000), http://edge.org/conversation/one-half-a-manifesto.

21 Sharon Grace, "Codes of Grace," *Mondo 2000* http://ctheory.concordia.ca/krokers/grace.html.

PART V: The Resistance

1 Dietrich Bonhoeffer, *Dietrich Bonhoeffer: Witness to Jesus Christ* (Fortress Press, 1991), pp. 267-8.

2 Aldous Huxley, *Brave New World Revisited* (RosettaBooks, 2010), Chapter 12.

3 Bruce Levine, "How TV Zombifies and Pacifies Us and Subverts Democracy," (Oct. 30, 2012), http://brucelevine.net/how-tv-zombifies-and-pacifies-us-and-subverts-democracy/.

4 David Hinckley, "Americans spend 34 hours a week watching TV, according to Nielsen numbers," *NY Daily News* (Sept. 19, 2012), http://www.nydailynews.com/entertainment/tv-movies/americans-spend-34-hours-week-watching-tv-nielsen-numbers-article-1.1162285.

5 John Schwartz, "Name That Freedom," *The New York Times* (Oct. 23, 2010), http://www.nytimes.com/2010/10/24/weekinreview/24schwartz.html?_r=0.

6 Eric Lane, "Saving Democracy with Civic Literacy in America 101," *Utne Reader* (January-February 2009), http://www.utne.com/politics/america-101-civic-literacy-saving-constitutional-democracy.aspx#axzz3GzBVfBIC.

7 Rebecca Riffkin, "Public Faith in Congress Falls Again, Hits Historic Low," *Gallup* (June 19, 2014), http://www.gallup.com/poll/171710/public-faith-congress-falls-again-hits-historic-low.aspx.

8 Lydia Saad, "Government Itself Still Cited as Top U.S. Problem," *Gallup* (Jan. 15, 2014), http://www.gallup.com/poll/166844/government-itself-cited-top-problem.aspx.

9 Jon Clifton, "Americans Less Satisfied With Freedom," *Gallup* (July 1, 2014), http://www.gallup.com/poll/172019/americans-less-satisfied-freedom.aspx.

CHAPTER 32

1 John Lennon, "Revolution" (Apple, 1968).

2 Aldous Huxley, *Brave New World and Brave New World Revisited* (Harper Perennial, 2005), p. 340.

3 George Orwell, *Nineteen Eighty-Four* (Knopf Doubleday Publishing Group, 2009), p. 74.

4 Aldous Huxley, *Brave New World and Brave New World Revisited* (Harper Perennial, Modern Classic, 2005), p. 333.

5 Aldous Huxley, *Brave New World and Brave New World Revisited* (Harper Perennial, Modern Classic, 2005), p. 333-334.

6 Henry H. Lindner, *"On The Matrix: It's Meaning and Relevance to These Pages,"* http://henrylindner.net.

7 Henry H. Lindner, *"On The Matrix: It's Meaning and Relevance to These Pages,"* http://henrylindner.net.

8 George Orwell, *1984* (Harcourt Brace, 1980), pp. 234-35.

9 Aldous Huxley, *Brave New World and Brave New World Revisited* (Harper Perennial, Modern Classic, 2005), p. 336.

10   Jordan Michael Smith, "Vote all you want. The secret government won't change," *The Boston Globe* (Oct. 19, 2014), http://www.bostonglobe.com/ideas/2014/10/18/vote-all-you-want-the-secret-government-won-change/jVSkXrENQlu8vNcBfMn9sL/story.html.

11   "Madison Debates (July 11, 1787)," *The Avalon Project* (Yale Law School), http://avalon.law.yale.edu/18th_century/debates_711.asp.

12   Aldous Huxley, *Brave New World and Brave New World Revisited* (Harper Perennial, Modern Classic, 2005), p. 339.

13   Aldous Huxley, *Brave New World and Brave New World Revisited* (Harper Perennial, Modern Classic, 2005), p. 339.

14   "Albuquerque residents attempt citizen's arrest of police chief," *The Guardian*, (May 8, 2014), http://www.theguardian.com/world/2014/may/08/albuquerque-police-citizens-arrest-chief-protests.

15   Justin King, "City Council Tells Police They Have 60 Days to Plan to Destroy or Remove MRAP," *The Anti-Media* ((August 28, 2014), http://theantimedia.org/city-council-tells-police-they-have-60-days-to-plan-to-destroy-or-remove-mrap/.

16   Michael Lotfi, "Michigan Nullifies NDAA's Indefinite Detention," *Washington Times* (Dec. 27, 2013), http://communities.washingtontimes.com/neighborhood/american-millennial/2013/dec/27/breaking-news-michigan-nullifies-ndaas-indefinite-/. *Also see* "The State of the Nullification Movement 2014," Tenth Amendment Center (June 2014), http://tenthamendment.wpengine.netdna-cdn.com/wp-content/uploads/2014/06/state-of-the-nullification-movement-2014.pdf.

17   Orlando Patterson, *Freedom: Freedom in the Making of Western Culture*, Vol. 1, (Basic Books, 1996), p. 9.

18   Erich Fromm, *On Disobedience: Why Freedom Means Saying "No" to Power* (Harper Perennial, 2010), p. 5.

19   Erich Fromm, *On Disobedience: Why Freedom Means Saying "No" to Power* (Harper Perennial, 2010), p. 5.

20   Erich Fromm, *On Disobedience: Why Freedom Means Saying "No" to Power* (Harper Perennial, 2010), p. 53-54.

CHAPTER 33

1   James M. Washington, ed., *The Essential Writings and Speeches of Martin Luther King, Jr.* (Harper, San Francisco, 1991), p. 292.

2   Erich Fromm, *On Disobedience: Why Freedom Means Saying "No" to Power* (Harper Perennial, 2010), pp. 5, 12.

3   Hannah Arendt, *Crises of the Republic* (Harcourt, Brace and Company, 1972), p. 76.

4   "Dogs, Kids and Clubs," *Time* (May 10, 1963), http://content.time.com/time/magazine/article/0,9171,830260,00.html.

5   James M. Washington, ed., *The Essential Writings and Speeches of Martin Luther King, Jr.* (Harper San Francisco, 1991), p. 290.

6   James M. Washington, ed., *The Essential Writings and Speeches of Martin Luther King, Jr.* (Harper San Francisco, 1991), p. 293.

7   James M. Washington, ed., *The Essential Writings and Speeches of Martin Luther King, Jr.* (Harper San Francisco, 1991), p. 293

8   James M. Washington, ed., *The Essential Writings and Speeches of Martin Luther King, Jr.* (Harper San Francisco, 1991), p. 294.

9   James M. Washington, ed., *The Essential Writings and Speeches of Martin Luther King, Jr.* (Harper San Francisco, 1991), p. 294-95.

10   James M. Washington, ed., *The Essential Writings and Speeches of Martin Luther King, Jr.* (Harper San Francisco, 1991), p. 297-98.

11   James M. Washington, ed., *The Essential Writings and Speeches of Martin Luther King, Jr.* (Harper San Francisco, 1991), p. 298.

12 Erich Fromm, *On Disobedience: Why Freedom Means Saying "No" to Power* (Harper Perennial, 2010, p. 23.

13 Erich Fromm, *On Disobedience: Why Freedom Means Saying "No" to Power* (Harper Perennial, 2010, p. 53.

14 James M. Washington, ed., *The Essential Writings and Speeches of Martin Luther King, Jr.* (Harper San Francisco, 1991), p. 240.

15 Viktor E. Frankl, *Man's Search for Meaning* (Beacon Press, 2006), pp. 110-111.

16 Viktor E. Frankl, *Man's Search for Meaning* (Beacon Press, 2006), pp. 65-66.

17 James M. Washington, ed., *The Essential Writings and Speeches of Martin Luther King, Jr.* (Harper San Francisco, 1991), p. 64.

18 James M. Washington, ed., *The Essential Writings and Speeches of Martin Luther King, Jr.* (Harper San Francisco, 1991), p. 66.

19 James M. Washington, ed., *The Essential Writings and Speeches of Martin Luther King, Jr.* (Harper San Francisco, 1991), p. 66.

20 James M. Washington, ed., *The Essential Writings and Speeches of Martin Luther King, Jr.* (Harper San Francisco, 1991), p. 69.

21 James M. Washington, ed., *The Essential Writings and Speeches of Martin Luther King, Jr.* (Harper San Francisco, 1991), p. 70.

22 James M. Washington, ed., *The Essential Writings and Speeches of Martin Luther King, Jr.* (Harper San Francisco, 1991), p. 65-68.

23 James M. Washington, ed., *The Essential Writings and Speeches of Martin Luther King, Jr.* (Harper San Francisco, 1991), p. 71.

CHAPTER 34

1 Aldous Huxley, *A Brave New World Revisited* (Harper Perennial, 2005), p. 333.

2 Frantz Fanon, *Black Skin, White Masks* (Grove Press, 1967), p. 194.

3 John Lennon, "Strawberry Fields Forever" (Capitol, 1967).

4 Marlon Brock, "10 Prison Security Techniques Being Implemented on the American People," *Police State USA* (Feb. 11, 2014), http://www.policestateusa.com/2014/prison-security-american-people/.

5 Marlon Brock, "10 Prison Security Techniques Being Implemented on the American People," *Police State USA* (Feb. 11, 2014), http://www.policestateusa.com/2014/prison-security-american-people/.

6 Dustin Slaughter, "The Murky Legality of Philadelphia Police Department's License Plate Reader Program," *The Public Record* (May 28, 2014), http://pubrecord.org/nation/11262/murky-legality-philadelphia-police/.f

7 Marlon Brock, "10 Prison Security Techniques Being Implemented on the American People," *Police State USA* (Feb. 11, 2014), http://www.policestateusa.com/2014/prison-security-american-people/.

8 Marlon Brock, "10 Prison Security Techniques Being Implemented on the American People," *Police State USA* (Feb. 11, 2014), http://www.policestateusa.com/2014/prison-security-american-people/.

9 *Florence v. Burlington*, http://www.scotusblog.com/case-files/cases/florence-v-board-of-chosen-freeholders-of-the-county-of-burlington/.

10 Marlon Brock, "10 Prison Security Techniques Being Implemented on the American People," *Police State USA* (Feb. 11, 2014), http://www.policestateusa.com/2014/prison-security-american-people/.

11 Marlon Brock, "10 Prison Security Techniques Being Implemented on the American People," *Police State USA* (Feb. 11, 2014), http://www.policestateusa.com/2014/prison-security-american-people/.

12 Marlon Brock, "10 Prison Security Techniques Being Implemented on the American People," *Police State USA* (Feb. 11, 2014), http://www.policestateusa.com/2014/prison-security-american-people/.

13 Marlon Brock, "10 Prison Security Techniques Being Implemented on the American People," *Police State USA* (Feb. 11, 2014), http://www.policestateusa.com/2014/prison-security-american-people/.

14 Marlon Brock, "10 Prison Security Techniques Being Implemented on the American People," *Police State USA* (Feb. 11, 2014), http://www.policestateusa.com/2014/prison-security-american-people/.

15 Marshall McLuhan, *Understanding Media: The Extensions of Man* (New American Library, 1964), p. 34.

16 Jonathan Lethem, *They Live* (Soft Skull Press, 2010), p. 42.

17 Joshua Rothkopf, "Empire of the Sunglasses: How 'They Live' Took on Republicans and Won," *Rolling Stone* (Oct. 27, 2014), http://www.rollingstone.com/movies/features/how-they-live-took-on-the-republicans-and-won-20141027.

18 Jonathan Lethem, *They Live* (Soft Skull Press, 2010), p. 82.

19 Jonathan Lethem, *They Live* (Soft Skull Press, 2010), p. 127.

20 Jonathan Lethem, *They Live* (Soft Skull Press, 2010), p. 127.

21 Rod Serling, "Deaths-Head Revisited," *The Twilight Zone* (Nov. 10, 1961).

22 William Shirer, *The Rise and Fall of the Third Reich* (Simon and Schuster, 1960), pp. 69, 70.

23 William Shirer, *The Rise and Fall of the Third Reich* (Simon and Schuster, 1960), pp. 69, 70.

24 John W. Whitehead, "Losing Moses on the Freeway: An Interview with Chris Hedges," The Rutherford Institute (June 23, 2005), https://www.rutherford.org/publications_resources/oldspeak/losing_moses_on_the_freeway_an_interview_with_chris_hedges.

Index

About the Author

JOHN WHITEHEAD is an attorney and author who has written, debated, and practiced widely in the area of constitutional law, human rights, and popular culture. Widely recognized as one of the nation's most vocal and involved civil liberties attorneys, Whitehead's approach to civil liberties issues has earned him numerous accolades and accomplishments, including the Hungarian Medal of Freedom and the 2010 Milner S. Ball Lifetime Achievement Award for "[his] decades of difficult and important work, as well as [his] impeccable integrity in defending civil liberties for all."

As nationally syndicated columnist Nat Hentoff observed about Whitehead: "John Whitehead is not only one of the nation's most consistent and persistent civil libertarians. He is also a remarkably perceptive illustrator of our popular culture, its insights and dangers. I often believe that John Whitehead is channeling the principles of James Madison, who would be very proud of him."

Whitehead's concern for the persecuted and oppressed led him, in 1982, to establish The Rutherford Institute, a nonprofit civil liberties and human rights organization headquartered in Charlottesville, Virginia. Deeply committed to protecting the constitutional freedoms of every American and the integral human rights of all people, The Rutherford Institute has emerged as a prominent leader in the national dialogue on civil liberties and human rights and a formidable champion of the Constitution. Whitehead serves as the Institute's president and spokesperson.

Whitehead writes a weekly commentary for *The Huffington Post, The Blaze,* and Lewrockwell.com, which is also carried by daily and weekly newspapers and web publications across the country and is available on The Rutherford Institute's website (www.rutherford.org). Whitehead is the author of some twenty books, including the award-winning *A Government of Wolves: The Emerging American Police State* (2013), *The Freedom Wars* (2010), *The Change Manifesto* (2008), and *Grasping for the Wind* (HarperCollins/Zondervan, 2001), the companion documentary series to the book of the same name, which also received critical acclaim. The series was awarded two Silver World Medals at the New York Film and Video Festival.

Born in 1946 in Tennessee, John W. Whitehead earned a Bachelor of Arts degree from the University of Arkansas in 1969 and a Juris Doctorate degree from the University of Arkansas School of Law in 1974. He served as an officer in the United States Army from 1969 to 1971. He lives in Charlottesville, Virginia.